# The Cole Story

L-R Top Row: Tom, Greg, Jason, Freya, Marvin, Michael
Middle Row: Cura (Marvin's sister), Lisa, Mayumi, Mimi
Bottom Row: Andrew, Michaela, Marcia (BooBoo), Quincy

# The Cole Story

A Chronicle
of the Marvin and Mimi Cole Family

## assembled by
# Marvin M. Cole

Grateful Steps
Asheville, North Carolina

Grateful Steps Foundation
CREST MOUNTAIN
30 Ben Lippen School Road #107
Asheville, North Carolina 28806
Copyright © 2022 by Marvin Cole
Library of Congress Control Number 2022943915
Cole, Marvin M.
*The Cole Story*
All images are from the author's
private collection unless otherwise specified
ISBN 978-1-945714-66-5 Paperback

Lyrics of The Battle Hymn of the Republic by Julia Ward Howe on page 299 are not under copyright.
Our use of lyrics of "Old Dogs, Children and Watermelon Wine" by Tom T. Hall on page 263 is
underlicense by a Creative Commons Attribution-NoDerivatives 4.0 International License
Our use of lyrics of "Big River" by Roger Miller on pages 258 and 262 are underlicense by a Creative
Commons Attribution-NoDerivatives 4.0 International License
Permission has been requested from Lyric Find for use of the Lyrics on page viii of "Circle of Life" by
Tim Rice, the song composed by Elton John.
Permission for use of Christmas paper "Christmas Tartan" as a border for cards on pages 16-19 has been
received from Ella and Viv Paper Company.
Scripture quotation on page 286 is from *New Revised Standard Version Bible: Anglicized Edition*,
copyright © 1989, 1995 National Council of the Churches of Christ in the United States of America.
Used by permission. All rights reserved worldwide.

Printed in the United States of America
at Lightning Source
FIRST EDITION

All rights reserved. No part of this book
may be reproduced in any manner whatsoever
without written permission from the author.

www.gratefulsteps.org

To Mimi—daughter, sister, wife, mother, grandmother, great-grandmother and a joy

## CONTENTS

| | |
|---|---:|
| *Preface* | *vii* |
| Little Bits of Who and What Assembled Marvin | 1 |
| Miriam Joyce West Cole – Call me Mimi | 47 |
| Snapshot Reflections of My Life – Colonel Thomas G. Cole, US Army (Ret) | 85 |
| A Snapshot of Memories – Lisa's Chapter | 151 |
| Michael's Point of View | 181 |
| Riverboating Intermission | 201 |
| Cole Review by Bob Greenberg | 209 |
|   Greenberg Afghan Wedding | 222 |
| As College President | 227 |
| Marvin The Teacher – by Rob Watts | 245 |
| My Neighbor – With Responses by Bari Haskins Jackson, IM Nur (Martin), and Doug Wingeier | 257 |
| My Huckleberry Finn Education | 295 |
| *About the Author* | *307* |
| *Acknowledgments* | *310* |

# PREFACE

When I finally reached the "Coming of Age" stage of my life—somewhere in my mid-70s—I began to think about how little I knew about my parents, grandparents and great grandparents, not to mention my ancestors from Ireland, Scotland, England, Germany or Timbuktu. I was informed that my Great-grandfather John Cole had fought in the War Between the States, and I first wondered was he with the North or the South since people in the Western part of North Carolina were divided or did not care about the issues. I chastised myself for not having the resourcefulness to ask my parents and grandparents about their lives, their values, and to learn of their good and bad experiences. I would like to know their opinion of the issues of their time and about what was going on in the world and their world. Those stories are lost.

Thus this book. It is a collection of memories, beliefs, thoughts, activities, even some facts, and especially about or by significant people and events that might help grandchildren and beyond, and friends, have some insight into the lives of this Cole family. Another impetus was Granddaughter Marcia Wheaton naming a best song at one of our Florida vacations from the Judds: "Grandpa, Tell Me 'Bout The Good Old Days."

When a child is born, thinking parents—after checking to see if all fingers and toes are in proper order—give thought to what this miracle that is our child will become. The range is phenomenal. Andrew H. Miller—in his book *On Not Being Someone Else*[1]—speaks of the "fundamental condition . . . of being this single self among many possible selves . . . one person among all the people I might have been." He quotes anthropologist Clifford Geertz: "One of the most significant facts about humanity may finally be that we all begin with the natural equipment to live a thousand kinds of life but in the end have lived only one."[2]

What happens along the way—the tweaks of significant others, events, experiences, particularly in the early years—has a tremendous influence on the life and happiness out of a thousand possibilities. We only know the tweaks by looking back and seeing those things that gave direction and purpose to our life. This memoir is an attempt at the tweaks that affected the Cole Family.

---

[1] Miller, Andrew H. *On Not Being Someone Else: Tales of Our Unled Lives*. Cambridge, MA. Harvard University Press. 2020
[2] Geertz, Clifford. American anthropologist.

"Circle of Life" from the *Lion King*
lyrics by Tim Rice, composed by Elton John.

From the day we arrive on the planet
And, blinking, step into the sun
There's more to be seen
Than can ever be seen
More to do than can ever be done …
There's far too much to take-in here
More to find than can ever be found
But the sun rolling high through the sapphire sky
Keeps great and small on the endless round

In the circle of life
It's the wheel of fortune
It's the leap of faith
It's the band of hope
'Til we find our place
On the path unwinding
In the circle, the circle of life …

# 1

## Little Bits of Who and What Assembled Marvin

**J. Basford (Bassie) Cole** (1868-1946) Grandfather, farmer.
**Ella Cole** (1866-1946) Grandmother, school teacher. Grandmother Ella loved to read books. Grandfather Bassie collected pennies from the community to pay the preacher at Snow Hill Methodist Church who came every third Sunday.

Top right Marvin on leave with parents Clyde and Margie Cole

Margie and Clyde listening to the radio at Christmas time. Dad loved listening to the news back when it was genuine, not the propaganda cult-producing muddle heard in the 1990s until the 2020s.

# Little Bits of Who and What Assembled Marvin

Telling "who I am" is a bit difficult for many of us because of fear that someone might think we are bragging, "tooting my own horn." As a boy, for me to say something good about myself would bring on scowling looks from my parents. They were persistent in the message, "Don't get above your raising," and the aspect of damaging my self-concept was not part of our culture at the time.

But Will Rogers did say "It ain't bragging if it's true."

On the other hand, so many times I have attended funerals of friends and acquaintances and learned for the first time who these people were. And I think, if I had known what was revealed in the eulogy, I could have had some good discussions with that person, asked some questions, shared experiences. Why do we have to wait until someone dies to find out who they are? But we have to find out from someone else . . . at his or her funeral.

Here in brief form are some of the stimulus events and people of my life as well as responses to typical biographical questions to attain at least one view of this questionable person named Marvin. You learned by reading *The Red Badge of Courage*[3] that Stephen Crane demonstrated that one does not know who he or she is until faced with a crisis. To get closer to really knowing someone would take kaleidoscopic views by the person as well as many people with whom that person has been affiliated. And one would get a different picture with each turn of the kaleidoscope. Herein is the account from my present kaleidoscopic view.

## *Early Years*

Marvin Mallonee Cole was born in a little shack across the road from Pole Creek Baptist Church in Candler, North Carolina, on August 8, 1932. Some say that my questionable behavior in later life was a result of being born that close to a Baptist Church. This was three

---
3 Crane, Stephen. *Red Badge of Courage*. NYC, NY. D Appleton and Company. 1895.

years after the Great Depression, and I was part of the fall-out. In the *20th Century Day by Day* reference book, the slot for August 8, 1932, is not even listed, indicating nothing of significance happened on that day. I suppose that is one reason there has been no statue or commemoration erected on the shack site near Pole Creek Baptist, only briars and scrub oaks.

Mother knew that day that I would soon be appearing and walked two miles to find a neighbor to go tell my father to bring the doctor. The doctor's name was Dr. John Rich, a country doctor who delivered a lot of babies in his career. I remember as a lad going to his office with my father who went to get a flu shot. In the reception room of a two-room building, I saw stacks of magazines and medical brochures cluttering an old dining-room table. The rooms looked like they had never become acquainted with a dust cloth, much less a broom in months . . . or years. Dr. Rich had to press hard with the flu-shot needle, making a depression on my father's arm because that needle had been used so many times that it was very dull. My father—an eight-to-ten-hours-a-day carpenter, accustomed to lifting two-by-ten lumber planks—winced when the needle finally broke through the skin. I was happy I was not eligible for the flu vaccine.

I grew up in an abandoned public school house my father had purchased it in 1938 for $500. It sat on 2.5 acres on Hookers Gap Road in Candler. The name of the school was Snow Hill, and my father attended there until he completed his formal education in the eighth grade. The ceilings were high, and the floors were rough.

I received a tricycle one Christmas and remember riding it under the framework set up for my mother making quilts.

My Father Clyde Mallonee Cole built houses early in his career and then became Foreman for the Bordner Construction Company in Asheville, and my Mother Margie Norma Morgan Cole, was a homemaker. They both attained an eighth grade education. Opportunity for further education did not exist at the time.

My mother was born in the Dix Creek section of Leicester, North Carolina. After she had completed the eighth grade, the teacher continued to bring books for her to read because she knew my mother was a learner. Driving through Candler today, I see several homes my father built, and he was well known for his cabinet-making abilities. Before starting a new house, he figured out how many two-by-fours, two-by-sixes, and other lumber he needed to complete the house. He was baffled that I had troubled with arithmetic in grade school. My sister, Cura, and I had wonderful parents who disciplined but never approached abuse. My father was the choir director at Snow Hill Methodist Church for many years and my mother sang in the choir.

As a boy, I rarely went to Asheville and did not need or want to go. It cost twenty-five cents to take the bus to Asheville on the Pisgah and Leicester (P&L) line, but my mother went every month or so and she brought me books from the Brown Bookstore. These were usually Zane Grey books about hero cowboy types in the West. But what I remember were his vivid descriptions of the landscape of the area. There is a scene in *Wanderer of the Wasteland*[4] in which a very thirsty man, while struggling to get through the desert and crawling along, was bitten in the face by a rattlesnake. I struggled with him as he worked through his recovery and overcoming the bad guys.

We did not have such a thing as a vacation while I was a boy because we were not that far removed from The Great Depression and Mom and Dad concentrated on just getting biscuits

---
[4]Grey, Zane. *Wanderer of the Wasteland*. New York City, NY. Grosset & Dunlap.1923.

and gravy on the table. The closest thing to a vacation came when Snow Hill Methodist Church went on a Sunday picnic to the foot of Pisgah, and another year we picnicked at the Pink Beds on the Blue Ridge Parkway.

During warm weather, I spent my days doing chores my father left for me to do, like pulling weeds from the garden for the hogs and cleaning the chicken house and placing the contents on the garden. (This was part of my pre-college liberal education to learn that chicken manure makes excellent fertilizer.) After chores on some days, my friends Wade Caldwell and H.B. Rogers and I might build a pond in the creek or play "Cowboys and Indians" in the woods. My horse was a broom handle with a leather strap tied at the top for the bridle. In the summer months, shoes were worn only to church on Sunday. During high school, I milked a cow named Blondie before school and in the evenings. My mother made butter from the milk, as well as buttermilk. My only sex education from my parents was one summer morning my father told me to take Blondie to Mr. Fred Wright's bull "to get her fixed." The only other sex education was from the dirty jokes the boys passed around at school.

My main profession in life was in education, although that was the farthest thing from my mind throughout high school. I took agriculture/shop courses in high school because most jobs in the area were farming, logging or working at the local Enka Rayon Plant. The Agriculture Teacher, Mr. J.B. Edwards, chose Neil Anderson, Wade Caldwell and me out of thirty-some students to compete in the cattle judging teams and seed judging competition for which we traveled to N.C. State University for the finals. We were also chosen to compete in the Parliamentary Procedure competition. These activities were scary for me at the time, and I only recognized their significance to my growth later in life. Mr. Edwards was a good teacher, but I did not recognize at the time that perhaps he saw potential in the three of us as well as he was trying help us to build-up confidence.

My father took an active interest in my schooling. Even though he could attend school only through the eighth grade, he wanted my sister and me to go to college. I think his interest was unusual in that regard as I learned from fellow classmates. He made me take typing in high school and that course was the cause of a lot of good things, including jobs in my future.

There were two other boys in that typing class, competing our typing skills with a room full of girls. It was a lovely setting but wasted on me because of my fear of girls. Of the other two boys in the typing class, one became a colonel in the army and the other, a successful engineer in Connecticut. Taking high school typing in the late 1940s was not considered a "manly" thing to do, whereas in today's world, jobs are difficult to find if one cannot type on a computer keyboard.

Fifty-three students graduated in my class at Candler High School in 1950. Ninety-eight students graduated in our ninth-grade class three years earlier. It was typical then for about half the ninth grade class to drop out prior to graduation. Four boys and no girls attended college. But that high school typing class made it possible for me to get a super job in the U.S. Air Force by helping me type my own term papers in college and by my typing Mimi's term papers in college and my writing love letters to acquire a wife. Unfortunately, Mimi kept those love letters, shows them to our children and quotes from them on any occasion of need. Some are pretty disgusting.

## *Military*

Looking back, all my work positions have been learning experiences, and each helped me to prepare for the next position. My first job was straightening bent nails from my father's carpentry. After one year at Mars Hill College, I entered the U.S. Air Force in 1951 at the height of the Korean War. McCarthyism was intensive in Washington and widespread elsewhere. Eugene McCarthy was a Senator from Wisconsin who kept lists of people who were supposedly Communists. He was feared and he ruined the careers and lives of a lot of people before he was confronted and proven as a fake and evil person. But those in the military were trained to hate and always be on the alert for communists.

After basic training in Texas, we were counseled on our specialty schools for the work we were to be doing for the next four years. I looked at the big map on the wall of the Personnel Sergeant's office of all the "Specialty Schools" and looked for the one closest to Asheville, North Carolina. I wanted to get as close to home as possible. That school was Military Police in Augusta, Georgia (Fort Gordon), and I informed the sergeant that was the school I wanted. He stated my scores indicated I could do well in other areas, but I insisted I had always wanted to be a policeman. One of Mimi's favorite stories is how I worked four years as a policeman and never arrested anyone. But I had a lot of friends.

So I was put on a train to Georgia. At that time in 1951, the Korean/Chinese Communists were overrunning the United States' air bases in Korea, and the Air Police were trying to prevent the assaults with .45 caliber pistols. So the Air Force sent their prospective military police for infantry training at an Army Base. We had done some crawling in Texas, but the crawling in Fort Gordon got serious. We crawled with an M1 Rifle whereas in Texas we crawled with a Carbine. If a speck of dust was found in a rifle barrel by the drill sergeant, then that airman slept with his M1 that night. If one referred to his M1 as a "gun" instead of a "weapon," then he was to do a number of push-ups, determined by the whim of the drill sergeant. We experienced crawling under live machine gun fire with threats that any raising of the head could be disastrous, and if a speck of dirt was found in a weapon's barrel at the end, then the airman cleaned it and was ordered to go through the live fire range again. It occurred to me that I had joined the Air Force, and so far, I had few opportunities to view the sky because my nose was creating a little indention in the sand. But there was only one person to blame for saying he wanted to be a policeman.

After graduating from Military Police School and made to feel like I could handle all bad guys, the Air Force sent me to Lockbourne Air Force Base in Columbus, Ohio, and there I spent the winter guarding airplanes and looking for communists. Some nights the temperature was fourteen below. We dressed in wool parkas and bunny boots and stood under bomber and fighter jet wings four hours on and four hours off for twenty-four hours. Then we had two days off with the first day spent sleeping.

I hated that winter weather and said, "I am smarter than this," so I volunteered to go to Korea. My geography lessons had not covered the weather in Korea. But the military being the military and fortunately for me, sent me to London, England, to a base named West

Drayton, which happened to be a former British Military Prison.

There were no planes on the West Drayton base. And because my father had made me take typing in high school, I was assigned an office job in police headquarters. My job required a Top Secret Clearance, so an FBI personage was sent to check on me and that provided a little excitement on Pole Creek. My father was asked what Marvin had "gotten into" and if he was in trouble. My mother wrote to me asking what was going on with the Air Force and me.

The West Drayton base was only a few blocks in size with the personnel in the main building developing and analyzing pictures that the U.S. U2 planes were taking while flying over Russia and other places. One of those planes, taking off from Peshawar, Pakistan, was shot down by the Russians, and the pilot, Gary Powers, was captured as a spy. Anyway, my job, along with William Pollitz from Davenport, Iowa, for three years was to type the applications for secret, top secret, and crypto secret clearances and obtain fingerprints for personnel developing and analyzing those U2 pictures. Sometimes at night I was awakened by CIA officers and English Police to type up statements by some airman accused of murder or other serious crimes. So I had good worthwhile work and exciting experiences in the Air Force.

The military experience was also a good learning experience for me. I really was not ready for the study habits required for college, and the military helped me mature and obtain a broader outlook on life. I see it as my first college experience, or at least pre-college. It assisted me in learning a lot about people, and particularly about good values and bad habits. At our stage in development as human beings, I wonder about the proper development of young people who have not experienced the education of the disciplined.

I learned in the Air Force that Catholics did not have horns as I had been taught at church. Our first son is named for two Catholic friends—Thomas Pillion from Pittsburg, Pennsylvania, and Gilbert Paulin from Bridgeportl, Connecticut—who had "love thy neighbor" values. I learned to live, work, sing and play with Black People and confirmedwhat Huckleberry Finn had learned— that black people inside are the same as white people.

I began to realize that some who quote from the Bible may be speaking on what they want to believe rather than what Jesus wanted believed. A major part of my religious education was the importance of beer and wine in the South as an accepted characteristic of being Christian while the real meaning of "my brother" was not on the agenda. I found that other areas of the country did not consider the consumption of alcohol as a major avenue to Christianity. The English friends at The Cherry Tree Pub in West Drayton could spend a couple of hours chatting while sipping on one pint of lager beer. The Americans, particularly, it seems those from the South, seem to seek manliness with the single source of chugalugging. What is that about? Who is civilized? Who is educated?

## *Western Carolina University*

After the military, I was led by a brown-eyed girl to Western Carolina (College then and University now). Since our Flag Football team at West Drayton had gone to the finals in England, some of the team thought we would be fabulous in college ball at home. I was a

Center, weighing in at 210 pounds wet and found myself at Western Carolina with college linemen looking very tall and wide. Making the third string, I found myself used as a lineman for the first string to practice against and facing an All Conference Little All American Guard. Before the season was over, I told the coach that I might be better as a sports writer for the college newspaper.

The brown-eyed girl named Mimi and I met through the courtesy of best friends Ed and Mary Jo Bumgarner, his sister. They arranged the date, and Ed and his girlfriend Lorena Smith picked us up for a double date to a movie. My first impression of Mimi was that she was a little chubby because she wore the crinoline slip under her skirt that was popular at the time—it was supposed- to make one look like Scarlet O'Hara. The crinoline was a stiff undergarment, which made the skirt have a cone shape, and it is no longer in vogue, thank goodness. Mimi's weight at the time was 110 pounds.

Since I had one year of college at Mars Hill, and had taken some University of Maryland courses in England, I entered Western Carolina as a sophomore. One of the requirements that year was to complete a speech course. This was an attempt to try to eliminate the "twang" in us mountain Southerners and saying such expressions as "I liked to died" and "I wus waiting on you." But I was so shy and bashful that I told the brown-eyed girl I had rather drop out of college than have to get up before people and speak. But the 110-pound, brown-eyed girl shamed and strong-armed me into taking the course.

Mimi and I dated steadily while attending Western Carolina until one day she decided perhaps she should look around a little to see if I was the right one for a husband. She stopped our dating. My life became the source of the themes of some many country songs. I went home over the weekend and went to see Mimi's mother. I told her that Mimi had decided to cease dating me. Mimi's mother, Catherine Candler, did not hesitate to give me advice. She told me to pick the prettiest girl I could find, a homecoming queen if possible, and date her and then we will see what happens to Mimi. I took Catherine's advice and asked the Homecoming Queen for a date and she accepted. Later Mimi was furious when she found out her mother had conspired against her.

Of course, word got around the dormitory about my date because Mimi and the Homecoming Queen lived on the same dormitory floor. On the day I was to have the date, we had what was called "The Assembly" where all students were required to attend to hear speeches and lessons, from some person selected by the Administration. I was sitting in my assigned seat at The Assembly when Mimi came from behind and dropped a note in my lap. The note said "I am all yours," and it was signed "Mimi."

I never heard whoever was speaking that day. But I had a problem in that I had made a commitment for a date with the Homecoming Queen that night. So I got with Mimi after the Assembly and told her I had to honor my obligation. She said she understood, but I had a miserable day that day feeling those horns of a dilemma. Meanwhile, in the dorm, Mimi and friends were planning some dirty tricks for the unsuspecting Homecoming Queen. I will not go into the details because I want this to be a decent book, but just remember the admonition that "Hell hath no fury like the fury of a woman scorned." The poor Homecoming Queen was innocent of the whole matter. When I returned her to her dorm that evening I did tell her that Mimi and I were getting back together. She understood. She was a nice lady. So gentlemen, when you fail to understand a lady, remember to seek help from her mother.

When she was 4 years old, Mimi's father died as a result of an appendicitis operation. The medical people at the time did not know of the importance of exercise following an operation. Later, Catherine West, with daughters Norine and Miriam (Mimi), married Coke Candler who became a very successful Chairman of the Buncombe County Commissioners for eighteen years. Coke and Catherine then had two more children, Mary Catherine Candler Swayngim and Eddie Candler. Coke was a graduate of Duke University and Captain of the Duke basketball team although he did not make the first string in basketball in high school. There is a lesson there for us deliberate contemplative types.

One summer evening I went to the Candler home to pick up Mimi for our usual movie outing. Mr. Candler met me at the door and said "Son, I want to show you something." So he led me upstairs to Mimi and Kitty's room which depicted the floor, bed posts and chairs with dirty clothes, dresses and undergarments, and the room would make a tornado be proud of its results. And Coke just looked at me and said: "I just want you to know what you are getting into."

Mimi and Kitty were animated in their displeasure at their father. But Coke was pleased. I was too enamored with Mimi to understand Coke's gesture. So I had a prospective father-in-law who was striving to give me warning, and a mother-in-law who schemed to make her choose me over others to get Mimi out of her hair. At least that is how I interpret it. I was blessed to have good in-laws.

In our junior year, I was still shy but was persuaded by a group of students to run for president of the student body. So I had to make a five-minute speech along with the other candidates. In spite of my "shaky legs" speech, I was elected to President of the Student Body and Student Senate, and that experience established the course for my lifetime career. I wanted to become a Dean of Men, because I admired the person in that position very much. His name was Howard Aldmon, and he later became Vice-President of Student Affairs at The University of Tennessee.

There is an interesting story about how Dr. Aldmon came to Western Carolina. After high school, he was granted admission to the University of North Carolina and was driving a friend to Western before going on to Carolina at Chapel Hill. Upon entering Western's campus, Howard immediately fell in love with mountain setting and decided to attend college there. Consequently, according to my assessment, he attained an academic education and avoided what he would have received at the University of North Carolina.

The brown-eyed girl and I dated throughout our sophomore and junior class years, attended the dances and ball games, made occasional visits to the drive-in movie theater and sang in the Baptist Church Choir. Mimi had grown up attending the Hominy Baptist Church, and I attended Snow Hill Methodist Church, so it was obligatory on my part to teach Mimi the Christian religion as opposed to the Baptist practices. Mimi sang in the College Chorus and was one of the soloist's for church and for the operettas and other musical programs at the college. I was Sport's Editor for the Western Carolinian college paper and manager for the

Welcoming Eleanor Roosevelt at the Asheville Airport while President of the Student Body at Western Carolina College (University). Mimi and I drove her back to Asheville the evening after her speech at Western. We had been told to provide a pillow and quilt for her to sleep in the car on the way back. When we passed through Canton, she raised up and said "What is that awful odor?" We informed her about the paper plant, and that was one of Mimi's favorite stories. Mrs. Roosevelt served as first lady of the United States for four terms from 1933-1945, championing poverty alleviation, access to education and civil rights. She traveled to the European and Pacific front lines of World War II.

college baseball team under the renowned Coach Jim Gudger. Again, my father's insisting on my taking typing in high school came in handy in typing Mimi's term papers. One never knows what courting tactics will come in handy someday.

When I ran for President of the Student Body, we had a square dance on the square as promotion as well as signs printed. One sign stated "Roll with Cole" and some were printed out on small Post-it-note-size squares. One rather shapely coed girl placed the sign on her posterior on tight jeans and rolled up and down the sidewalks to class and elsewhere. Mimi had some misgivings about those maneuvers.

I took my responsibilities as President of the Student Body very seriously. A lot of time was spent in preparing for meetings and the various activities. Dancing was a major activity on campus, and we were able to bring Buddy Morrow and his Band of Renown for a whopping cost of one thousand dollars. We also had The Four Freshmen and we built a club house on college property on Lake Glenville among other things.

It gave me a lot of encouragement at the end of the college year when some administrators thanked me for making their job easier for that year.

In the summer prior to our senior year, Mimi finally coerced me into marriage. She has another version of the coercion theory, but I will keep quiet because I know it is rude to interfere with another person's story. We were married by Pastor M.D. Smith in Hominy Baptist Church on June 4, 1957, on a very rainy evening. Because of the rain, I wore an extra pair of shoes and clothes and carried my wedding attire to dress when I got to the church. The shoes were left at the church while we went on our two-day honeymoon to Little Switzerland on the Blue Ridge Parkway. Word was received later from Pastor M.D. Smith that a certain Methodist could find his shoes at the bottom of the Baptistery. I did not succumb, but I knew he was joking.

We moved into a one-room furnished apartment owned by a history professor and his wife, Dr. and Mrs. H.P. Smith, on the hill that had been unofficially named by students as "Buzzard's Roost," where faculty had houses. At the end of the fall quarter, the Director of the Student Center resigned and the administration asked me to take that position on an interim basis. The Student Center consisted of a small, two-storied building, which contained a snack bar, a television room for students to watch Yogi Bear and twenty-some tables—which were in constant use for students playing bridge— a pool room and a dance floor. My employment saved the college money and time spent searching for a Director and Mimi and I became rich. I received $2,800 a year plus a two-room apartment in the building free of charge. Since we were now nouveau riche, we purchased a new English Ford and sold the 1948 Pontiac my father had given me when I returned from military service.

Son Thomas Gilbert Cole was born January 20, 1959, and Marcia Elizabeth Cole was born October 14, 1960, while we were living in the Student Center. Since Pampers were a couple of years away from being invented, we used cloth diapers, which meant almost constant washing and drying. We had no dryer and had to string up a wire outside our apartment. Since we were in the middle of the campus, the Librarian Ms. Lillian Buchanan took offense to diapers hanging in this august academic institution. So we had to get a wooden rack and place it on the dance floor after the students had departed in the evening. Ms. Buchanan was trying to instill in us mountain rapscallions a sense of propriety that I did not fully comprehend at the time but an understanding came later. She was correct in her efforts.

After graduation in 1968, I continued as Director of the Student Center and taught The Psychology of Adjustment, which was an ostentatious title for a three-quarter orientation class for freshmen. The quarter system in colleges was divided into fall, winter and spring, roughly three-month periods as opposed to the two-semester system. While performing these duties, I also obtained a Master's Degree in Counseling in preparation for my hopefully becoming a Dean of Students.

## *Indiana University*

Some professors and administrators encouraged me to pursue a doctorate. You can believe that during all my college years I had in the back of my mind that this country boy had not intended to go to college at all. Frequently the question of, "Marvin, are you supposed to be here?" ran through my mind. So I am thankful that some professors and administrators kept encouraging me to progress in education. These promoters prompted me to attend Indiana University with the reasoning of getting a different perspective from a setting other than the South.

Mimi's cousin operated a coal truck in which he ran back and forth from the Northern coal mines to North Carolina. So we employed him to move our small belongings from Cullowhee to Bloomington, Indiana. The cousin tried his best to wash the coal dust off the truck bed before obtaining our collection of "hand-me-downs" for the trip to Bloomington.

We had housing in some old converted Army barracks with the overgenerous name of Hoosier Courts. The rent was $50 per month including utilities. Mimi made $110 a month as a teacher assistant, and I made $100 as a graduate assistant. We scraped through with my mother seeming to know when we were getting short and sending us $10 in the mail. We would go to the grocery and buy a bunch of beans.

Indiana University was different in many respects. Outside the University I found that mid and southern Indiana had attitudes regarding race similar to those in Georgia. Indiana University became one of the first state universities to admit women. In 1895, Marcellus Neal became IU's first African-American graduate and in 1919 Frances Marshall became IU's first female African-American graduate. So Indiana University was at the forefront of being an "educated college."

Herman Wells became President of IU in 1938, did wonders for International Education, and was a model university president. I will give you one example. During the civil rights period of the 1960s, many African-American students from the South attended Indiana University because they could not be admitted to colleges in Southern States. The stores and restaurants in Bloomington, where Indiana University is located, refused to serve the Black students. So President Wells informed Bloomington stores that if they did not serve their Black students, then he would place the whole city "Off

Limits" to all University students. The city admitted African-Americans. Now that is a college president!

## *Pakistan*

During my second year at Indiana, for some reason, the administration and professors at the School of Education asked if I would consider working a couple of years at their project at the University of the Punjab in Lahore, in the country then named West Pakistan. My "good" friends often remark that IU wanted to send me somewhere else because they did not know what to do with the Pole Creek anomaly.

I went home to our old army barracks apartment and told Mimi of the request and asked if we should take the job.

Mimi was not sure she had heard of Pakistan and had misgivings about the word Lahore. The next day she looked it up in our *Worldbook Encyclopedia* and found the average lifespan in Pakistan was 27 years. She was age 26 at the time, and that had a dampening effect on her interest. That day the administrators talked me into taking the job. I felt like it was something of a compliment to be selected, but the kids were not impressed when we all had to take a bunch of vaccine shots, traveling to Indianapolis to get a Yellow Fever vaccination, close our Hoosier Courts apartment, get passports and make travel plans.

We spent two good experience years in Pakistan at a salary of $7,500 per year and free housing. We were rich again. I was Administrative Assistant to the Director of the Institute of Education and Research. We had twelve teachers from the United States as well as some Pakistani professors. Our purpose was to offer a Master's Degree program for Pakistani teachers.

A very important personal benefit was making some good Pakistani and American friends. We made lifetime friends of Mohammed and Iqbal Nawaz. We experienced Mark Twain's assessment, "Travel is fatal to prejudice, bigotry, and narrow-mindedness, and many of our people need it sorely on these accounts. Broad, wholesome, charitable views of men and things cannot be acquired by vegetating in one little corner of the earth all one's lifetime."

During our last year in Lahore, I collected data for my doctoral dissertation evaluating the graduates of the Institute by mailing out questionnaires and visiting the former students in various provinces of the country. It was after one of those visits that I came down with "Dengue" or "Sand Fly Fever," sometimes called "Break-Bone Fever." I spent a miserable, feverish, clammy week shaking in bed.

Before departing for Pakistan we were informed that having servants would be a necessity. That sounded pretentious to me, what my mother would call "highfalutin'," which to her would have been close to being a sin. So we delayed that decision until we arrived and found the outside temperature of 114 degrees and no air conditioning in the kitchen. Mimi did not delay a decision. We employed a cook for kitchen work, a "bacha" for cleaning house and an "ayah" to take care of Lisa and Tommy. Mimi had a job teaching fifth grade at the American School. We were in a new house in the

Gulberg section of Lahore, but when the dust storms came through, every room in the house was covered with dust even with all the windows and doors closed tightly. We were glad to have a bacha. The bacha was also useful for discouraging beggars and snake charmers from entering our premises.

Tommy and Lisa had non-parental planned or approved but interesting language lessons with the bacha named Pierre and the cook named Joseph. It is amazing how quickly children pick up the indecent language in any country. But one incident involved Lisa instructing the bacha. My sociology courses did not include the various terms for bathroom activities, but our families had made use of the term "Shoo Shoo" since "defecation" was not in the Pole Creek or Beaverdam vocabularies, and other terms were not acceptable in Methodist philosophy. Children seem to have an attraction to unmentionable bathroom-type words, probably because their public use is frowned on by parents and therefore must be something to treasure. Lisa was age 3 and 4 while we were in Pakistan, attended a childcare school in one of the American homes and was alert for learning unmentionable words. These were shared with the Pakistani members of our household.

One of the American families living about a block from our residence was having a big dinner party one evening and asked for Pierre to come assist with the serving of the food.

When we arrived in the living room already half full of guests, Pierre greeted with "Hello, Tommy. Hello, Lisa." And then in a rather loud voice, he said "Lisa, Shoo Shoo" and then laughed with Lisa. Mimi and I were struck dumb, and the other guests had understanding looks and smiles on their faces. We had a family confab when we returned home.

One of Mimi's favorite stories before we left Bloomington when Lisa was just over a year old was when the neighbors at Hoosier Courts at IU complained that she was peeing in the plastic wading pool. For you younger parents still learning about "life after kids," these are the kinds of stories from parents your children love for you to tell others, particularly in their teenage years.

One day the cook came to us and said, "Memsahib, Sahib, children are at the gate saying bad things to people walking by. We went out to find Tom with a baby blanket wrapped around his head like a turban and Lisa in a makeshift robe.

They were shouting, as we learned, the words "Ji-kum-dum-jow," which in Urdu/Punjabi means "Go to hell." We were appalled; we had learned some market Urdu words but had not reached that elevated level. So apparently one of our staff had taken liberties with language lessons for Tom and Lisa.

We were very conscious of the behavior of "the ugly American" while overseas, wanting to live up to our own principles, but not wanting to embarrass Indiana University, United States Agency for International Development (USAID) or the United States. The culture was very different, and some Americans could not adjust and had to be sent home. We tried to stay clear of any activities that would cause the American Ambassador to send us back to the United States. We certainly did not want the word out that our children were telling people of our host country to go to hell.

Dear Friends:

The Coles have spent an exciting, but busy five months in Pakistan. Mimi has a full-time teaching job at the American School and Marvin is enjoying learning the ropes and frustrations of his first job as an administrator. Tommy and Lisa are busy with things children do their age as well as learning this new language faster than their mother and father.

Although we have not been in Pakistan long enough to really "know" the culture and traditions, we will give you a little picture of what we have learned from others concerning Christmas in this part of Asia.

The 25th of December is a holiday in Pakistan but most Pakistanis will be celebrating because it is Jinnah's birthday. Jinnah is considered by many to be the Father of Pakistan. He expounded the theory of a separate Muslim state vigorously until India and Pakistan became two nations in 1947.

The buildings and many homes are lighted for this occasion, and the people are in a very light-hearted mood much like you find in the United States. So the Muslim and Christians share a common holiday on the 25th of December.

I will mention several Christmas customs hurriedly. Small bands come to your door and play and sometimes sing what they call Christmas music. This custom has almost evolved to our halloween. Although the groups will not attempt the trick we hope, they most assuredly will ask for the treat. Santa will visit the American children this year on a camel for their parties. As most of you know, we have a chokidar which guards our home at night. Tommy has expressed his concern that the chokidar knows that he is to allow Santa to come through our gate.

Also, many of the people who have provided certain services for us, i.e., mailmen, telegraph boys, garbage collectors, et cetera, will all come by to say hello, but mainly to collect "Bakhshish". Bakhshish is related to what we call a "tip". Most Americans try to leave their home at Christmas time and go to India and one reason they give is to avoid these nuisances.

The Coles will stay in Lahore this year at Christmas time. This is the first time we will have a one family Christmas since we have always spent this season in North Carolina with our families. We have a six foot tree which we ordered from Sears because blue spruce is hard to find in Pakistan. Marvin, as usual, is late in buying a present for his wife, although he has unsuccessfully attempted to persuade his wife that her present for the next five years was the three days we spent in Hawaii on our way to Pakistan.

As we have expressed to you before, our views and perspectives have changed considerably from our short stay in this very different culture. As an example, we have a better understanding now of the manger scene which all of you will see during the season. Formerly, it was quite difficult to picture a manger scene in the middle of some large city or in a Church. But here we see the (modern) donkeys, camels, straw huts, etc, and can more readily picture the manger scene, although we are many miles from the actual setting.

Although many of you will be wishing for snow this year, this wish is useless here. Our flowers will be blooming all over the yard and we will probably have vegetables from our garden. The temperature is now in the lower 60's or upper 70's and we will probably spend Christmas day in our yard playing with children's new toys.

We are enjoying good health and having a wonderful experience with these wonderful people. The last five months are probably equal to two years college work for each of us.

We wish you a wonderful holiday season and will be thinking of you.

Yours
Mimi
Marvin

Tommy

Lissa

## *Indiana and Morehead*

After two years of learning and growing in Pakistani ways, we returned to Indiana in 1965, and I was assigned to work as Assistant to the Dean of the School of Education while completing my graduate work. Philip Dean was a mathematician by education and a wonderful person who did not allow being a Dean to make him pretentious. I completed my studies, defended my dissertation and graduated in 1966 with a Doctorate in n Education.

I phoned my parents that I had completed my doctor's degree and graduated, and my father asked if I "could cure a sick horse." My father had a bit of a sense of humor.

My mother wrote me a letter expressing "happy for you" and some words expressing the need to always remember where I came from. Her advice was consistent with her goal for me to be a decent human being to all people, and I hope she has never been disappointed with the results of the education she gave me. My parents blessed with a real higher education.

## *Morehead, Kentucky – Atlanta, Georgia*

I interviewed and was made Dean of Institutional Programs—faculty referred to me as "Dean of Other"—at Morehead State University in Kentucky where the president was a former Kentucky legislator and the minister of the local Church of Christ. Talk about three potentially enormous egos. Our values did not coincide, and he reminded me of Abraham Lincoln's words ". . . if you want to test the character of a man, give him power." After two years in Morehead, in 1968, I had learned how not to be a college president. It was a very valuable lesson and one of the stages preparing me for future positions in higher education.

Son Michael Patrick Cole was born on February 16, 1968, and two weeks later we moved to Atlanta with two other disenchanted Morehead State Deans and a Chemistry Professor to open a new "Harvard of the South" higher education institution named Atlanta Baptist College.

We were successful in opening the college and acquiring 310 students the first year. I spent every Sunday soliciting students in the spring and summer by visiting Baptist churches in the area. But the Board of Trustees wanted to get rid of the Minister at the large Baptist church in Atlanta and made him President of the college. So the preacher-president problem continued as we had a person with a good prayer but who had no administrative experience at a college. That and the lack of financial support and fundamentalist philosophy closed Atlanta Baptist College, and it was given to Mercer University in 1970 for their Pharmacy School.

I fell out of love with preachers. As a result of the Morehead and Atlanta Baptist experiences, I said to Mimi, "I never want to have a preacher in our home until we have known him or her for at least ten years and can attest to the legitimacy, but still keep a wary eye." I felt betrayed then but feel now that was immaturity on my part as I expected a minister to be different from ordinary people in behavior, wisdom and values. Now I know they are just ordinary people. I do not condemn any religion and believe that all major religions are still learning to be what they should be. I teach Sunday School occasionally at the Methodist Church and attend regularly, but one of my shortcomings is a prevailing need to keep a wary but helpful and hopeful eye on preachers as well as college presidents. Hillary Clinton made a true statement with "It takes a village to raise a child." I would add that it takes a village to continue raising an adult. Perhaps there has been too little emphasis on the responsibility of church members to raise their pastor.

## *Afghanistan*

With the demise of Atlanta Baptist College, I sent my resumé to Dean Thomas Schreck at Indiana University, stating I was seeking employment in case he knew of openings. It was on the Dean's desk when a USAID Official came to Bloomington to review the University's recommendation to fill a Student Affairs Advisor position at Kabul University. University personnel had already selected possible candidates before my resumé arrived. The official rejected the University's chosen person so Dean Schreck picked up my credentials out of the In-Box on his desk and said "What about this guy?"

After reviewing my resumé, the Director said, "That's the person we want," so the Dean phoned and asked if I wanted to work at Kabul University in Afghanistan. I know not why or how the Director chose me just by looking at paperwork.

Mimi had to go back to the *Worldbook Encyclopedia* to find out about our prospective new home. In 1970 we went forth for three years and another wonderful learning experience in Asia. When England was in the position to acquire nations around the world, they took over and ruled India for about a hundred years before departing in 1947. At that time, the subcontinent was divided into India (mostly Hindu) and West Pakistan and East Pakistan (mostly Muslim). Later East Pakistan became Bangladesh.

During the hundred-year period of rule of India, England built roads, improved education and government systems and achieved further modernization. Therefore, India benefitted from the English domination. But when England entered Afghanistan, they were repelled and were never able to take over the Afghans. To this day, Afghanistan does not have a railroad and the only paved road in the country was built in the 1960s by the United States and the Soviet Union. So we talk about how bad empire building is, but in this case, Afghanistan is still much more primitive than India or Pakistan.

Books and articles have been written about Afghanistan being the graveyard of empires. Some of the invaders have been the Greek Empire of Alexander the Great, the Mongol Empire led by Genghis Khan, Maurya Empire, Timurid Empire of Timur, Mughal Empire, the British Empire, the Soviet Union and others. At present the United States has had a military presence in Afghanistan for twenty years that has been reported as our longest war. Presumably, we are there to prove that all the other empires were wrong and we know how to do it. But we will not develop Afghanistan with military endeavors. A military presence intensifies Afghan resistance.

From my non-State Department-educated opinion, we were making progress early in 1973 with several educational and agriculture programs from several universities in the United States under the auspices of USAID, as well as significant Peace Corps personnel. But the main purpose of the United States Government at the time was our presence prevented Russia from getting closer to a warm water port. We were preventing Russian expansion. Our goal was not altruistic. Then the Soviet Union broke up and was no longer an expansion threat, so we withdrew our educational programs.

Russia then moved in and stayed for ten years before being expelled by Afghans with United States military assistance. Then the weapon supplies the US provided the Afghans were used by conservative Islamists to obliterate any semblance of progressive advancement in the country. Women and children suffered most. The vast majority of Afghans remain illiterate, unhealthy, poorly housed and survive day by day with only one hope—that being in Allah.

The U S military presence in Afghanistan only intensified their resolve to fight and remain regressive and certainly did not indicate that the United States Government was interested in improving the country. Education (without indoctrination), health and agriculture programs are the only way to be serious about helping the Afghans.

So our entrance into Kabul was a step back in time. One physical example is that the wall around our house in Lahore, Pakistan, was only about four feet tall, while the wall around our home in the Karta Se section of Kabul was two feet wide, ten feet tall and had broken glass protruding from the cement on top of the wall. We had a locked gate and a guard housed on the premises. The Ambassador from the United States told Americans not to leave town unless with a caravan of cars.

There were four of us on the Indiana/USAID program. My job was to advise and develop Student Personnel programs.

I worked with the Kabul University Vice President for Student Affairs and sometimes worked with the President.

The Chief of Party was Dr. Taul Miller, who was an Economics Professor at Indiana.

A short time after we had arrived in Kabul, Indiana University sent another team member who became a very important part of the team and remained a close friend of the Cole family. His name was Robert (Bob) Greenberg, and Mimi and I were asked to sponsor him until he got established in Kabul. Bob was raised in Chicago and graduated from Carleton College in Northfield, Minnesota, a small private liberal arts college with an outstanding reputation. I was not equipped to compete with his brains, but he put up with me. He had spent two years in Iran with the Peace Corps during which time he became quite fluent in speaking Farsi. Therefore, he was called on frequently as an interpreter.

After picking up Bob at Kabul Airport and introducing him to his new living arrangements, we took him home for dinner. And this event presented us with a story we have recited to others for years. It demonstrates how naïve Mimi and Marvin were, and still are in many ways, regarding religious customs and ... well, the list would be too long. We served ham, completely disregarding the obvious fact that Greenberg meant Bob could be Jewish. Serving ham in Afghanistan was a delicacy. Bob ate the ham and drank the wine, and it occurred to us only later that we had made a significant *faux pas*. He did not tell us that evening, and we brought it up to him later when a wavering flash of "duh" passed through Kabul.

Actually, Bob turned out to be more Methodist than Jewish anyway. My various religious experiences with participants over the years have taught me to be understanding, which many would not tolerate. One of the quotes attributed to the great philosopher Yogi Berra is, "I do a lot observing by watching." Well, by watching, I cannot distinguish the difference in the behavior of any of the major religious groups. I will know that one has superiority over another when I see a difference in attitudes and actions come Monday morning.

The game of chess was born in or near Afghanistan. Researchers have been unable to determine if the game was born in Northern India or Afghanistan. They do feel confident that the birth was in the mountainous area around the sixth century. (Pakistan was a part of India until 1947).

Nevertheless, Afghans are fond of chess and Mimi and I occasionally had chess parties at our home involving Afghans, Americans and interested Europeans. The Farsi word for chess is "shatranj." It was noted that the Afghans moved the chess pieces very quickly compared to the slow and contemplative process observed in the United States.

Anyway, Greenberg and I began playing chess soon after his arrival in Kabul, and we played frequently after work hours. For over two years, I could never beat him. Bob and Mimi would gossip nonchalantly while I was concentrating intensely on the game, hoping the chatting would distract him. But it was to no avail. I even went to his home when he was sick with hepatitis to play, and he still beat me. That was one of Mimi's favorite stories to tell anyone who visited.

For the most part, we never felt the danger that many stories reveal about Afghanistan. But there was one incident that had me literally shaking. When the students went on strike, the Kabul University President asked me to help him with the technical side of giving a speech in the main dormitory. The dormitory was built by the United States and was the largest and most elaborate building on the campus. The students were either allowed, or the university did not have the power to stop, possession of guns and knives in their rooms.

The president asked me to tape a speech for him and play it from a hiding place at a certain time at the dormitory in the evening. The speech involved his persuading the students to stop the protests and return to classes. He came to my house to tape the speech, which was about twelve minutes long. He had arranged with the Dormitory Director for me to set up the tape recorder at 4 p.m.—hiding me in a locked room adjacent to the meeting room—and play the tape at 8 p.m.

It is interesting to note that the President did not have the trust in his personnel or the proper equipment to speak to his students. But the Dormitory Director hid me behind a locked door, with only one door exiting that room and that was to the meeting room where the students were to gather for the speech, and I waited for four hours reading Frank Herbert's *Dune*, while wanting the time to fly so I could get home. The President had sworn me to secrecy, so I had not informed the Indiana Chief of Party about the request.

Around 7:30 p.m., I began to hear the students gathering outside my hiding place. The noise increased up until my turning on the speech. After the President had finished,

I shut off the recorder and was going to wait until the crowd dispersed. But they failed to disperse. They did not leave the room, and I was stuck to wait. Various people started speaking in Farsi, and soon I began to recognize through my limited Farsi words like farangi, which is a scornful word for an outsider. I knew they were talking about me in my hiding place.

So for the next couple of hours, the Director and the "protest leaders" harangued each other with the leaders reporting to the crowd, and I felt blessed that I did not know what was being said. But I understood the protestors wanted me to be presented to them for reasons I did not wish to contemplate. During that time, the President spoke to me on the phone three times, expressing concern and apologizing but told me he was afraid to call in the Police or Army because it would give the protestors further ammunition. To say the least, I was uncomfortable and felt my knees shaking, and I had nothing to defend myself with but an Akia Reel to Reel Tape Recorder. I did wonder if I would be able to get out of this predicament unscathed.

The Director's name was Sher, which means lion in Farsi. Sher was a Pashtun or Pathan, a tribal group who lived in Pakistan as well as Afghanistan. The name Pashtun denotes honor, goodness, bravery, loyalty and dignity. They are renowned and respected fighters and battle to the death over three things: wealth, women and land. Tribal vendettas can continue for decades. The Pashtuns are the Hatfields and the McCoys of hillbilly land in the United States.

So finally Sher, the Pathan, grabbed the main leader of the protest and put a big knife to his throat. He told another leader to take Dr. Cole to his car, and if he was harmed in any way that the main leader was dead. This was announced to the group, and I was escorted through the crowd with them spitting on me and throwing chairs my way, but I was not physically harmed. I was amazed that I could drive away.

When I arrived home in the middle of the night, Mimi was in bed and said, "Where in the world have you been?" I was still in a shaky way, but told her that I did not want anyone to ever hear about what happened to me that night. I was pleased the President had kept it secret, but ten minutes later the phone rang and a man named Arnold Shiffendecker of the CIA in Afghanistan asked me what was going on in the dorm at the University. Apparently, the CIA had a scout at the dorm meeting. The next day the *Kabul Times* had an article about a spy in the dormitory at the university the preceding evening. We had a good laugh at that fake news, but I had another title to add to my resume.

***

In the work at Kabul University, we developed, from what we could determine, the first Academic Record form (Permanent Record) for recording courses and grades on one sheet. Prior to this, the records had been kept on a separate sheet of paper for each semester for each student, stacked together. A string was pulled through the stack with a needle to keep them together, and then it was placed on a shelf. I also wrote the first Kabul University Catalog of Courses with a lot of help from Bob Greenberg. This was initially printed in English and then translated into Dari. (Farsi is the general Persian language used in most Middle Eastern

Indiana University Chancellor Herman Wells at our home for a dinner in Kabul, along with Lisa, Mimi, and neighbor Whitten.

Bubba was our house guard. He cried when we departed Afghanistan – not a pleasant memory for us because of his uncertain future.

Mimi and Lois Hendrix painting a house that became the first dormitory for women at Kabul University.

Tom, Mimi, Lisa (holding Myart), Mike and our German Shepherd Princess. They are standing in front of our house and the tallest sun flowers we have ever seen.

countries, and Dari is the same as Farsi. The Afghan government changed the name from Farsi to Dari in 1964. Pashto is also widely spoken in Afghanistan).

Looking back, the projects we worked on in Afghanistan seem so simple, but change was difficult and the work was slow. An example would be in getting something printed in English at a printing press where the typesetters only know the Afghan languages. Proofreading was rewriting almost each page. So a couple of months' work turned into nearly a year. Advances were made for the women at the University as a result of the Indiana project. In our "Afghan" room in Candler, we have a picture of the first woman admitted to Kabul University. The wives and men of the Indiana Team cleaned up and refurbished a house, which became the first dormitory for females. Unfortunately, when the Americans departed Afghanistan in the late 70s, the Russians moved in, and I have longed to hear if any of our efforts to improve Kabul University remained.

I wonder sometimes if the university personnel from the United States didn't obtain more benefits than the Afghans.

The experience had a significant impact on our lives and how we view others. Our three children learned the joys of friends from many sections of the United States as well as England, Germany, Italy and Afghanistan. In addition to the Indiana Team, we had professors from the University of Wyoming and other institutions on various projects in the country. At the American International School of Kabul (AISK), we had over three hundred students. In order for the high school to engage in athletics, teams were formed from USAID, American Embassy, Peach Corps and CIA. We played on Friday since it was a non-work day because it was a religious worshiping day for Muslims. We then worked on Saturday, but had Sunday off. The Friday games were a rather big event for the Western World people as we had crowds representing several countries at the playing field and hotdog stands, beer, and cheerleaders from the high school.

But there was no television or radio during our three years in Afghanistan. As a consequence, Tommy and Lisa learned the joys of reading. Bob Greenberg found daughter Lisa crying in her room one day and when Mimi and I asked what was the matter, she put her book down and replied through tears "Old Yeller just died."

We would occasionally drive our car from Kabul through the Khyber Pass to Peshawar, Pakistan, where we stopped at the closest bookstore—there were no bookstores in Afghanistan—and told the kids to buy all the books they could carry. They still enjoy the good habit of reading. Television and radio can in no way compete for the benefits and joy of reading good books.

While in Kabul, we took advantage of some good travel opportunities. A group of Americans were going to Russia, and Mimi and Lisa went with them to visit Moscow and Leningrad with a stop at Tashkent. Later, Tom and I went on a trip to Nairobi, Kenya. Tom was age 14 and progressing into the disgruntled attitude that age group requires. It seems my main communication with Tom at this period in his life was to say no. So I told him at the beginning that I was not going to say no to him for the entire trip. But he did not ask for anything outlandish. Tom had a good brain and a good heart and just had to get through the teenage disorder.

We visited the Zoo in Nairobi and other tourist spots in the city. After a couple of days, we spent the night in Treetops just outside of Nairobi. As we entered the area, a guard with a high-powered rifle met us to walk us to the hotel, which was on stilts. We were told not to say a word, to keep quiet on the walk. We saw water buffalo with notable horns were eyeing us on our route. Tom was impressed. I was just nervous. That night, we were awakened by the hotel staff each time herds of elephants, lions and zebras came through to get refreshed at a water hole.

The next day we took the train from Nairobi to Mombasa, stopping to spend the night at Tsavo National Park for more animal visits and looking at Mount Kilimanjaro and feeling like Hemingway travelers (except Hemingway had amoebic dysentery when he was in the area). This was a trip of a lifetime and a rewarding and very beneficial father-son time together.

All in all, life was good for the Cole family in Afghanistan. We had good friends, and I felt the work was meaningful. I am very thankful to Indiana University for providing us two great experiences that helped us `grow in two foreign cultures. We spent two years in Pakistan and three years in Afghanistan. The University paid for multiple copies of my dissertation for distribution to USAID, State Department, and anyone else interested. On the personal side, I felt the years overseas gave us a broader perspective for multi-cultures and peoples, and I am very grateful for that experience.

It is a bit of irony that when we left Afghanistan in 1973, we left a country where we had a tall compound wall around our house and where we could travel out of town only in a caravan of Americans. But the news we had from the United States by way of news magazines and letters was that our country was burning and everyone was rioting. I felt relatively safe in Afghanistan, but I had misgivings about coming home to the United States.

## *Atlanta Again*

In 1973, as we began preparations to leave Afghanistan, we received a letter asking if we were interested in a dean's job at a new campus of DeKalb College in Atlanta.

And we were. We were scheduled to return to Indiana and work at the Gary Campus of Indiana University, but were a bit skeptical of the area.

The same week we received the Atlanta job offer, we received a letter from the bank saying our house in Atlanta was in arrears for several months. We quickly sent the bank the money. We had sold the house at 3786 Evans Road on a lease/sale agreement in 1970, assuming we would not return to Atlanta. But the couple who purchased the house apparently packed and moved away in the middle of the night as reported by the neighbors who stated they believed our former home dwellers were with the "Southern Mafia." So all of a sudden we had a home and a job in Atlanta, and I couldn't help but feel like someone upstairs was looking after us.

We returned to Atlanta in July 1973 to our old home at 3786 Evans Road and a job on the South Campus of DeKalb College. I was Dean of Students for one year, Academic Dean the next year, and then Executive Dean of the campus for five years. It was a low-point in the "human being world" when White flight was rampant in South Metro-Atlanta because Black people were moving into the area. On the South Campus, we went from seven percent black in 1973 to seventy percent Black Students in 1980.

DeKalb college was a unit of the DeKalb school system at the time under the Board of Education, and the County Superintendent was our administrative head. I was repeatedly informed by the School System Administration that when the forty percent Black-White ratio was reached on the South Campus, I was to prepare for protests, fights and demonstrations.

Thank goodness for previous experience. As a boy, my mother visited and helped the only Black family living in our area in Candler. My mother also was friends with the only Cherokee family in the area, working with Mrs. Corn to make lye soap in a big black pot at the edge of the woods. My mother practiced "neighbor." Sister Cura and I were never taught to hate Black, Native American, White or any other people. We were never taught to hate, but local culture's education, experience and religion had not progressed to the point that they could fathom that Blacks and Whites could sit side by side in church. Such conditions in those days were never mentioned.

I had only positive experiences with Black Airmen in the Air Force. We worked, played sports and partied together, and it made me understand why WWII Black soldiers felt a sense of treason when returning home to abuse after fighting for their country. How could White people not see the inhumaneness and ignorance in taking that stance—particularly those who classified themselves to be Christian?

While at Indiana University in the 1960s, many Black students were enrolled because they could not get into the universities in the South. During my first semester, one of Mimi's remembrances was my inviting a couple of classmates for lunch one Saturday to study for an upcoming sociology test. One student was a Catholic Priest and the other an African-American, and Mimi was totally unfamiliar with either category. Mimi remembered the pastor at Hominy Baptist saying to her sister, Norine that he would rather preach her funeral than for her to marry a Catholic. But love interfered and Norine married LeRoi Moore and never went back to Hominy Baptist Church.

When I was a boy, my father employed from the construction firm where my he was foreman. a Black person to do some work at our home one Saturday. At lunchtime my father invited the gentleman to have lunch with us.

But that Black person would not sit down at the same table with White persons. That affected me. How sad, and what a lesson!

And of course, the previous experience of work with different cultures and people in Pakistan and Afghanistan, and a desire for the backward Pole Creek boy to succeed, helped give me the confidence to believe we could make good things happen at South Campus. The constant reminders about forty percent Black Student Body would mean trouble made me want to prevent those repercussions. The Black Faculty and Administrators met with me in the Conference Room, and I asked for their help in guiding our policies and procedures. I told them of the prediction from the Superintendent's office, asked for their advice, and to tell me if I misinterpreted, misled or made any decisions that thwarted or frustrated healthy Black-White relations.

We never had any problems.

While still Dean of South Campus, I was working in my office at 5:00 p.m. on a Friday afternoon when a phone call came from the Chairman of the Board of Education. He said, "I have phoned all the campuses of the college, and you are the only dean working." I think that impressed him, but he did not know that it just takes me longer than most to get the job done. But my work habits instilled by my father may have been one reason in 1981 that I was named president of the college. My mother might not like me saying it because it could be bragging, but I think my being able to get along with everyone was also a factor.

We had four Liberal Arts campuses and a Technical school, 18,000 students and a pretty good reputation. Many of our adjunct faculty were professors from Georgia Tech and Georgia State University who would teach evening courses at DeKalb and earn an extra $7,000.

While Dean of the South Campus, I received a great gift in my education from the faculty. We had an innovative group of faculty who designed a multidisciplinary approach for several subjects. For one of the segments, they asked me to sit in on a panel discussion of *Adventures of Huckleberry Finn*. I think the faculty wanted to show the students that the Dean could read and write.

Sister Cura had given me *Huck* when I was about 13 years old, but I had to reread the book. I was surprised at how I viewed the book as a boy and the completely different things I observed when reading it as an adult. That reminds me of a Mark Twain quote: "When I was a boy of 14, my father was so ignorant I could hardly stand to have the old man around. But when I got to be 21. I was astonished at how much the old man had learned in seven years." (Actually, Twain's father died when Twain was 12 years old, so here he was using what Huck called "a stretcher.")

I learned even more by listening to the English teachers explain what was really happening in the novel. Mark Twain said to his friend Dean Howells that to "understand my stories, you have to read between the lines." English teachers help us non-English college majors read between the lines. So I kept asking the English faculty questions about Mark Twain and Huck Finn and they finally said since you are so enthralled with Mr. Twain, and since you resemble him in appearance, why don't you do a Hal Holbrook Twain impersonation?

That was in 1976, and I started by memorizing "What Stumped the Blue Jays?" followed by a twenty-minute segment of Huckleberry Finn. It took me a couple of months to learn a twenty-minute piece while adding the gestures, eye and head movements, and the slow walk. It was time consuming, and demands of my college work kept interfering with my becoming Twainized. Mike was about age 9 and would check the script as I recited it, and I could tell that this was not the most exciting activity for his evenings. But even today he retains some knowledge about Huck Finn. Fortunately, my secretary Katherine Martin, who became Assistant to the President, was an English/Drama major and a very demanding drama coach. She would stand at the back of the gym during practice and yell at me "I can't hear you" and then fuss if I got a line in the wrong place.

Ella Montgomery, a Black lady on the South Campus, took an interest in my Twaining. She took me to the Mall one day, and I purchased a somewhat-white suit. It had a little yellow color but was good enough for Wednesday night church service programs, which were my trial runs at the time. A Rotary Club member was at one of those services (Civic Clubs are always desperate for a program), and he asked me to do a Twain program for the Rotary. This led to a performance at a Joint Georgia Tech/University of Georgia Foundation meeting, and that led to my having a little more confidence. But in all of these, I was nervous as a cat in a dog kennel. Some years I had over thirty performances, and I really never totaled them, but the grand total had to be close to one thousand or more over a thirty-eight-year span.

Most performances, lectures on Twain, some summers for a week at an Elderhostel, were for as little as a cup of coffee at some places, ten dollars in others, and the most I made was two thousand dollars at a Country Club. I performed as Mark Twain in over twenty states and those included Medical Conventions, Nurses Conventions, a convention at the Hilton Hotel in New York City, and the Delta Queen, Mississippi Queen, American Queen riverboats on the Mississippi River, Bell of Louisville on the Ohio River, and the Delta King on the Sacramento River in California. After the performance at the New York City convention, I put on street clothes, and Mimi and I walked over to Broadway where I quoted a Twain line to her there on the sidewalk, and said, "Now, honey, we can say I performed on Broadway."

But for the next forty-four years, and with continuous practice and studying, I had the joy of impersonating the man who critics say is the Father of American Literature. Before Twain's works, all the authors in the United States copied the patterns of European authors. Mark Twain brought Americanism to America's literature.

*Adventures of Huckleberry Finn* has encountered a lot of criticism for being a racist book, mainly because of the use of the word "nigger" for 212 times. But these critics miss the meaning of the book. The "N" word was the only word used in 1885 in describing a Black person. The term African-American had not been invented. *Huck Finn* is the first book written depicting a Black man as a hero (staying with a wounded Tom Sawyer when Jim knew he would be captured for doing so), and mainly, a Black slave and a White boy became friends. How can that be a racist book? Those who know and write about Twain's works know that the book is not about racism, but about freedom. And in this case, it is not about freedom of Jim from slavery, but about Huck escaping from a racist culture to embrace a Black person as a friend. The book raises the question as to whether we can put aside what we have been exposed to all our lives and do what is right by accepting our neighbor the Black Person. Today, many have not reached that level of humaneness or that requirement for Christendom.

The outcomes of the Federal election in 1876 resulted in Federal Troops being withdrawn from the South and therefore the white supremacists began harassing and killing Black people in the daytime as well as their previous practice of murdering only in the nighttime. That same year Twain began working on Adventures of Huckleberry Finn.

My mother and many mothers expressed the admonition to "not get above your raising." Mark Twain says in *Huck Finn* that you s*hould* get above your raising, forget unscrupulous attitudes and actions, and become a genuine human being. Educated people should be adaptable to change, and it does not take a college degree to become educated. But people have to continuously work to attain that status throughout their life.

## *After Atlanta*

I retired in 1994 and Mimi retired in 1995. Our Atlanta house was put on the market in 1995. Our basement was a collection of filing cabinets containing of a lot of office paperwork—in case I was ever sued—Mark Twain scripts and journals, my father's electric saws and hand carpenter tools, some lumber and flower pots. We worked at getting the house in shape, and I worked on the yard to get it to look as good as the neighbor's. But I never got around to cleaning the basement. One afternoon the real estate agent came by with a client and went through the house while Mimi and I sat on the patio. After a short time, the client and agent came out and said he wanted to purchase the house. Mimi blurted out, "Have you seen the basement?"

But the client was not concerned about the basement. He liked the yard and asked one question: "How is the karma of the house; is it a happy house." We answered that we had been very happy in the house and that our children were happy.

He bought the house, but we took our home with us and moved to North Carolina and into my grandparents' log cabin—built in 1895—while our new house was being built just up the creek. We were happy in the cabin also, but Mimi did long for a thermostat in the wintertime, particularly when the fire went out of our wood-burning stove. Although I had been in education all my working years, I failed completely in teaching Mimi the joys of splitting wood for the stove. But she excelled in convincing me that her mother had not taught her to wash dishes and that was the job of the husband. Once our good friends Bill and Norma Crews visited my family in Candler, and Bill asked my father if he ever washed the dishes. My father replied, "No, it makes me nervous."

Our new home had a living room twenty-six feet wide and in an octagon shape—like the study Mark Twain had in Elmira, New York, where he wrote *Tom Sawyer* and *Huckleberry Finn*. Our walls were decorated with several Twain pictures and our book collection contained over three hundred by or about Mark Twain. One picture, of which I am pleased, was a picture of Hal Holbrook and me while we were attending a Mark Twain Convention at Elmira College in New York.

In 1997, Shelley Fisher Fishkin published *Lighting Out For The Territory*,[5] which is about Mark Twain and his teachings. The title was taken from the last words Huck spoke in his book. He said, "I better head out for the territory, because Aunt Polly is

---

5. Fishkin, Shelley Fisher, Lighting Out for the Territory, Oxfords, England, Oxford University Press, 1997, p.163.

planning to adopt me and civilize me, and I can't stand that. I've been there before." This is in reference to the trip down the river whenever he and Jim stopped at a town and encountered civilization and frequently became involved with dishonest and deceitful people. So late one night I was reading Fishkin's book and encountered these words in the chapter on Twain Impersonators:

> Occasionally part-time Twain impersonators get bitten by the bug and decide to ditch "real life" altogether. That's what happened to Marvin Cole in 1994. Then President of DeKalb College, the third-largest college in the Georgia University System, Cole resigned his job and dedicated his life to impersonating and studying Mark Twain. He was proud that during his thirteen years as President, DeKalb had doubled its enrollment and employed more minority faculty than any other college in Georgia, but he was also committed to the higher education Twain was capable of providing. "I believe so much in what Mark Twain was trying to do and say," Cole told a reporter. "He said we are hypocritical people who don't know how to live with each other. I don't think we've progressed over the years in learning to become humane, and because of the increased diversity in our country, if we don't learn how to live together, we can become another Bosnia. I guess my act serves as both entertainment and a warning."

I was so surprised to read Fiskin's words that I wanted to wake Mimi and read it to her, but I did not want the bruises that would result. I did not become rich doing Twain, at least moneywise. I reported the income on my Income Tax and the preparer expressed concern some years that I spent more on performing Twain than I earned and he feared the IRS would consider it a hobby. The last white suit I purchased cost $2,300 and I can't even wear it to church for fear people would confirm a weirdness already suspected.

My real pay cannot be calculated. I performed Twain a lot at Wednesday night church services and nursing homes at no charge. But one day a lady at the cash register at Jesse Israel & Son's Garden Center told me that her mother had heard my Twain program at the nursing home and that she "had laughed more than she had in ten years." That makes all the study and practice time worthwhile. I did not make a lot of money lecturing and performing Mark Twain, but the smiles and laughter, making people happy, and hopefully giving the real meaning of *Huck* and Twain has made me rich.

When the COVID-19 plague came to the United States, it brought a halt to Twain performances. The year 2020 was the 100th anniversary of women's right to vote. A symposium on the anniversary was being held in Cashiers and a Professor from Western Carolina University asked me to speak on Mark Twain's view of women voting. Twain was a big advocate of women's rights, and I spent a considerable amount of time preparing for a forty-five minute presentation. But alas, it had to be cancelled because of our COVID-19 gift from China. Although Washington seemed to view China as a big enemy, it was funny that everything we purchase has a "Made In China" label. But that is one gift for which I wish China had adopted a more selfish attitude.

After my retirement in 1994, Dekalb College became Georgia Perimeter College and is now one of the Schools of Georgia State University. I was Dean for eight years, President for thirteen years, and retired in 1995. The faculty raised money for Mimi and I to have a forty-three-day vacation in New Zealand and Australia. What a gift! I took a five-day walk called "Milford Trek" in New Zealand across a mountain with patchy snow while Mimi stayed in the hotel drinking wine and reading trashy novels. In Australia, we attended an opera at the big Opera House and took a four-day train ride across Australia from Sydney to Perth and back. It was a fabulous experience, and it was made more wonderful by traveling with a fantastic companion. At night we would cut the light out in our cabin and look out on the desert to view kangaroos leaping across the countryside. On our way back, we stopped at Alice Springs and then at Uluru, known as Ayers Rock. The hotel roused me up at 4:30 a.m. one morning and (while Mimi stayed in the hotel continuing to read trashy novels), I, with a number of others climbed the huge monolith famous for its gorgeous auburn hue. The early morning hours were necessary because of the heat. Uluru was visited by hundreds of thousands of tourists every year. Mimi and I will be forever grateful to the faculty of DeKalb College for giving us the pleasure and learning experience of visiting New Zealand and Australia.

We moved into our new home in 1997 and have enjoyed it tremendously. We live on twenty acres originally purchased by my great-grandfather prior to the Civil War and on which he raised wheat, corn and vegetable crops. Originally it was seventy-five acres but was split up and given to the heirs. Daughter Lisa with husband Greg and son Andrew built a home on the property, and son Tom moved in with us in 2016. Son Michael lives in Cartersville, Georgia, and is Director of Finance and Payroll at Dalton State College. But now our kids are trying to reverse their proper roles by treating their parents as teenagers. Mimi and I hear "Where have you been?" "Do you know it is after 10 p.m.?" "Did you take your medicine?" "When did you change the oil in your car?" "You should not be plowing a garden at your age," on and on. I tell you, children can be a pain when you obtain your mature years. Try to stay away from them if you can.

## *Incidentals*

A favorite biographical question is, "What is the greatest challenge mankind faces?" My quick all-encompassing answer is "ignorance." Ignorance means lacking knowledge or experience—uninformed. Knowing the truth can help one make proper decisions. If unaware of the circumstances, how can one come to the proper conclusion? If one knows the disease, one can determine the cure. If one does not know the best product, how can one know what to purchase? If one does not know if the preacher or prospective congressperson is a good person, how can one know if he or she should listen to him or her? Oxford Philosophy Professor John Alexander Smith in 1914 made what I believe is the best definition of being educated: "Nothing that you will learn in the course of your studies will be of the slightest possible use to you in after life—save only this—if you work hard and diligently, you should be able to detect when a man is talking rot, and that, in my view, is the main, if not the sole, purpose of education."

Martin Luther King Jr. reminded us that the educated person is incomplete without character. He told us to be wary of teachers who "... impart knowledge and thinking skills but fail to cultivate compassion and integrity. The most dangerous criminal may be the man gifted with reason, but with no morals." To me, an educated person knows that to fail to love one's neighbor leads to destruction.

My current interests include my family, friends, books, would love to play old people's tennis, gardening, storytelling, learning more about Mark Twain, music, my Serendipity Sunday School Class and church Journey Book Group, and doing my little bit for the homeless people at Haywood Street Congregation in Asheville.

My current bucket list would include keep learning, travel the Danube on a riverboat, take trips on Mississippi riverboats, and visit the western part of the United States. If I could go back in a time machine to visit, I would like to watch Peter's face when he stood there with two fish in his hands before a crowd of five thousand people and Jesus saying, "Feed Um."

To date my best novels and non-fiction books are *Adventures of Huckleberry Finn* by Mark Twain, *To Kill A Mockingbird* by Harper Lee, *Walden's Pond* by Henry David Thoreau, *Man's Search For Meaning* by Viktor Frankl and *The Grapes Of Wrath* by John Steinbeck. My most favorite movies are *To Kill A Mockingbird*, *Out Of Africa*, *The Cowboys*, *Zulu*, and *The Sound Of Music*.

I am most grateful for a Mimi, a wonderful family, having been born into a good family, reasonable health for age 90, having a lifetime of wonderful experiences in education, good friends, our home, and being able to continue a relationship and learning how humans can become humane to other humans.

To close, I give a quote from author Mark Sullivan in a book I really enjoyed titled *Beneath a Scarlet Sky.*[2] An old man named Pino Lella says to his young friend Carletta, "You know, my young friend, I will be ninety years old next year, and life is still a constant surprise to me. We never know what will happen next, what we will see, and what important person will come into our life, or what important person we will lose. Life is change, constant change, and unless we are lucky enough to find comedy in it, change is nearly always a drama, if not a tragedy.

But after everything and even when the skies turn scarlet and threatening, I still believe that if we are lucky enough to be alive, we must give thanks for the miracle of every moment of every day, no matter how flawed. And we must have faith in God, and in the Universe, and in a better tomorrow, even if that faith is not always deserved."

---

.2. Sullivan, Mark. *Beneath a Scarlet Sky.* Seattle, WA, Lake Union Publishing, 2018.

Friends are a major source of one's education, whether in the dormitory or in the cornfields. We do not have pictures of all our friends, but these depict the quality of Cole friends. They helped make us who we are.

Ed and Lorena Bumgarner – Friends from Candler High School days.

Flora Devine: Vice President for Legal Affairs at DeKalb College. She was exceptional in character and as a team member, and gave enormous knowledge and assistance for legal matters in a trying time.

Fred and Barbara Hill. Fred was Executive Vice President at DeKalb College. He was solid as a rock as a friend, devotion to helping other people and building a better college.

Bill and Norma Crews

The US Air Force was in my opinion a significant part of my early education. I had one year of college at Mars Hill but the military gave me the experience of discipline and teamwork. More importantly, It taught me that people "not like me", like Catholics, Black people, and Yankees, when I got to know them, were people "just like me." This learning had not been a part of my Sunday School training. Two of those people are pictured on this page, Thomas Pillion from Pittsburg Pa. and Gilbert Paulin from Bridgeport, Connecticut. Both Catholic, they gave me new insight into Christendom. The big lesson was to beware of how some people interpret the Bible. Our first son was named for Thomas Pillion, on the right, and Gilbert Paulin pictured below.

Thomas and Mary (Chickie) Pillion

Gilbert Paulin

Top: The Journey Group from Central Methodist Church – Asheville pictured in 2014. Seated: Dr. Jerry Cook, Mickey Cook, Mimi, and Dan Patterson. Standing: Ann and Logan Merritt, Marvin, Lee and Amy Loy, Dell and Sherman Dillard, and Glenda Patterson. Doug and Carol Wingeier were also members of this group. As of November, 2021, this group has been meeting and discussing *Biblical Principles and Current Society* since September 2006. The only thing approaching disagreement was Dell Dillard expressing the outrageous opinion that the University of North Carolina had a better Academic Program than Western Carolina University. I am not sure what chapter of the Bible caused Dell to make such a statement, but I suspect Job. However, the group forgave him.

Bottom: The "Once a Year Bridge Playing Attempters" of Georgia. Front: Norma Crews, Mimi, Floy Cross, Elma Hill, Wendall Cross. Back: Bill Crews and Dr. Arthur Codington.

Jim Moore in a jealous pose, envious of the handsome dude on his shirt. Bill Crews, Marvin and Randy Pierce testing the swing on the Cole's back porch during their visit in April 2022. Bill was Vice President of Student Affairs at DeKalb College and Randy was the chief administrator of the Gwinnett Campus, later becoming President of Highlands College in Rome, Georgia. Below: Storytelling friends Shella Kay Adams and Gary Carden with Mr. Twain.

The Cat's Meow: Lisa and Kimberly; Patricia and Lisa; Melissa and Lisa; Lisa, Michaela and Jake; and Tiger. Tiger preferred not to be seen in a picture with Lisa.

When Tom moved to the mountains, he became interested in a certain kind of chemistry. Our friend and neighbor Ken Henson was his teacher.

Left: Doug and Steve Swayngim, LeRoi Moore, And Tom.

At the Cole family vacations, many times located at Mexico Beach in Florida, each evening we would have "school" in the way of a study of a book, discussion of a movie, a trivia night, and other "kinda" education activities. The pictures on this page depict Lisa with the book we studied one year. Lisa was the discussion leader for this event. Also, Tom is pictured with the Tee-shirt obtained for that year and the bottom picture shows our evening out at a local restaurant.

"Literature is never dull when Marvin Cole is around. With the perfect timing of a stand up comedian and the flair and fervor of an evangelist, Cole entertains an audience with recitations of tall tales and short anecdotes.
—*Tharon A Giddens*
*Atlanta Journal Constitution*

"I think you capture the spirit of Mark Twain as he would have wanted. You have the rare talent of speaking to every single person in an auditorium. You look the part, you act the part – you are Mark Twain."
— *Robert B Williams*
*Kennesaw State University*

"Tom Sawyer will never be the same."
— *Doug Lipman*

"Twain made the statement that '...in all his works he was either preaching or teaching.' Marvin Cole continues that course of action with his presentations."
— *Sandra Gudger*
*Founder, Asheville Storytelling Circle*

### Performances
Root-Ta-Peg
Building Privies
What Stumped the Blue Jays
My Grandfather's Ram
Tom Sawyer Whitewashing a Fence
Adam and Eve (with Mimi Cole)
Stories from Afghanistan and Pakistan

### Lectures-Dramatization-Discussion
What is Huck Finn About
The Other Side of America's Best Humorist

### Experience
American Personal and Guidance Convention – NYC
Tellabration of Asheville – Featured Teller
Data Research Convention – St. Louis
State Legislature – Georgia
English Teachers of Georgia – Calloway Gardens
Elderhostel – Dalton State College (five consecutive years)
Steamboats on the Mississippi –
*American Queen, Delta Queen, Mississippi Queen*
University of Kentucky – *Belle of Lousiville*, Ohio River
Sacramento River – *Delta King*, California
American School Counselors Convention – Atlanta
Georgia Tech and University of Georgia Foundation
Georgia State University

Numerous chuches, nursing homes, civic clubs,
high school and college English classes,
and fund raising programs for various organizations

For more information:
Marvin M. Cole
165 Ridge Road, Candler, NC 28715
828-665-7674
samtwain1@aol.com

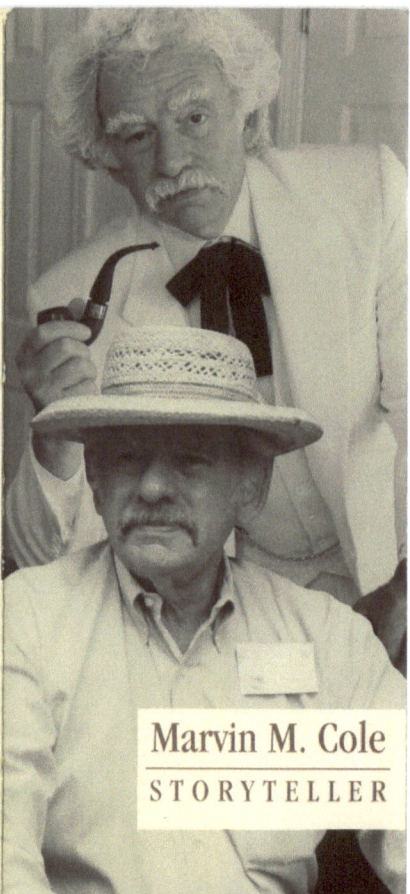

## Marvin M. Cole
### STORYTELLER

## Tall Tales & Short Anecdotes...

Marvin tells stories of past and present from Appalachian sources, mountain tales, stories originating in the Western United States, riverboat tales, and experiences derived from his five years of living in Afghanistan and Pakistan. Most of his repertoire is taken from the works of Mark Twain. In fact, six hours of Twain is available from his over twenty years of study and research, but you do not have to listen to all of it at one time.

Discussions following performances are welcome unless it is in a theater setting. Questions are welcome.

Cole is a member of the Asheville Storytelling Circle, the National Storytelling Network, and the Southern Order of Storytellers in Atlanta. His goals in storytelling are to help people laugh and enjoy life, and particularly to look at how we can understand and appreciate other people.

### Marvin's Own Tale

Marvin Cole grew up in an abandoned schoolhouse on Hookers Gap Road in Candler, NC about twelve miles from Asheville. The area is called "Pole Creek" for individuals needing a more high sounding sophisticated domiciliary location. He presently lives on the farm acquired in the middle of the nineteenth century by his Great-Grandfather.

Although he grew up listening to stories, telling them before a group did not come easy. He almost dropped out of college in the sophomore year because of a required speech course. Shyness was overriding any thought of speaking to more than two people at a time. But a girlfriend and present wife shamed him into taking the course, and a year later he was elected President of the Student Body at Western Carolina.

Although a lot of his stories are from the works of Mark Twain, he also tells stories about the mountain people of the Appalachian area and other tales.

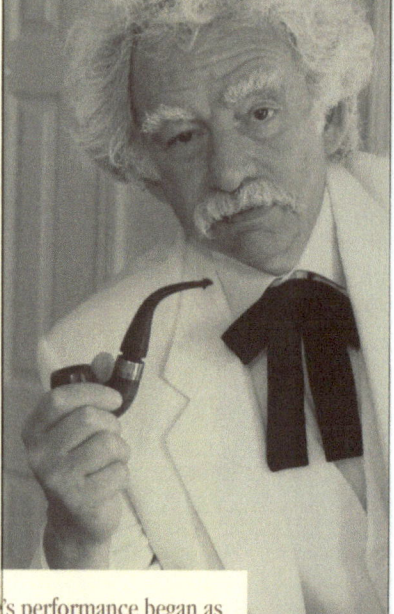

"Cole's performance began as he stepped onto a dark stage illuminated only by the small flame from a match to light his Twain-like corn cob pipe."

L-R Top Row Mayumi, Lisa, Greg. Second Row Tom, Mimi, Marvin, Mike. Third Row Jason, Marcia, Freya

# 2

## Miriam Joyce West Cole: Call Me Mimi

# Miriam Joyce West Cole: Call Me Mimi

I was born on July 3, 1936, in Clyde, North Carolina, which is a few miles west of Canton. My parents were Walter West and Catherine Haynes West. I suspect that my ancestors were German, Scotch and Irish, like most people living in the Appalachian Mountains. My father, a mechanic, died when I was 6 months old as a result of a blood clot following an appendectomy.

In 1940, my mother married Coke Candler from Candler, North Carolina. They first met at a square dance when my mother was visiting a friend in Candler. Two weeks later, they married.

The newlyweds returned from getting married in South Carolina and picked up my sister Norine and me to return to a new home in Candler. My Grandmother Haynes woke me up and told me I was to meet and go home with my new father. They said later that I said, "I do not want a new father and just let me sleep." But I was bundled up and put in the back seat of Coke Candler's new Ford automobile. On the way home, I peed on my new father's leather-seated Ford. I did not remember such things, but they are the kinds of things adults remember and tell about their children. Such matters of private heart, mind and bladder upset parents at the happening but later turn out to be on a list of very funny things to tell friends.

So I was raised in "Old Candler Town." The town part consisted of two grocery stores, a pool hall and several homes. Young ladies were instructed not to enter the pool hall. One reason was that young men used to hang around the door and whistle at girls passing by.

My Step-Father Coke Candler was a graduate of Duke University. He taught math and was the coach at Sand Hill High School. Although I never got to know my biological father, I considered Coke Candler as my father, and he disciplined me accordingly. He was a good father to me.

Mimi preparing for a DeKalb College Faculty Reception.

6/16/82 THE DEKALB NEWS/SUN PAGE 5 C

### Choral Guild Sings At College

William Noll, right, conductor of the Choral Guild of Atlanta, accepts the congratulations of Dr. Marvin Cole, president of DeKalb Community College, following a performance at the south campus. Mr. Noll has achieved distinction as a symphonic conductor, a pianist, and a choral director. Both he and the choral group are gaining a national reputation as a result of several successful eastern tours.

"If one had to name a star for the night, it would be the chor... the Choral ... of Atlanta, which thund... magnificently and precisely under the direction of WILLIAM ...

**WILLIAM NOLL**
Music Director and Conductor

**Proudly Announces Its**
**1985   SEASON   1986**

The Choral Guild of Atlanta in Symphony Hall, 19...

---

Dear Mimi,

Just a note to tell you that we enjoyed your solo last Sunday. "How Great Thou Art" has special meaning for Frank and me and you do it so beautifully, as you do all your solos. We are so fortunate to belong to a church where there is so much talent.

Sincerely,
Mary Stallard

---

Christmas, 19...

Dearest Marvin & Mimi,

Just a note to thank you both for all of your kindnesses & support throughout the year. My person... the arts of Atlanta are greatly blessed by your s... Sincere best wishes for all of the Coles for 1981

Most since...
William

**thank you**

My father's success at Sand Hill caused him to be named Athletic Director and Coach at the Enka Rayon Plant that was built by the Dutch in 1928. The Enka Plant and the Canton Paper Mill were two major economic factors in building the middle-class in Western North Carolina. Industrial plants were being built in many states. They had gymnasiums and sponsored the professional basketball and baseball teams of that period. These teams were a major source of entertainment for the community. The Enka gym was sold out when the Harlem Globetrotters came to play.

So my new father was doing well and building a good reputation in the community as Enka Coach when in 1941 the Japanese attacked our country. He joined the U.S. Navy and became an officer providing physical training for navy recruits at Occidental College in Los Angeles. My mother and 2-year-old sister, Kitty, accompanied him to California. My older sister, Norine, and I lived temporarily with our grandparents. I am told that in that setting I became very spoiled, but I personally believe that people making such statements were exaggerating.

When my father found an apartment in Los Angeles, he sent train tickets for Norine and me to come to be with the rest of the family. The train ride was a new and interesting experience. Norine was about 13 years old but looked older. She was a beautiful young lady. The train had many soldiers and sailors as passengers and Norine's being so attractive rendered a lot of attention. Norine was appreciative of the attention but was annoyed by her little sister who was also looking for attention. I made statements with a decidedly Southern twang that embarrassed Norine, who repeatedly tried to get me to shut-up. But she failed because I was enjoying the game.

We lived in Los Angeles for two years and then my father was transferred to San Diego, and we lived in a house in Descanso, which is a small town in the Cuyamaca Mountains. Descanso is a Spanish word meaning "rest from labor."

My pestering Norine on the train was only basic training for future annoying tactics, particularly with boyfriends. Following WWII, one evening after we had returned to Candler, Norine was in the living room of our home listening to a suspenseful story on Fox Radio Theater. So I sneaked in the room, crawled behind the sofa and right at a crucial moment in the story I unplugged radio. If one needs an example of vehement fury, Norine's actions exceeded the requirements.

My expertise in the art of harassment apparently reached professional level after Norine began dating LeRoi Moore. One day Roi was riding down Candler School Road with his Uncle Jack who saw me walking on the side of the road. Uncle Jack said, "There is your girlfriend's sister."

LeRoi immediately said, "Run over her."

***

One of my jobs as a child was to empty the chamber pots every morning. Sometimes, or many times, I would forget, and the pots would become quite full until my mother discovered my negligence. But when one starts a working career cleaning chamber pots, the other downsides in life smell like roses.

As a child, I loved to sing. At the time, we had an outhouse for a toilet and usually I sang while sitting on the pot with the door wide open. Our Aunt Mabrye and Bryon Brenton lived next door and one day, Uncle "B", as we called him, walked by and said, "Good Morning, Mimi."

Through the open door, I replied, "Good Morning, Uncle B," and then kept on singing to the world.

*\*\*\**

Experiences in my youth that influenced my adult life revolved around parents who encouraged education. I have enjoyed good music all my life and have been a soprano soloist in many church choirs.

I began singing solos in church and at funerals while still in high school.

My principal in school was Mr. Dan Cooke. Mr. Cooke had an interest and appreciation for music and art and because of my singing placed me with the high school chorus when I was still in the eighth grade. He also arranged for me to take voice lessons from a professional musician. Voice lessons continued throughout college and many years of my life as I sang with the Atlanta Choral Guild and Embry Hills United Methodist Church Choir in Atlanta.

My favorite vacations as a child were trips to the western part of the United States. My father was an enthusiastic and very capable trout fisherman so our trips involved trout streams and camping out. My mother, sister Kitty and I got to see a lot of wonderful scenes, but we were joyous when we had to spend a night in a motel.

I graduated from Candler High School in 1954 and entered Western Carolina (college) University with a major in Elementary Education. Although tempted to major in music, my very astute voice teacher in Asheville informed me of the difficulties and sometimes despicable activities one has to go through to succeed in the professional world. Therefore, I decided to become a teacher and at the same time participated in the college chorus, musicals and operettas, as well as church choir. After Marvin and I began dating, some of our movie and dining money was earned from my singing at weddings and funerals.

When I was home for the summer from college, Kitty and I shared a bedroom upstairs in our home in Candler. After Marvin and I had been dating for a while, he came to pick me up for a date one summer evening and my father asked him to accompany him upstairs. Coke led Marvin into our bedroom where Kitty and I had dispersed our underwear, blouses, skirts and other paraphernalia on the floor, bedposts, the bed and closet doors. It was a mess, but a typical teenage scene. My father looked at Marvin and said, "I just wanted you to know what you are getting into."

Kitty and I were first shocked, then aggravated, then angry at my father. Kitty was furious. I think Coke was trying to teach Kitty and me a lesson more than he was warning Marvin.

My father treated Norine and me as his own children and yet a bit different than Kitty and Eddie whom he fathered. I always called him "Father" or "Daddy" because he was the only father I knew. However, Norine called him Coke because she remembered her biological father. Coke left it up to us. But he gave chores to Kitty like picking and breaking beans and working in the garden but did not give me such assignments. I have wondered if he sensed that my music interests and garden-work did not complement each other. But there was no question about the love and concern Coke Candler had for his wife and four children.

***

Marvin's good friend in high school was Ed Bumgarner and my friend and roommate my freshman year was Ed's sister Mary Joe, whom everyone called "Jody." Ed and my other good friend, Lorena Smith, daughter of Hominy Baptist Church's pastor Rev. M.D. Smith, were dating. In June 1955, Ed, Jody and Lorena conspired to have me go on a blind date with Marvin. Marvin had just been discharged from four years in the U.S. Air Force and just returned from three years serving in England. I was not dating anyone and had no prospects, so Marvin told later that he was the final resort for my dating anyone. We had a good evening, and so I decided to give the poor boy a chance. I figured that culture prevalent on Beaverdam should give someone from Pole Creek an uplift.

We dated all summer while I worked at the Buncombe County Court House and Marvin assisted his father as a carpenter-helper. We continued dating as we attended Western Carolina for our sophomore year and junior year. Marvin had previously attended Mars Hill College for one year and had taken University of Maryland courses in the Air Force.

During our junior year after we had dated for over a year, I decided we should break up for a while and test the waters to see if we were serious. Marvin was hurt and told my mother that Mimi had decided to date other boys. My mother instructed Marvin to go back and date the prettiest girl he could find, a homecoming queen if available. So Marvin did that. I was furious with my mother for conspiring against me. But, I hate to admit, it worked, and I cannot say that I lived to regret it, but I am still peeved that my mother collaborated with Marvin.

We married the summer after our junior year. Marvin had been elected President of the Student Body and we had an exciting year with presidential duties. Because of his work as Student Body President and the Dean liking my solos (I sang in the Cullowhee Baptist Church he attended), Marvin was given the job as Director of the Student Union when a vacancy occurred. We lived in a two-room apartment in the Student Union while Marvin continued as Director, teaching Orientation Classes all year and working on his Master's Degree.

Tommy and Lisa were born while we were living in the Student Union. Therefore, they claim they were intellectual giants since they attended college during their first two years of life.

Faculty members and administrators encouraged Marvin to obtain a doctorate, and we ended up with his attending graduate school at Indiana University in Bloomington, Indiana. We lived in an old Army barracks remodeled for eight apartments. The rent was fifty dollars a month. Marvin got a job as Graduate Assistant to a Professor, which paid $100 a month, and I got a part-time job teaching pre-school at the University Laboratory School at $110 per month. We paid a lady in the downstairs apartment to baby-sit Tommy and Lisa. It is fortunate we had not been accustomed to sumptuous living. We looked forward to paydays because that meant we had meat for dinner. Beans became very important.

During the second year at Indiana, Marvin came home from his job at the School of Education and said to me, "Mimi, I have been recommended for a job with Indiana University overseas. How would you like to work in Pakistan for a couple of years?" I immediately asked, "Where is it?" Thus began my research of Pakistan. I read that life expectancy in that Asian country was twenty-eight years. I was age 27 at the time, and the prospects of going to Pakistan took on a negative effect.

I decided I did not want to go to Pakistan, and that same day Marvin came home saying he had told the Dean yes and gave a departure date. Marvin was very excited about the job, so I decided I would go if it was that important to him. One thing that made an impact on both of us was that the pay was $7,500 a year and free housing. We had looked forward to eating more than that one meat per month.

Dr. Stoner, a professor at IU, and his wife had spent two years in Pakistan working on the Indiana project. They spent a lot of time with us telling us about Pakistan and a lot of things we would experience. They did this with enthusiasm, which helped me switch to a more positive attitude.

Tommy was age 4 and Lisa age 2 when we traveled to Chicago's O'Hare International Airport for departure to Pakistan. While in the waiting room, a young man dressed in a Navy uniform came in, and Tommy immediately burst out with "I'm Popeye the Sailor Man." Bystanders applauded, but the young sailor stomped out with a very unpleasant look on his face. Tommy was unaware he had offended anyone.

We moved into a new, furnished house that was larger than any we had ever lived in before. We were advised to have household help because of the extra preparation for good sanitation and the fact that it was 114 degrees outside and the kitchen was not air-conditioned.

We settled into a routine. Marvin began his new job as Assistant to the Director of the Institution of Education and Research at the University of the Punjab. Dr. Ernest Horn, the Director, and his wife, Doris, were great friends and advisors as we learned the ways of this new culture. They lived about a block away from our home. I recall one time Marvin asked Ernest to come help in the selection of a carpet. Bargaining for most purchases was a standard and refined art in the Asian culture. So Ernest got down on his knees and thoroughly examined the carpet, counting the stitches, as the best carpets had not more than twelve stitches per inch. That is just one phase of the process of buying, with the seller's expecting a series of haggling and they seem disappointed if the buyer accepts the first price.

In the fall of 1963, Tommy started kindergarten at the American School, and Lisa was in a pre-kindergarten school administered and taught in a home by a spouse of one of the Indiana Team members. I taught fifth grade at the American School for two years.

It was important to us that our children be courteous and respectful to our servants and all Pakistanis. One afternoon, our houseboy named Piarah came to me and said, "Tommy and

Lisa are outside the gate saying rude things to people passing by."

When I got there, I saw Tommy in a homemade turban yelling at people. Tommy was in a turban made out of his blanket, and Lisa was dressed in an oversize sari. They were yelling the same thing: "Je Qundum Jowh" in the Urdu language. I asked Piarah what that meant. Reluctantly, he replied "Go To Hell." They did not learn those words from their parents or at their schools, so it must have come from the servants. That evening we had a family conference.

One of our lasting impressions was the poverty we saw—the worst poverty we would ever see until we worked in Afghanistan. We developed an appetite for curry, rice, lamb kabobs and chapatti bread. A good learning experience was learning a different culture and religion. That helps one to know his or her own culture and religion. A lifetime of good feelings was attained with our developing a friendship with Dr. Muhammad and Iqbal Nawaz who moved to the United States and lived in Cincinnati. The Cole family relished the together and communication times with Nawaz and Iqbal and their children Salman and Sara. Marvin said he learned a lot from Nawaz.

Sara became a successful psychiatrist. She recently told about her question to her father, "Why is the country next door to Pakistan far more progressive than Pakistan?

Nawaz replied, "Because Pakistan chose to educate only half its population and not educate the women. That is the reason we moved to the United States." That was Nawaz—a gentle, loving gentleman. We were fortunate to have the experience that Indiana University gave us because it positively affected the rest of our lives.

At the end of our two-year tour, we visited Germany and England on our way back home. Marvin wanted to visit his old Air Force Base in West Drayton, England. While there, he took us to a pub called The Cherry Tree about a block from the base. This was ten years after Marvin was stationed there, and as we walked in the door, the barman looked at Marvin and said, "Long time no see." I guess that says a lot. Marvin still remembered his name as Charlie Nailard.

***

We moved back to Bloomington, Indiana, for Marvin to finish his final year on the doctorate. Tom was in the third grade and Lisa in the first grade at the University School.

After completing his degree in 1966, Marvin was offered a job as Dean of Institutional Programs at Morehead State University in Morehead, Kentucky. One of the bright things about our living in Morehead was the birth of our son Michael Patrick.

Morehead was a lovely town and had good people, but the leadership was more political than academic, and Marvin was unhappy with the values of the President. So he accepted a job as Dean of Students at Atlanta Baptist College in Atlanta. It was exciting to be in on establishing a new college, but the finances were not available, and again Marvin was wary of the values of the President. The college was given to Mercer University as a Pharmacy School and we were again in search of a job.

So in 1970 Dean Thomas C. Schreck at Indiana University phoned Marvin and asked if there was interest in a job as Advisor in Student Affairs in their project at Kabul University in Afghanistan. And we were interested. The US/AID Official had turned down other candidates and selected Marvin. I am still perplexed as to why. But they did not ask me.

So we were off to Afghanistan with three children this time. We stopped this time in Hawaii, Hong Kong and Bangkok. And we had peculiar feelings when the pilot announced that we were flying over Viet Nam.

The first morning that we awoke in Afghanistan in our new residence in a ten-foot walled compound with a security guard, we heard loud announcements from the street. They became familiar sounds each morning as vegetable sellers progressed through the streets with donkeys with sidesaddles full of potatoes, tomatoes, melons, and other vegetables. You would hear "Bonji Rumi" for tomatoes and "Catchalou" for potatoes. But that morning a donkey let out a huge "hee haw" and all of a sudden a wide-eyed 2-year-old Michael was crawling into our bed and saying "What's thata Mommy."

It was far more peaceful in Afghanistan in the early 1970s than it has been up to the 2020s. Kabul being an Embassy City offered many activities and nationalities. The two older children attended the American International School of Kabul (AISK) and both participated in sports activities.

The American School had students from several countries although the majority were citizens of the United States. The AISK Community wanted the students to experience the normal school activities, which included athletics. So representatives from the U.S. Embassy, Peace Corps, U.S AID, and other agencies formed teams that played flag football in the fall and softball in the spring on Friday afternoons. It seems small potatoes compared to U.S. Friday nights, but it was a big occasion for the American and International communities with cheerleaders from AISK and with the U.S. Embassy selling hot dogs and hamburgers and cold drinks.

Marvin designed the first catalogue of courses and first permanent record report of student grades for the University. The Indiana group worked on an old house—cleaning and painting, which became the first women's dormitory at the University. About five years after we departed Afghanistan, the Americans left and the Russians moved into the country. The Afghans did not know peace since that time, and we often wonder what happened to the work we did, the friends we made, and the servants who probably had the best paying job of their lives while working for Americans.

Tommy and Lisa had a good deal of freedom to go from place to place during the day as long as it was in close proximity to our house. They learned enough "street Farsi" to get the message across. Tommy loved to go to the street vendors and get kabobs and naan (flat bread). Naan was baked in a big clay pot placed in the ground with a fire at the bottom. The flat dough was slapped against the wall of the pot where it stayed and cooked. The naan-maker would know when to reach down and obtain the cooked piece with a flat shovel-looking tool before it fell into the fire.

One afternoon the children and I needed to go to obtain groceries and planned to go by taxi. Taxi drivers were always anxious to get American fare because the pay was better and less haggling than they had to go through with the Afghans. As I hailed a taxi, Tommy hailed another one at the same time. The two came rushing to us and wrecked right in front of us. They began yelling and fighting each other. At that time one of our servants came out and encouraged us to come back inside the compound. He told us that the police would come and would demand money from foreigners just because we were present. Such are the stories we have of living in another culture. Such are the stories that make us compare with events in our own country and hope that we can always strive to improve our civilization.

The International Community in Kabul mounted two productions during our tour. Casting was done by auditions, including the orchestra that consisted of about ten people, some of whom could manage to stay in tune most of the time. The Director was Sally Lewis who was wife of the Charge d'Affaires or Resident Representative Samuel W. Lewis, who later became Ambassador to Israel.

The first production was Brigadoon and the second was H.M.S. Pinafore. I played and sang the role of Fiona in Brigadoon and Josephine in H.M.S. Pinafore. Marvin was Stage Manager and played the role of bartender Frank in Brigadoon and the role of Dick Deadeye in H.M.S. Pinafore. The house could seat only about seventy-five, but we packed it for both performances for seven nights each. Sally lost hair from listening to the only person available to play the bagpipes. He was just learning to play, and the screeching was out of this world.

The International Community and some Afghans were a very appreciative audience as such theater performances were not common in Afghanistan. Most of the Afghan entertainment consisted of listening to someone playing the sitar and/or drums.

I have often heard Marvin tell Mark Twain's statement about travel:

> Travel is fatal to prejudice, bigotry, and narrow mindedness, and many of our people need it sorely on these accounts. Broad, wholesome, charitable views of men and things cannot be acquired by vegetating in one little corner of the earth all one's lifetime.

I can only agree with Mr. Twain's thoughts.

Our experiences in Pakistan and Afghanistan made a good deal of difference in the continuing outlook of the Cole family about people and things and circumstances. We are fortunate that a lot of our women and men in the military and Peace Corps have experienced cultures other than the corner of the world in which they were born.

At the end of the three-year tour we returned to Atlanta where Marvin was Dean of Students, Academic Dean and eventually President of DeKalb College. During his presidency, the 16,000-student college went from county control to become a unit of The University System of Georgia. It is now an integral part of Georgia State University.

My profession in the teaching field involved kindergarten and elementary school at the Laboratory School of Indiana University, the American School in Lahore, Pakistan, and elementary school in the DeKalb School System in Atlanta. I finished my teaching career with DeKalb Board of Education as a kindergarten teacher for ten years at Ashford Park Elementary School. My years working with young children provided a very rewarding experience when considering job satisfaction.

Atlanta offered many musical opportunities for me that I greatly enjoyed. For years I sang with The Choral Guild of Atlanta, Atlanta Opera Chorus, and The Southeastern Savoyards and have had the good fortune to participate with choral groups two times in Carnegie Hall and in Florence Italy. I was soprano soloist with Embry Hills United Methodist and Morningside Presbyterian churches. I enjoyed taking voice lessons throughout this period and singing under the direction of William Noll.

***

Retirement in North Carolina beginning in 1995 has been enjoyable. Living in a log cabin Marvin's grandparents built in 1895 was a new experience. In the wintertime it gave me a new appreciation for a thermostat. Building our new home was exciting, and we are greatly enjoying it, sitting on the back porch and listening to a nearby creek. Spending more time with relatives has been wonderful, and I have enjoyed attending many of Marvin's Mark Twain performances.

Our daughter, Lisa, her husband, Greg, and our grandson Andrew built a home on the property and our son Tom lives with us. Tom is becoming quite a chef in our kitchen. His salmon dishes are outstanding. Son Michael works as Director of Finance and Payroll at Dalton State College in Dalton, Georgia. We enjoy the company of our children.

My current interests are my children, grandchildren and great grandchildren, my friends, reading, crossword puzzles, cooking, cooking television shows and music. The highest item on my bucket list is good health. My favorite movies are *Gone with the Wind, Out of Africa, Rebecca, Shenandoah,* and *To Kill a Mockingbird.*

One more significant fact about my life is that on numerous occasions, I have been asked the question, "What is it like living with Marvin?" And my response is, "I get a lot of sympathy from people."

Marvin and I have been blessed with many meaningful experiences and blessed with a long and happy marriage.

# BIOGRAPHIES

**LYNNETTE TALOVICH ANDERSON** (Hansel) is the choral director at Campbell High School (Fairburn) and soloist at Covenant Presbyterian Church. She holds the B.M. and M.M. degrees from West Virginia University where she had lead roles in *The Medium* and *The Rape of Lucretia*. She was also a soloist with the WVU orchestra in Haydn's "Paukenmesse" and as a 1971 "Young Artist Competition" winner. For the past four seasons she has sung in the chorus of the Atlanta Opera and continues her vocal studies in the studio of Elizabeth Colson.

**THOMAS ANDERSON** (Music Director) has served as conductor for all DeKalb Music Theatre productions since *Brigadoon*. Dr. Anderson is conductor of the DeKalb Symphony Orchestra and serves as chairman of DeKalb's Division of Fine Arts and Professor of Music. He has been a member of DeKalb's faculty since 1967

**JIM BRADFORD** (father) is a fellowship graduate of Manhattan School of Music in New York with a performance degree in opera theatre. He performed leading roles with the Manhattan Opera Theatre under Gian-Carlo Menotti and Leo Taubman. He has performed as a soloist at Town Hall in New York, with the Atlanta Symphony, and the Birmingham Civic Opera Association, and in numerous performances of opera and oratorio in the Atlanta area. A former regional winner of the Metropolitan Opera Auditions, he has performed other operatic roles including *Le Nozze di Figaro, Don Giovanni, Gianni Schicchi, The Crucible* and *La Boheme*. He has been a member of DeKalb's faculty since 1966.

**MIMI COLE** (mother) is a graduate of Western Carolina University and currently a graduate student at Mercer University of Atlanta. She is a teacher with the Dekalb School system. Before coming to Atlanta she sang Fiona in *Brigadoon* and Josephine in *HMS Pinafore* in community theatre productions. In Atlanta she has sung with the Choral Guild of Atlanta, the Southeastern Savoyards and the Atlanta Opera. She is a soloist at Morningside Presbyterian Church and continues vocal study with Elizabeth Colson.

**JANE GALLOWAY** (Witch) is a private voice instructor and is employed by Zee Medical. As a former adjunct faculty member at DeKalb College, Jane performed the roles of the Countess in *The Marriage of Figaro* and the Countess in *A Little Night Music* at North Campus. We last saw her on this stage as Maria in *West Side Story*. She has toured the Southeast with regional opera and theatrical companies. Jane has been extensively involved with children's opera and theatrical companies. Jane has been extensively involved with children's opera and is very familiar with *Hansel and Gretel* having previously performed the roles of Gretel and the mother.

**JENNIFER JENKINS** (Director, Set and Lighting Designer, Technical Director) has degrees from Dekalb College and the University of Georgia. She gained professional experience with the Harlequin Dinner Theatre, The Center for Puppetry Arts and on film crews for *Greased Lightning* and *The Prize Fighter*. She is in her seventh season as technical director at DeKalb College.

This look toward Hansel and Gretel was natural for Mimi since it had been used for many years directed to Marvin ... along with the stick.

| CAST | |
|---|---|
| Peter, a poor broom maker | Jim Bradford |
| Gertrude, his wife | Mini Cole |
| Hansel, their son | Lynnette Talovich Anderson |
| Gretel, their daughter | Lori Medlock |
| The Sandman | Chris Patton |
| The Dew Fairy | Evelyn Sponaugle |
| The Witch | Jane Galloway |

One of the many attributes in having children is having grandchildren and great grandchildren to spoil with no discipline responsibilities.

TOM WITH GRANDCHILREN SAGE, LEVI, MAGUIRE, KAI AND LINCOLN.

Above: Enjoying the nightlife in Australia.
Below: Sixtieth Wedding Anniversary. People kept saying to Mimi that they admired her stamina in surviving without doing him in.

- Enjoying life after retirement.
- At Marcia "The Boo Boo's" wedding reception in Peachtree City, Georgia.
- Mimi dancing with boyfriend.

Mimi and Marvin lived in the cabin from 1995-97 while our new home was built just up the creek. Marvin's Grandparents Basford and Ella Cole built the cabin in 1885. Marvin inherited 23 of the original 75 acres that included the home place. In the early 1930s the government ruled that every home must have a toilet either inside or out. Prior to that time most rural people, including my grandparents, accomplished nature's call in the woods or what was called "chamber pots". So President Roosevelt initiate a Works Public Administration (WPA) wherein 8.4 million people were employed to go around the country building bridges, outside johnnies, and various art and other projects. My grandfather had a healthy mistrust in the government, and after I was age twenty-something my Mother said that he stated: "Well, they can make me build it, but they can't make me "s---" in it. I am grateful that my grandfather sent those "be wary of government" genes down to Marvin.

In the 1940s, my father built a kitchen, dining room, and bath room to the cabin. Some may feel such a move would remove the elegant ambiance to the home, but my father said he had no use for the good old days.

After we moved out of the cabin it was used by family members including Jim and Karen Moore with Clint and Tanner, Janie Moore Brown, Steve and Maryann Swayngim with Rebecca and Josh, Jon and Kelly Deel, and Lisa and Greg Slocum with Andrew.

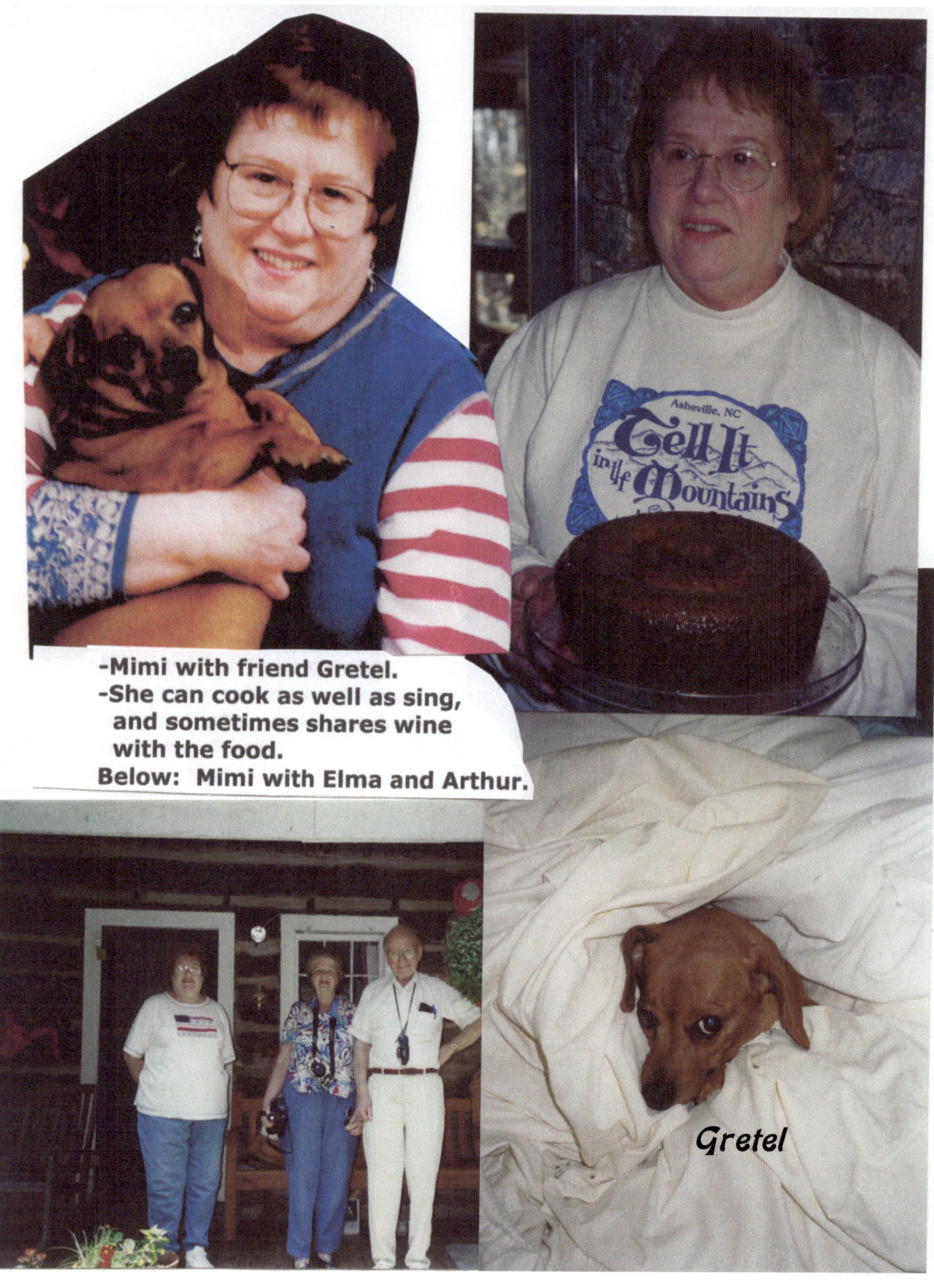

- Mimi with friend Gretel.
- She can cook as well as sing, and sometimes shares wine with the food.

Below: Mimi with Elma and Arthur.

Gretel

Above: The three sisters of the Coke and Catherine Candler family, who married the underfed but loved trio.. Below: LeRoi Moore, Robert "Bob" Swayngim, and Marvin. By some coincidence, Roi, Bob, and Marvin were centers on the high school football team. Perhaps that is a sign of political stance or that they had enough sense to know to which backfield person the ball should be centered to in a Single Wing Formation.

Above: Our three great nephews, Jeff Candler, Jim Moore, and Doug Swayngim, who played good blue grass music as members of the Dog House Band.

**DOG HOUSE BAND**

JIM AND KAREN MOORE, TWO OF OUR ROUGE RELATIVES.

NEPHEWS JEFF CANDLER, AND JIM MOORE. TWO OTHER NEPHEWS, MIKE MOORE AND DOUG SWAYNGIM, WERE MEMBERS OF THE BAND. MIKE DIED IN 1988 AND DOUG DIED IN 2019. MIMI AND MARVIN WERE BLESSED WITH WONDERFUL NIECES AND NEPHEWS.

Janie and Terry; again; Doug and Cindy; Janie and her kids and grandkids.

Doug and Cindy Swayngim

Mimi on her 60th wedding anniversary with Becky and Tony Candler, and Avery Squitieri.

Miriam Joyce West Cole emphatically declared in no way were these two pictures to appear in this book.

# *MIMI*
## EULOGY

Tomorrow is Mimi's birthday. Her 86th.

When we were living in Kabul, Afghanistan,
a friend came over after work one evening
    and happen to mention the festivities
        of his twenty-first birthday.
Then he asked Mimi about her birthday party
    and Mimi replied that she did not have
        a twenty-first birthday party.
The friend was dismayed that she had been deprived
    of such a significant event in one's life.

So he began scheming with others . . .
. . . he Americans in Kabul were always looking
    For a chance to get together
        to have a touch of home.
And thus, Mimi had a 21st birthday party
    in Afghanistan
        at the age of thirty-five.
That was fifty-two years ago
    and that friend was Bob Greenberg,
    who became a member of our family.
He retired from the University of Tennessee
    and was going to be here today
        but he and his wife Kathy
            were attacked by Covid.

But Mimi would be smiling at you today for coming
    to her eighty-sixth birthday,
        and she would appreciate your smiles.

She would also be a bit bothered because
    she was not one to seek attention.

But she enjoyed happy gatherings.

This week, one of Mimi's high school classmates said
she remembered Mimi as "JOLLY" --
    full of merriment, pleasant.

Socrates informed us that
    THE UNEXAMINED LIFE IS NOT WORTH LIVING.
Mimi operated under the philosophy that
    THE UNLIVED LIFE IS NOT WORTH EXAMINING.


We first met on a blind date
    arranged by our friends in 1955.
Double dating,
    we went to the Plaza Theater
        on the Square in Asheville to see a movie.

I had just returned from three years in the Air Force
    stationed in England.
I was a bit worried because
    I was a Pole Creek country boy
        and she was the step-daughter of the
Chairman of the County Commissioners.

**My English Language usage was atrocious…**
   on the level of "Shucks Far" and "I ain't gonna",
      "wait"n on you" and "I liked to died."

**so, to me, this was uptown girl dating backward boy.
She later told friends that**
   there was no other prospects in Candler  --
      that it was a desperation effort.

**Mimi was amused at my Southern mountain talk**
   mixed with a slight British accent.

\*   \*   \*

**She was taking voice lessons and sang very
sophisticated music … music from La Boeheim…**

**Would talk about Puccini and Renata Tebaldi.
And I was not sure she could reach**
   my level of singing
**NINETY-NINE BOTTLES OF BEER ON THE WALL.**

**And she never did.**

**But she raised me up to appreciate finer music.**

**She taught our kids to appreciate music.**

One time in Atlanta when our children were teenagers,
    Mimi talked about the attributes
        of the Nutcracker Suite.
Son Tom later
    In fulfilling the requirements of being an
        obnoxious teenager,
referred to it as the "BUT CRACKER"
    and boy was there ever a lecture
        on the hours and years it took to prepare
            and perform Tchaikovsky's masterpiece.

Of course, as is common with such faux pas,
    that very serious comeuppance at Tom's expense,
        became a family funny story
            often mentioned through the years.

We were pleased when our grandkids
    would ask to watch and listen to the movie
        Amadeus – about the life of Mozart.
We watched it at least one time every year.

But, in time, with proper training,
    patience, tender care,
        and proper nourishment,
Mimi learned from my carefully researched tutelage,
    the finer facets of music by
        Eddie Arnold, Ray Charles, Johnny Cash
            and on rare occasions …,
                Willie Nelson.

The two of us… fit together.

The family has been aware in recent weeks
    of Mimi's putting things in order.
She knew she was NOT going
    to be around much longer.

We would cry together.
She had her lists of things to be done.
She told me to get someone to help me
    clear her clothes and things from the house.
….Asked me to say <u>The Lord's Prayer</u> with her.

Lisa was present when she gave a "bless list"
    and named people she wanted blessed.


The Alzheimer's which had been creeping around
    for over a year
caused her to have
    different personalities
        particularly during the last month.
Sometimes she would yell at me to "get out"
    and often thought I was a medical assistant --
        not her husband.

As many of you know,
    Alzheimer's is a disturbing disease …
        for the family as well as the patient.
    There were humorous moments ---
One night she told me not to let the children see
    that we were sleeping together,
because she was a married woman.

Then, as this strange dementia
    disease exhibits its mysteries,
she would LATER REALIZE what she had done,
    It would come back to her,
        and she would want hugs and apologize.

She was in one of those bad moods
    when Ann and Logan Merritt came to stay with her
        when I had an appointment.
    They were dear friends.
        She told them to get out.

So in the hospital, she ask
    that we asked Ann and Logan for forgiveness.

TEN YEARS AGO, she hung the telephone up
    on a relative who was criticizing her son.
She asked that we ask that person to forgive her
    … for hanging up the phone.

After eighty-six years of living,
    If that level
        is the best you can come up with
    as the worst things you have done in your life   …

Well, I think of Peggy Lee's
    "If that's all there is, then lets go dancing."

We were never big outspoken
     religious demonstrators,
but only sickness prevented our going
       to church and Sunday school.
I guess we were suspicious
     of street corner yelling religious people
        and tried to live under a philosophy that
     **JESUS DID NOT REQUIRE A BUMPER STICKER**
       to show who he was
          or what he did.

But one could tell,
     when Mimi did NOT have concerns
       about WHO was listening,
         or who she might offend,
          or being accused of being pretentious,
     all of those mountain inbred inhibitions,
…one could tell how deeply she felt about religion.

---

When Mimi was having a bad day
     and I could not offer any food or drink
       to please her, ….
that all changed if one of her children, grandchildren
     or a friend would walk into the room.

The appreciation she had for her in-house family
     and extended family,
       was phenomenal.

When I walked into the hospital room
    and her eyes adjusted to focus on me –
those eyes would brighten up
    and the sweetest smile
        would come on her face.

And if that isn't love …

A life of love and grace.
    What else is more important?


Your presence honors us.
Thank you for what you mean to us.



Marvin M Cole
July 2, 2022

# 3

## Snapshot Reflections of My Life
## Colonel Thomas G. Cole, US Army (Ret.)

# Snapshot Reflections of My Life
# Colonel Thomas G. Cole, US Army (Ret.)

If I could change the time-period in which I was born, would I? All in all, I have had a wonderful life with over 62 years of good experiences and am grateful that I have. I do not say this in a bragging way, I say it because I was fortunate enough to be born in the time period that I was. My siblings, Lisa and Mike, and I had wonderful and loving parents who taught all their children right from wrong and to treat all people with dignity and respect. My father's career was in Education. As part of his continued pursuit of his Doctorate, we had the opportunity to live in Pakistan (1963–1965) and Afghanistan (1970–1973). Because I was born in 1959, these overseas assignments had a major impact on my life. No, I would not change.

Not only was I blessed with my parents (Marvin and Mimi) but my own family as well—my children (Jason, Freya, Marcia and Michaela) and their mother (Mayumi). We had many unique experiences that shaped my young adults into the folks they are now.

I believe one of the impacts of living overseas in my adolescence was the decision to join the Army after completing my Associate Degree at DeKalb College. I had been accepted to the University of Georgia to work on my Bachelor's Degree, but I did not feel I was ready. As such, I decided to join the Army in 1980 and to receive some education benefits upon my discharge (the new GI Bill). With one break in service and the opportunity to complete my Bachelor's Degree, I returned to the Army and eventually made it my career. I had found my calling, but it was not easy on my family with multiple moves within the U.S. and overseas and the multiple temporary assignments taking me away from home. As such, their leaving friends and schools and going to new schools and new locations was hard on them. However, I believe because of all the moves, my son (Jason) and daughters (Freya, Marcia and Michaela) learned to adapt to new environments, different people,

1980 at Stone Mountain, Georgia, the day before Tom entered The Army. Photo taken by Tom Stowe.
**L-R Lisa, Marvin, Michael, Mimi, Tom**

cultures, ethnicities...wherever they went. They made friends and still have many of them to this day. Being half-Japanese gave the children a head start on cultural adaptation from the beginning. I am so proud of them for their acceptance and respect of all people and the great adults they are today.

With this background, the following writing presents the Snapshot Reflections of my life from the beginning until my Army retirement.

**Birth/Early Years:**

I was born in 1959 at Mission Hospital in Asheville, North Carolina. Both of my parents were from Candler, NC (a town west of Asheville), as were both their parents. Because we had extended families in Candler, we would, at least once a year except when overseas, come back to visit. The first year of my life, I do not seem to recall much for some reason. My parents and I lived in "married housing" at Western Carolina University while Dad was finishing his Master's Degree and Mom started raising children.

In 1960 Lisa was born, and we stayed for one more year until we moved to Bloomington, Indiana, where Dad began working on his Doctorate Degree at Indiana University. We stayed in Indiana until 1963 when Dad was given the opportunity to work at the University of the Punjab in Lahore, Pakistan. This was a joint project between Indiana University and U.S. American International Development (USAID).

My time in Pakistan was between the ages of 4 and 6 so I have a few memories of my time there:

> The heat. It was not unusual for daytime highs to reach 120 degrees and above. We had Mango trees in our walled compound... Most houses had walled compounds with barbed wire on the top or what we called concertina wire in the Army. I ate so many mangos one day, right off the tree but forgot to wash my face. Because of all the acidity in the mangos, I had sores all around my mouth in a few days.
>
> One day I heard music outside the wall and walked outside. There was a man playing a flute to a dancing Cobra and working for tips. I watched from a distance.
>
> I was in the house and heard a shriek. The housemaid had been taking clothing from the wire on top of the wall and slipped off the ladder and had laid open her arm from hand to past the elbow while bleeding profusely. I was shocked to see so much blood. She was rushed to the hospital.
>
> I began my love of curry and associated dishes although I did not eat the curry as spicy hot as most Pakistanis do.
>
> We took a trip to India; the Indian border is close to Lahore. We visited New Delhi, many towns along the way, and the Taj Mahal. I again ate a lot of curry.
>
> We were eating at a very proper British five-star restaurant in New Delhi that included gloved waiters. My sister had an accident, a loose bowel movement on the pillow under her and on top of the chair. So, the white-gloved waiter

(L-R) Top Row: Tom, Jason, Mayumi  Second Row: Quincy, Marcia, Freya
Third Row: Michaela

very properly removed the pillow, to the horror of the surrounding tables, and replaced it while my mother rushed Lisa out of the restaurant.

One Christmas I was given a full-dress Marine uniform, and I thought I looked sharp. It may have been an indication of something in my future.

In 1965 our tour in Pakistan ended and we moved back to Indiana.

## Back to Indiana:

While in Indiana our apartment (previous WW II housing) was in walking distance from the Indiana University football stadium. I remember going to some games with Dad and blowing a big, long, red plastic bugle supporting the Hoosiers.

I was outside the Indiana apartment one day playing while Mom was washing dishes as she was looking out the window. I was having a good time playing with friends and suddenly had to pee, so I proceeded to do so on a tree. The next thing I know is Mom came running from the other side of the apartment, freaking out about me peeing outside. I remember thinking, "What is the big deal?" I was busy.

**Morehead, Kentucky:**

In 1966 we moved to Morehead, Kentucky, where Dad began work at Morehead State University. Morehead was a small, quaint town where just about everything was in walking distance from our house. A very safe and great place for a child to grow up.

My friend, his father and I decided to go for a walk one day to the lake. I had been up there on several occasions and noticed how many snakes were in the water or near it. So being 7 years old, I looked and gawked at everything except what was in front of me. I then started hearing a rattling sound and suddenly heard, "STOP!" My friend's father grabbed me by the shoulder. He said, "Don't Move!" Right in from of me was a very mature rattlesnake all coiled up. The father, from behind me, very slowly picked up a big rock and dropped it on top of the snake. I did not spend much time at that lake anymore.

*** 

One of my biggest treats in Kentucky was to watch cartoons on Saturday mornings while eating my new favorite food, Lay's potato chips.

In the winter, I walked home from school one day across a bridge when I noticed a speeding car with teenagers driving by with one of them hanging out the window. The next thing I knew I was hit in my left temple with a snow ice-ball with the same size and feel of a baseball. I almost fell in the creek below and remember thinking, as a 7-year-old, "Why did he do that?"

Once I was at school surrounding the teacher's desk with several other students. Being curious as most kids were, I reached and picked up something from the teacher's desk. The next thing I knew, the teacher slapped me in the face while yelling, "Don't touch things without permission." I do not think she ever made Teacher of the Year.

We adopted a dog named Brownie . . . a sweet lovable mutt who loved all of us. One day, Mom, Lisa and I were starting to walk downtown, and Brownie wanted to come as usual. Before the walk, Brownie had been enjoying a nice bone and started walking after us with the bone. The problem was he wanted to go on the walk with us but still enjoy the bone, but it would always come out of his mouth and fall to the street. After the third drop, Brownie growled at the bone on the street and proceeded to follow us.

We were coming back from a trip to North Carolina, and we were in a rural Kentucky town getting gas late at night. While Dad was filling up, I went into the gas station to get a Snickers bar and proceeded to pay for it. The attendant was sitting at a desk facing outside when I tapped his shoulder to pay for the candy bar. He suddenly whirled around and slapped me. He was deeply sorry, and I got the candy bar free. I have always wondered had he been robbed before or suffering some sort of PTSD? I was getting tired of being slapped.

One of my treats in Morehead was to eat at the Eagle's Nest restaurant and eat the turkey open-face sandwich with gravy. My other treat was going to the movie on Saturdays where for a dollar, I could watch the movie, have some popcorn and a Coke. Years later Dad revealed that Mike was probably conceived while I was gone from home during one of these very encouraged movie sessions. I am not sure where they sent Lisa.

As we were close to Cincinnati, Ohio, Dad, friends of his and I went to watch my first professional baseball game between the Chicago Cubs and Cincinnati Reds. My love for baseball began.

One day I heard a song on the car radio. I really liked it, by an artist named Herb Albert. I asked Dad if he could get me the record, and the next day I had *Casino Royal* by Herb Albert and the Tijuana Brass. The love of jazz began right there.

**Georgia:**

In 1968 we moved to Doraville, Georgia, a suburb of Atlanta. Dad took a position at Atlanta Baptist College, now an off-campus center of Mercer University. This was the biggest American city I have ever lived in, and I began to root for the Atlanta Falcons and Braves. I also played little league baseball and fantasized about playing at Atlanta Fulton County stadium. I hope one day the "Falcons" will win a Super Bowl.

I had to go the dentist one day. We went to a medical complex with several offices to include another dentist. The other dentist's name was Dr. William D. Kay, and I remember telling my mom this was not a good name for a dentist.

When we moved to Georgia, we brought with us a barely used 1966 Pontiac Bonneville. The car was made for a GM executive, and it was equipped accordingly. It also had a 455 horsepower engine, and it eventually became my first car ... probably not a wise decision for a newly licensed driver, but I only had to replace the tires a few times. Prior to me getting my license, Mom, like all moms, took us here, there and everywhere. My mother had just obtained her license a year prior and was still pretty antsy every time she went out. Mike and I were being driven somewhere that day when she stopped at a stop sign prior to executing a right turn. As there was gravel on the road and maybe a little too much on the gas when Mom turned right, she burned some good rubber. She did not appreciate it when I yelled from the back seat, "Get it, Mom!"

> **Some new experiences while in Georgia:**
> • Going to a Braves' game and almost catching a fly ball.
> • Going to another game and having all my baseball heroes playing: Hank Aaron, Phil Niekro, Willie Mays and Willy McCovey. It was Braves against the San Francisco Giants, and with the exception of Phil Niekro all of them hit a homerun.
> • Going to the downtown Atlanta Krispy Kreme and getting fresh hot doughnuts off the line and eating a dozen.

In fifth grade I fell in love with my teacher who was named Ms. Hogg ... she was anything but. A recent graduate of the University of Georgia, she was flat-out beautiful. She had a great personality and was exceptionally good to all of us. One day one of the boys in class asked to use the restroom down the hall. As he was leaving the class, Ms. Hogg reminded him of something as he was closing the door from outside the classroom. Because Ms. Hogg spoke, he stuck his head back inside while still closing the door thereby placing his head between the door and door frame. I remember laughing for ten minutes while she laughed too. Ms. Hogg also introduced our class to the Beatles; one day we played one side of the Beatles' *Abbey Road* (1969), and I was thereby hooked.

**Afghanistan:**
In 1970 we moved to Afghanistan where Dad took the position as the Assistant to the President of Kabul University. This was again a joint project between Indiana University and USAID. In 1970 Afghanistan was bordered by the following countries: Iran, the Soviet Union (Russia now), China and Pakistan. With the breakup of the Soviet Union, Afghanistan is bordered now with the following countries: Iran, Turkmenistan, Uzbekistan, Tajikistan, China and Pakistan. (In Farsi, "stan" means land.)

To add adventure to our new three-year tour overseas, we stopped in a few places prior to arriving in Kabul. We made stops in:

- Hawaii, where I developed an ear infection
- Manilla, Philippines, which I do not remember because I was in the hotel room recovering from the ear infection in the hotel room.
- Hong Kong, to include a tour to Kowloon, which was part of China because Hong Kong was still under British control.
- India was next where finally we took Ariana Airlines to Afghanistan.

Our house in Kabul was again a walled compound that came with two dogs from the previous tenant. Princess, the German Shepard, and Doingla, a fiery Dachshund. I had several turtles in the compound. Princess would run around the compound with the turtles in her mouth before gently putting them down. Doingla would lick the porch for hours while occasionally jumping up to snap a bee hovering above her head.

Lisa and I attended the American International School of Kabul (AISK) with an attendance of around three hundred students. The students came from many nationalities, including Afghan, Pakistani, Indian, Canadian, American and many others. It was a real cultural melting pot.

At the time, Television (TV) was nonexistent in Afghanistan. Radio was available but only if one wanted to listen to Farsi. When my sister and I started school, we pretty much stayed at school from early in the morning until 5:00 in the evening. School was over at the usual time, but we played sports after school all during the school year. I played everything, including baseball, softball, basketball, field hockey, indoor hockey with a rubber ball and flag football. For me this was idyllic life, and I was very happy.

Because of no TV, we read anything we could get our hands on. When raising my own kids, I did not let them watch TV on school nights because I wanted them to read. I was not popular with this decision, but all of them have an exceptionally good vocabulary and knowledge of a variety of subjects. I remember reading Ray Bradbury's *The Martian Chronicles* and *S is for Space* among many of his science fiction novels. About once a year, we travelled as a group to Peshawar, Pakistan, and stayed at the American Consulate staff house. But to get to Peshawar we had to go through the Kabul Gorge, Jalalabad, and the infamous Khyber Pass where the British Army was annihilated in the 1800s among other armies. We always made the trips to Peshawar in the daytime, especially during the transit through the pass. I later found out on all our trips many of the adults were packing a firearm. While Kabul was relatively safe, the rest of Afghanistan had dangerous areas, particularly to the Ferangi (Foreigners) for the ability to steal and other nefarious acts. We also made trips in Afghanistan to Ghazni, Kandahar and Mazar-i-Sharif, which is close to the Soviet Union (Russia). We also made a trip to the Bamiyan Buddhist statues, which were later shelled and destroyed by the Taliban in 2001.

As I went along with my family to Afghanistan from 1970 to 1973, I was the second generation of the Cole family to be in the country. Since then, my son, Jason, has deployed twice with a US Army Blackhawk Medevac unit as a Crew Chief. Jason is the third generation of the Cole family to have lived in Afghanistan.

Back to Peshawar. I had several favorite things to do in Peshawar including watching TV at night at the Consulate. I am not sure if this was a Consulate or Pakistani channel, but I do remember watching *Flipper* on one of these nights. My next favorite thing was to eat Water Buffalo steaks every night we were there. Finally, on one day of each trip we went to the London Book Store, which sold books and comics. My folks let us buy as many books and comics as we could carry, and we would immediately start devouring them. I have many fond memories of reading Archie and Richie Rich comics.

On another trip, we went to India. We stopped in Lahore to visit people we knew from our days at the University of the Punjab. On returning from India, we were stopped at the Indian side of the border with Pakistan. Note: Historically there have been tensions between these countries since the British gave up control of the territory in 1947 and West Pakistan, India and East Pakistan were formed. Now they are known as Pakistan, India and Bangladesh.

While we were at the Indian side of the border, all our passports were given to an official who then took them to the Commander of the post. The local official came out a few minutes later and asked for me and me alone to accompany him to see the Commander. I was around 12 at the time, and that day was my birthday. My folks were thinking, *What is going on?* They were somewhat worried. I walked in to see this huge Indian Sikh official who had invited me in to have a cup of tea with him because it was my birthday. After the cup of tea, the Commander walked out with me and said in very British-proper English to my mother, "Congratulations, Madam, on the anniversary of the birth of your son."

While not playing sports or while school was not in session, we would, as well as most of AISK, be at the American compound's pool and tennis courts spending the day swimming, taking tennis lessons and listening to Led Zeppelin, James Taylor and Carole King among several others. One day, having a severe lapse of judgment, maybe several days, I went into the commissary and took a can of Cheetos without paying for it. I do not know why I did not just pay for the Cheetos because I had the money. So, my father received a call from the Commissary Manager to inform him of what I had been doing. So, my dad put the worst punishment on me that I could have—he restricted me for two weeks at home. It turned out the punishment was not that long. At that time, I worked with wood and used a wood wedge to carve out my designs. As I was at the house, I did much more woodwork than normal. One day I hit a soft spot on the wood and the wedge went straight into my left hand below the index finger. Blood was flowing profusely, and I yelled, "Mommy!" like a little schoolboy. It took seven stiches for which I still have the scars today.

Afghanistan was like the Wild West and still is today. In the early 1970s, and during the Hippie generation, we had travelers come from all over the world. We called them WTs or World Travelers. Many of them came for the hashish and opium, which some say was the purest in the world. Many WTs died in Afghanistan from overdosing with this pure product. Sadly, the American Embassy was busy notifying family members back home of the deaths and arranging transport for burials back home. My friends and I could very easily have obtained the drugs, but we never did.

My friends and I had fun in other ways. If one had money, one could buy it. My friend Chops Zeller and I bought gunpowder and made our own bombs. We bought pounds of it, went into the desert and spent all day blowing things up. It was extremely fun until one day gunpowder went off in Chop's face and he was very severely burned.

***

The American community lived throughout Kabul, and we were all close. The adults as well as kids did plays, sports and dinner parties as we were all away from home but made our own America overseas. For instance, Dad played flag football and softball for the USAID. Several teams: the Embassy, the Peace Corps, AISK and others provided true community events.

Americans lived throughout Kabul and other cities, whereas the Soviets/Russians lived all together in a walled compound roughly about four blocks in size. One winter day a buddy and I were cold and hungry, so we stopped at a Kabob shop outside the Soviet/Russian compound to warm up and eat. Over some warm sugared tea, Kabobs and Naan we were talking with the proprietor, and he asked where we were from. During this conversation, the proprietor said, "Ruski Kuss Modar!" This is Farsi for Mother F___er. I always wondered for his next Russian customer if he told them "Amerikani Kuss Modar!"

One-year AISK was to visit the American school in Islamabad, Pakistan, for a sports festival. On the way there, we stopped in Torkham, a border town on the Pakistani border. We were going through the shops. A merchant was selling a pistol for about ten dollars. It did not matter that I was 12 years, only that I had the money. And he would also throw in the bullets. I almost bought it but then thought, No, Mom and Dad would **not** like it. Maybe I was beginning to mature.

We were in Kabul one day at a gas station, and an attendant tried to rip off my father for gas. My dad is a very non-violent person and never spanked me when I should have been whipped at some points, in a matter of speaking. The attendant was basically saying he was not paid when I saw Dad give him the cash. I was in the passenger seat waiting when I saw Dad pick up the attendant by his collar and say, "I paid for it." From the passenger seat I am saying, "Holy Shit."

During our stay in Kabul, an Italian man opened a pizza restaurant right down the street from our home. It was called "Totinos." One day some buddies and I decided to go check it out and get some pizza. All of us were around 12 and thought first with our stomachs and then our brains. During our ordering, when asked what I wanted to drink, I replied, "I would like a beer."

When he replied, "What kind?" . . .

Internally I was thinking, *Yes! Guess what the rest of my buddies ordered.* Thereafter, I ate many anchovy pizzas while enjoying the beer. Today I cannot stand anchovies, but I can still tolerate a beer.

I was a real pain in the ass during that time. But my parents kept on trying, and I will always be eternally grateful. My father is not only my father but my lifelong mentor and confidant. He never gave up on us. Two years into Afghanistan, he asked me and my sister, "Where would you like to go for a trip?"

I chose Kenya. Lisa and Mom chose Russia. Lisa is a year younger than I. Their first stop was in Tashkent (now Uzbekistan), then on to Moscow. During their time in Moscow, Lisa developed a bad cold and a Russian tour guide suggested some vodka upon the return to the hotel. I think the Russians suggest vodka for any situation. After a bottle and half, Lisa was feeling much better.

Dad and I left for Kenya via Mecca, Saudi Arabia, and then on to Nairobi, Kenya. We stayed in a hotel in Nairobi for a few days where I remember getting a bush hat and a new pair of white-with-blue-stripes Adidas sneakers. Some say Adidas stands for "All Day I Dream About Soccer." I always loved looking at the *National Geographic* magazines about animals on preserves in Africa. The first few days we went to local game parks surrounding Nairobi. On one of the local visits, we were in a car with the provided driver. We were on a dirt road with a male elephant on the left side of the car and the female elephant on the right side of the car. As this was mating season, the male elephant had his ears out and was snorting and stomping the ground . . . his instrument was also ready. At this point the driver said to my Father, "Saab, we must go now!"

The next adventure in Kenya was "Treetops." Treetops is on a preserve where one may stay overnight in a hotel built on treetops. To get from the entrance of the preserve to the facility, we walked with several armed personnel who were carrying guns well above the .22 Caliber level. One of the armed personnel said, "Among the most dangerous and relentless animals in Africa is the water buffalo." Directly in front of the facility was a large pond with lights highlighting the animals who came to drink. We could watch this from the balcony in our room or on the top floor while eating dinner or all night long. I was fascinated! The variety of animals that came was amazing, and that one night made the whole trip fantastic, as the whole week was.

On another tour, we went to Tsavo National Park. Like Treetops, we stayed the night in a cabin and Dad remembers drinking a gin and tonic while watching the animals. We could also see Mount Kilimanjaro in the distance from Tsavo. Mount Kilimanjaro is a dormant volcano in Tanzania. It is the highest mountain in Africa and the highest single, free-standing mountain in the world: 19,341 feet above sea level and about 16,100 feet above its plateau base.

The last highlight of the Kenya trip was the train ride from Nairobi to Mombasa, which is a city on the coast of the Indian Ocean. This was my first train ride, and it was overnight with a sleeper car. I remember going through areas and seeing animals while riding in the train. I also remember having one of the most restful nights in my life. If you have not taken a train trip overnight, I highly recommend it. From Mombasa, it was back to Kabul. I am forever thankful to my parents for this trip.

In 1972, we also went back to the US on Rest and Relaxation (R&R) as authorized per Dad's contract. My folks decided to go back to North Carolina and visit their extended family. Again, both of my grandparents lived within ten miles of each other in Candler, North Carolina. It was nice for all of us to see people we had missed over the last two years. I ate all the egg sandwiches I wanted from Nanny and Cura.

We returned to Afghanistan after two weeks. We stopped in Tehran, Iran, for refueling for our final flight to Kabul. I remember two things while waiting in the Tehran airport. First, I bought my favorite Iranian pistachios. They were red colored and had fine granules of salt on them . . . one day I hope to eat them again. The second remembrance is: I walked into the restroom and my brother, Mike, followed me in. I started my business, and the next thing I heard from Mike was, "I'm telling!"

I was thinking, *What is that little cheese-eater talking about?*

The next thing I knew, Mike was running out of the restroom yelling, "Mommy, Tommy is peeing on the wall!"

I later found out my mother was horrified, but my dad had calmly stated, "It's a urinal." Mike was 4 years old at the time and had never seen a urinal before.

I love knives and I asked my dad routinely to take me to a village named Cherikar, which specialized in knives and other weapons to include switchblades, brass knuckles, and switchblades with brass knuckles . . . these were my favorite—Panjobox in Farsi. So, I purchased several of all the above. I never had a problem with these until we are coming back to the US after completing our tour of work in Afghanistan. I had brought one of my brass knuckle/switchblades back on the return trip via Turkey, Austria, Scotland and England. From England we flew to JFK in New York. While at the airport ready to leave for North Carolina, a public announcer made a statement about weapons. I had not thought a thing about the knife the whole trip, but at JFK I was alarmed and told my dad. After the initial shock of my parents, my dad took the knife to get rid of it. He finally found a trashcan to dispose of it and found out the metal trashcan was empty. The knife hit the bottom with a tremendous clang that resonated in the airport . . . I imagine he almost had a coronary. My parents were extremely nervous until we finally boarded the flight to Atlanta. I still miss that knife.

**Back to the USA:**

In the summer of 1973, we returned to the United States and back to our old home in Doraville, Georgia. When I left the US in 1970, I was still in grade school, and when I returned, I was in high school. I left Afghanistan from a school of three hundred students (elementary through high school) to a high school in Doraville with over two thousand students. For basically three years, I had not watched TV, seen the most current movies and was pretty much out of touch with modern music. I saw no one from the core friends I had for the last three years. I had nothing in common to talk to anyone about. When asked where I moved from, I replied Afghanistan and more than a few people replied, "Where is that, Africa?" I left the USA a child and returned a young adolescent . . . I was in cultural shock in my country.

I felt like a foreigner in my home country. I could not sleep well at night and was internally imploding with cultural shock. I finally refused to go to school and did some other actions, which were really a cry for help. Through the love and patience of my parents, I started receiving counseling (heavy duty at first) and I finally started going back to school part-time and building up to full-time. It took awhile, but I came back to being a normal teenager to include having girlfriends, going to proms and just hanging out. I was not the greatest student, but I think my parents were just happy for me being in school and acting normal . . . as normal as a teenager can be.

For the rest of my high school years until the summer of 1977, I made some memories that helped shape me:

I continued to progress in school and life and was doing much better. I made some good friends by then (John and Steve Marchetti). They both had motorized scooters. I started bugging Dad if I could get one. Well, he did one better. The day I was to get my bike, I did not even know what I was getting, I was bugging him, "Can we go now to pick it up?" He had arranged for the Honda dealership to drop off the bike at home. So, while I was bugging him to go, I saw a truck out of bathroom window with a motorcycle on the trailer—a brand-new Honda XL 100! Eventually, John and Steve got the same model as well. We had a construction area near us where the plan was to build a hospital, but I guess the financing never went through. For the next three years, all of us and more, spent countless hours going around this dirt track called the Hospital. I believe this Honda XL 100 and friends helped me move on in life.

During this time, Hank Aaron (Atlanta Braves) was about to break Babe Ruth's homerun record in baseball. Dad offered to take me to the first game that season (a day game) to watch or go the next night. I replied, "Let's go the night game because nothing will happen the first game." Well, the day before we were going to go to the night game, my infamous decision came to haunt me. The first game (day game) the principal of the high school came on the intercom to announce Hank Aaron had just broken the record. We went the next night to the Braves night game, a cold and rainy April night, and Hank Aaron did not even play. No wonder I never win the lottery.

I graduated high school the summer of 1977 and really started to think, *What am I going to do now?* My peers were going off to college, the military, work and other pursuits. I finally decided to go to automotive mechanics school at DeKalb Community College that fall. I learned much about auto mechanics, and I also learned I did not want to do this for the rest of my life. I went to my folks and said, "I want to go to regular college at DeKalb and work for my Associate Degree." In the winter of 1978, I started regular college, although I had to take several remedial classes because of my less-than-stellar high school years. I had some great teachers who finally got me interested in learning and helped convince me that I could do this . . . and I did. I made the Dean's list several times and my confidence continued to build. For the next two plus years I continued to pursue my degree, and I had also been accepted by the University of Georgia to continue on for my Bachelor's Degree.

During this time frame, I had met some friends who had joined the Army, and I talked to them for hours. I also visited some recruiters from all services, and the Army seemed the best fit for me. I also learned some potential benefits for education I could receive upon leaving the service with an Honorable Discharge. I was still a little antsy about going to Georgia with its huge campus and student population, so I decided to put Georgia on hold, do an enlistment in the Army and go back to school. With the decision made, I enlisted and did not have to physically report until September 4, 1980, thus allowing me to complete my Associate Degree in Business. The degree also allowed me to come into the Army at the rank of Private First-Class (PFC), which when compared to the rank of Private, had a whopping difference in salary of about $20.00 a month, but I had a stripe on my sleeve.

My last class to earn my degree at DeKalb was Biology 102, which was called a mini quarter (two weeks long) compared to a full quarter of about three months long. We were in class six to eight hours a day and then of course I was studying afterward. This was a rough two weeks, but I made a "B" and was happy for it. An interesting side note to this class was the individual who sat next to me. He was a Master Sergeant in the US Army who was prepping for his retirement while I was 2.5 weeks away from induction into the Army. I thought this was rather ironic, even though I had no idea I would make a career out of the Army.

**The Army:**

Goodbye long hair, hello short hair! At the crack of dawn on September 4, 1980, my recruiter picked me up from our home in Doraville, Georgia, much earlier than my folks and siblings were normally up. It was one of those days I'll never forget. From there the recruiter took me to the Military Entrance Processing Station (MEPS) in downtown Atlanta, which includes recruits from all services. For most of the day recruits are physically examined, anywhere and everywhere. They must provide a urine sample, have blood tests and process a whole lot of paperwork. Once this is completed, all our paperwork was sealed and given back to us with the orders, "Do not under any circumstances open up this package." I was a Private First Class (PFC) because of my two years of college, as opposed to Private. So I oversaw the group and they put us on a bus to the Atlanta Airport where we caught a flight to Columbia, South Carolina, and specifically to Fort Jackson.

Fort Jackson was our first Army installation to receive our uniforms, boots and military gear and our first military haircut. The first military haircut was more like a sheep-shearing and came out of my pay. Two days later, we were waiting for the buses at about 9:00 p.m. to take us to Fort Benning, Georgia, outside of Columbus, Georgia, where I would go through Infantry basic training. The timing of the late-night departure was on purpose; the buses went through the night to arrive at the crack of dawn at Fort Benning and our barracks. Upon arrival, all the Drill Sergeants met each of the buses and with very nice greetings and very patient and kind suggestions, they told us to get off the bus now!

**Memories from Basic Training:**

Basic training for Infantry in 1980 was twelve weeks long. Because mine started in early September, middle Georgia was still extremely hot and humid without air conditioning in WW II barracks. The purpose of basic training was to break us down from a civilian mind frame to a military mind frame. Because of my college and rank of PFC, I was made a squad leader even though I was as brand new as everyone else. We learned to march, dress, how to address the Non-Commissioned Officers (NCOs) and Officers and learned other military protocols.

We were up at the crack of dawn and told to go to sleep around 10:00 at night . . . unless one had fireguard duty. We were always tired and when told, "Lights out," we heard snoring in about thirty seconds. We learned to take naps anytime we could. During transport on what we called "Cattle Cars," I learned to put my helmet on the butt of my M16 and sleep for ten-fifteen minutes or as long as it took to get to the training site.

While undergoing Rifle Marksmanship training at multiple shooting ranges, we would first have to take off the wooden covers over our shooting sites. This was not only to get eventually in the firing position, but also to check for snakes . . . which were prevalent on Fort Benning. Prior to any training event there were always safety briefings on shooting and other precautions such as regarding snakes and snake bites.

During one of the safety briefings prior to Rifle Marksmanship training, one of the Drill Instructors stated, "Now if any of you boys get snakebit between the legs you are s____ out of luck." We got the message and checked the shooting positions!

The Drill Sergeants always pushed us. Upon wakeup each morning, prior to chow and formation, each squad had cleaning duty to perform. There was never enough time to adequately perform these duties, and they knew it. There were four squads in an Army Platoon, and I was the third squad leader. We were about halfway through basic, and our Drill Instructor started with the first squad leader on why his cleaning duties were not performed to satisfaction one day. The first squad leader went on and on about not enough time to accomplish the duties. The Drill Sergeant relieved him. Same result for the second squad leader.

Next he came to me. I could see what was happening but was also thinking, *I am not going to get a leadership monetary bonus for this position.* I responded tiredly, "No excuse, Drill Sergeant."

To this he responded, "Good answer."

Guess what the fourth squad leader's response was?

We were doing Combatives (self-defense without weapons) one day within padded circular pits. With several platoons present, this took a few hours, and for some unknown reason, I was one of two left. I was not the biggest guy in the world at about 6'1" and at the time, at around 155 pounds. The Drill Sergeant who was the referee that day, was one of the biggest and meanest Drill Sergeants we had, and I had never seen him smile, much less laugh. So, when he looked at me and pointed at me to get in the center of the ring with this monster of opponent whom I was about to face, I was only thinking, S___! My opponent was from Mississippi, over 250 pounds with no fat and at least 6'3". He was also a middle linebacker on his high school football team. So, as I was walking up to my opponent and the Drill Sergeant, I said to my opponent, "Would you do me a favor today and not kill me?" When I heard the never-smiling Drill Sergeant and my opponent laugh, I breathed a sigh of relief. It was a merciful defeat.

In December 1980, I graduated from Basic Training and was an immensely proud Soldier. During Basic I was offered the opportunity to go to the Old Guard (Ceremonial Infantry Division in Washington, D.C.). Further down the line, I was offered Officer Candidate School (OCS), which was also at Fort Benning. At that time, one had to have only two years of college to be commissioned, but would need to complete a Bachelor's degree to remain an officer. I chose OCS. The next class for OCS was in the summer of 1981, so during that time period, I stayed in the same battalion, not as a trainee, but served duties as a Drill Corporal and the Battalion Commander's and Sergeant Major's driver. I learned much from these two individuals on my driving duties.

**Officer Candidate School (OCS):**

I reported to OCS in the early summer of 1981. OCS was on the garrison side of Fort Benning and really a little town as opposed to the part of Fort Benning I endured in Basic Training known as Harmony Church. Harmony Church was in a much more rural part of the post. Harmony Church was also the Headquarters (HQs) location for the Ranger School and had the Ranger Obstacle Course, which I would visit later in OCS. OCS was a way to become a Commissioned officer for those who did not go through the Service Academies or the Reserve Officer's Training Corps (ROTC). It was also a venue for those to apply for a commission who had the qualifying educational requirements or did not go through the aforementioned venues.

Because I was at the rank of PFC and because I was attending OCS, the Army promoted me to the rank of Specialist 5 to help with the added expenses of OCS. Rest assured, if I washed out of OCS, I would immediately be a PFC again.

As I was still fresh from Basic, was marching troops as a Drill Corporal and being in really good shape, I was confident. In OCS, the Tactical Officer (TAC) would get in one's face and play mind games. Some of the candidates were not used to this in-your-face approach and would literally shake in their boots or show other emotions, which would draw the added attention of other TACs. The pressure would only increase . . . they were trying to weed out the weak.

On one occasion, one of the TACs said, "Cole, you are the ugliest SOB I have ever seen."

I laughed and said, "Sorry, sir, but my mother already told me that." I had no more issues with the TACs in-your-face testing; they talked to each other because they saw I was not intimidated. I had issues with a TAC for another reason.

Fort Benning, at the time, was home of the Infantry—male only, OCS included females. I served later with many of my female candidates throughout my career who had much success. Note: Fort Benning is now home to the Armor and Infantry Schools. But at the time, being the Infantry school, all the training was infantry-centered to include weapons training, long marches with packs, learning to shoot heavy and light weapons and overnight tactical training.

OCS has an honor code the same as the Service Academies: "Do not lie, cheat, steal or tolerate those who do." We had several candidates dropped from the course for stupid lies when all they had to do was admit the offense and they would probably have been all right—minor offenses of course.

One such event happened to me. During Basic Training, I had developed a taste for Red Man chewing tobacco. About a quarter of the way through OCS, we had finished training for the day, and we were waiting for transportation back to the barracks. During OCS one was not allowed to use tobacco products of any kind. While enjoying some Red Man and my cheek was full as evidence, a TAC came out of nowhere and told me to write myself up for this offense.

This TAC Officer was not my own TAC officer, but he knew who my TAC was. Some may have thought, I'll just blow it off and nothing will happen. I thought on it, but not too long for two reasons: first, I was wrong in using the tobacco per established rules, and second, I was given a direct order to write myself up. I wrote myself up, and the next two weekends I was doing walking tours around the Infantry Center while my peers were getting a little "me time." I knew I was being watched from my peers and my TAC. If I did not complete those tours in the hot Georgia sun . . . I was gone. Later, upon graduation from OCS, my TAC (Captain Gomez) told me he had recommended me for a leadership award, but I had "too many walking tour incidents."

I thanked him for this and replied, "How about an award for the most walking tours?"

He laughed and said, "Not happening, Lieutenant."

One time, we were going to the field for a few days and the route where we were going ended at Harmony Church, my old stomping grounds of Basic Training. We marched around fifteen miles with full rucksacks and weapons. We started early in the morning with the eventual goal of negotiating the Ranger Confidence Course near Victory Pond in Harmony Church. With OCS, the leadership positions were rotated each week from Battalion Commander to Platoon Leaders.

I was a Platoon Leader that week. We were roughly two miles from the Ranger Confidence Course when the Candidate Battalion Commander was lost. He got on the radio and talked with the Platoon Leaders and frankly admitted he was lost; the TACs were also monitoring the radios. I then announced, "I know where we need to go. Let me take the lead, and I will get us there."

He did.

Prior to OCS, I could not get enough of running, so while waiting for OCS, I would run all the time, particularly in the Harmony Church area, so I knew it well. My platoon went forward, passing the others to take the lead, and I went straight to the Ranger Confidence Course. The Candidate Battalion Commander and my own TAC lauded me for my taking charge and my excellent map-reading skills, to which I replied, "Thank you, sir."

At the end of the day, I did not leave so cocky. While dropping from the One Rope Bridge on the Ranger Confidence Course, without permission from the Ranger instructor, yelling HOOAH, I hit Victory Pond over twenty-five feet below and promptly lost two of my front teeth when my jaw snapped shut. Because I did not ask permission to drop, I was ordered to do fifty pushups while spitting out the remnants of my two front teeth. Note: I was never a Ranger. I was in OCS, and the Ranger Confidence Course was part of OCS training. Rangers lead the way!

I graduated from OCS in September 1981 as a Second Lieutenant in the Signal Corps Branch of the Army. I was proud to have my parents in attendance, and I had my two front teeth fixed by that time.

## Signal Officer Basic Course (SOBC):

Upon completion of OCS, each new Officer proceeded to their branch-specific Officer Basic Course. The home of the Signal Corps is Fort Gordon, Georgia, which is outside of Augusta . . . the home of the Masters.

The Signal Officer's Basic Course (SOBC) was approximately three months long. Upon completion of SOBC one proceeded to his or her unit assignment or additional training as required. My original posting was to an Airborne Engineer Battalion located at Fort Bragg, North Carolina. I was not really thrilled with the location, but I did want to go Airborne (Parachute/Jump) school. During SOBC, we were visited from the assignment personnel. They were looking for volunteers for Korea. I offered, "If you send me to Airborne School first, I will volunteer for Korea."

They agreed and my assignment was changed.

I had been at Fort Benning for almost two years and had not been within a few miles of a female . . . at least those I wanted to keep company with. Signal Corps Officers were male and female, so our class had both. One day, I was walking back from the company HQ with a credit card application in my hand when a beautiful female officer in uniform said, "Don't do it; it could get you in trouble."

I did a double-take and looked behind me to see if she was talking to someone else. There was no one behind me. I was so stunned I did not say a word. Our class had two sections (flows) and she was in the other flow, but as a class we met as a whole.

A week or so later, we were having a mandatory class function at the Officer's Club on a Saturday night. I saw the beautiful soldier again. I finally found the nerve and asked her how her popcorn was? Her name was Mayumi Maguire. She was not wearing a uniform, but a very attractive white dress with colored patterns. I was immediately smitten, and we ended up talking for the next several hours. It was awkward at first when she informed me she was from Utah. I asked her, "Are you a Ute Indian?"

Mayumi looked at me like I was some uneducated hick from Podunkville and replied, "I'm Japanese."

This is a good life lesson. Do not assume people are from a certain place and guess their ethnicity, ask them!

Well, that night messed up everything! We ended up dating, and I fell hard for her. On a weekend trip to my parent's house, her stomach hurt the whole weekend. Monday, she went to the emergency room and found out she had an appendicitis, which could have burst the weekend before. Mayumi had emergency surgery, and I had the opportunity to spend many hours at Eisenhower Army Medical Center with her.

It then hit me one night, I am going to Korea, and she is going to Germany.

The bottom line is the Assignments Branch said, "We will not change orders unless you were married."

We were married on December 14, 1981, at Chapel # 5, Fort Gordon, Georgia. My orders were changed to Germany. At that time, females were not posted on the Demilitarized Zone (DMZ) with the Second Infantry Division in Korea. I did not regret this change of posting.

Our class organized the wedding for us, and both of our parents attended the ceremony. It was a little uncomfortable meeting her dad the first time because his daughter had just left home two months earlier. Mayumi's parents, James's "Mac" and Michiko Maguire, treated me like a son from the beginning. Mac was a retired Chief Master Sergeant with the Air Force. He met Michiko while stationed at Kadena Air Force Base, Okinawa, Japan. Okinawa is the birthplace for Michiko, Mayumi, and her sister, Kay, and brother, Jim.

Upon graduation from SOBC, we spent the Christmas holidays visiting her folks and her brother in Layton, Utah. Along the way we stopped in Salina, Kansas, to visit her sister Kay, and her sister's husband, Dusty, and their daughter, Charlotte. We brought Charlotte with us to Utah to see her grandparents. This was my first cross-country trip, and I really enjoyed it. After the holidays, we drove back to Fort Gordon where Mayumi prepared to leave for Germany via Charleston, South Carolina. I was to follow a month and half later after I completed Airborne School at Fort Benning. Airborne School was the longest three weeks of my life because I hoped I did not hurt myself and be recycled to another class that would delay my departure for Germany. I made it!

**Germany:**
After jump school, I stayed a few days with my parents before I took a bus to Charleston AFB, South Carolina, for military transport to Germany. As a newly commissioned Officer and Airborne graduate, I thought I was the "Cock of the Walk." I was checking in at Charleston AFB and a senior female Air Force NCO stated, "Excuse me, sir, but you look too young to be an Officer."

I had nothing to say, but my balloon had been burst. This NCO was not being mean or derogatory, just stating a fact . . . It was a humbling moment for me. It was not the rank I had, but what I had accomplished with it. In real world terms, I was just starting in the Army because everything prior was training.

Mayumi met me at Rhein-Mein AFB outside of Frankfort, Germany. Our unit's location was over an hour south in Heilbronn, Germany, 26th Signal Battalion, 93rd Signal Brigade, 7th Corps. Heilbronn was located over an hour south of Frankfort and thirty minutes north of Stuttgart. The Battalion's mission was to provide Corps Area communications via ultra-high frequency (UHF), very high frequency (VHF) and Microwave line of sight communications. Each company built two-hundred-foot towers, attached the aforementioned dishes on top of the towers to connect to our fellow companies and other communications requirements for 7th Corps. The towers were built by hand, meaning section by section, by specifically trained tower personnel. For our requirements one could not have communications without towers, so we were in the field way before the actual exercises began and were the last to leave. With exercises in the winter, aligning the dishes to the other sights were dicey, especially during frigid and windy conditions at two hundred feet above the ground. We normally rotated personnel every thirty minutes until we had established communications. I volunteered on more than a few occasions because we just did not have enough personnel. Note: In the early 1980s we were still in the Cold War with the Soviet Union. One day, I was on top of the tower with my Company Commander. He remarked, "You know if the balloon goes up with the Soviets, these towers are aiming stakes for their artillery and aviation . . . we are dead meat."

We stayed in a German Gasthaus (Guest House) for almost two months. I had been with my new bride for three-four days and then off to the field in tents . . . we were in separate platoons in diverse locations. That first year, we spent almost six months in the field on exercises. The Battalion Chaplain finally addressed the Battalion Commander—after two months in Germany—to let us have enough time to acquire housing. Both of us decided we wanted to live the German experience instead of living on base, and so we did.

We found a nice apartment in downtown Heilbronn that was ten minutes from Wharton Barracks where we worked. Along the way we could stop at the local Bakeri (Bakery) where all the pastries and bread were baked fresh every morning. Our apartment was within walking distance to fine eating establishments and the superb German food. The German Beer also helped.

**Additional German snapshots:**
When we arrived in Germany in the early 1980s, part of our orientation was to take "Head Start." Head Start is a program that taught basic German phrases to get somewhat functional in German conversation. The difficult part for Americans is that most Europeans speak three to four or more languages because of their geography and their acceptance of other languages and cultures. In Germany I found—among many other countries I visited or was stationed—if one tries to speak the local language, even if butchered, they appreciate the effort as opposed to being the Ugly American and demanding they speak English.

Mayumi and I went out to eat in Heilbronn one night, and I thought my German was getting fairly good. I was not hungry, but Mayumi was, so she ordered her food and I just wanted a salad because I had eaten pretty heavily earlier. So, I studied the menu, and thinking I understood my new profound knowledge of German, I ordered a salad. It turned out it was a garlic fruit salad. Now I love garlic, and I love fruit, but I do not like garlic on fruit. I was good, I ate what I could and took the rest home without any incident.

Mayumi and I were not in the field for a while, so we went to the Octoberfest in Munich, Germany, in the fall of 1982 with my Company Commander and his wife. I am sure I mentioned this before: Germany has the finest beer in the world and Octoberfest is not where one would go to quit drinking or to lose weight.

Mayumi did not drink but she had fun in her own ways. So, I was having a really good time at the Octoberfest in Munich, and as such I needed to relieve myself of some of this good time. I went to the restroom to take care of business. I came out of the bathroom, and was still feeling good on this great German Octoberfest beer when an Octoberfest waitress serving thousands of inebriated personnel pushed me aside. German women were not shy. Feeling pretty good on the aforementioned, this ticked me off as she almost took me off my feet, so I pushed her back, this lady carrying a tray of four heavy Octoberfest beer steins. She looked at me while still carrying the tray and pushed me back. I pushed her back; nothing was ever violent in these exchanges, but when she proceeded to put the tray full of four beer steins down to confront me, I decided right then and there no matter what happens I will not be looking very manly. I put my hands up in defeat and jogged out of there . . . she was tough! Bottom Line: Do not mess with the Ladies serving beer at the Octoberfest!

In Germany, the highways were called Autobahns and they did not have a speed limit. The left lane was the passing lane and the Germans let you know a half a mile out by blinking their lights to get out of the way. The only car we had at the time was Mayumi's green Chevrolet Vega, which protested even if it came close to 70 mph. We rarely spent time in the left lane as Mercedes Benzs, BMWs, Porsches, Audis and other auto makes blew past us like we were standing still. I also noticed BMW motorcycles in Germany and thought one day, *I'm going to get one of those.*

Later in 1982, Mayumi found out she was pregnant; we were incredibly happy. Before the birth, my sister and her new husband, Greg, came over to visit. We picked them up in Brussels, Belgium. On March 29, 1983, Jason Michael Cole was born at a military hospital in Stuttgart. Both of our parents came over to see our firstborn and we were happy to have them. Mayumi's folks came just a few days after the birth; she had to go back to the hospital because of an infection. I picked them up in Frankfort and took them to the hospital. Mayumi was discharged the next day. I took some leave and enjoyed Mac and Michiko's time in Germany. My parents came over a couple of months later, and we took some leave. We showed them some local sights and then ventured further. We took a trip from Heilbronn to Austria, Switzerland and Liechtenstein. We even bought some stamps. It was a wonderful trip.

After Jason was born, I was called by my Company Commander (CO) one weekend to inform me one of my soldier's sons was killed in an automobile accident outside of Wharton Barracks. The CO asked me to go down to our local medical unit to check on the soldier and see what assistance I could provide. I walked into the clinic and the deceased son (he was 5-6 years' old) was lying on a gurney as I walked in. The father was distraught and told me what happened. He was walking with his son outside of Wharton Barracks, and the boy saw something that interested him. He took off running and was hit by a car being driven by a German lady. The German lady did not realize the boy was still under the vehicle and alive. My soldier ran over to the lady, trying to tell her, "Do not move!"

But she thought he was attacking her. She panicked and floored the gas, dragging and killing his son in front of his eyes. This tragedy hit the whole community hard. It was arranged to have the soldier receive an emergency reassignment back to the US for him and his family. Two days later I drove him to Frankfort for his family's flight back to the US. This incident hit me hard personally because Jason was a toddler, and I could not imagine losing my child like my Soldier had. I have often wondered what happened to him and his family.

***

I had always wanted to run a Marathon (26.2 miles), and I finally accomplished this in 1983 by completing the Fulda Marathon. Mayumi and Jason were waiting for me when I crossed the finish line. We stayed at a really nice hotel in Fulda and marveled at the with thick, down blankets. The issue we had was Jason's upset stomach and his vomiting on the nice blanket. We worked hard to get it as clean as possible.

Later in 1983, we found out Mayumi was pregnant with our second child. On May 7, 1984, Freya Mignon Cole came into this world via a German ambulance because she was not as patient as her older brother. Mayumi had been in labor for 24 hours with Jason. Freya was born in a local German hospital in Heilbronn. Because Freya's newborn stay was in a German hospital, we received free diapers and other infant goods until we left Germany. Freya's birth was two and one half months before our departure from Germany.

This was a tense time in the Army because a Reduction in Force (RIF) was in process, and I was let go. I was devastated because I loved the Army. I believe my not having a Bachelor's Degree was the primary reason I was selected to leave. I then made it my mission in life to finish my degree and get back into the Army. Because Mayumi was still in the service, we made our plans for her next duty assignment at Fort Gordon, Georgia.

I have many wonderful memories of our time in Germany. We went there with two of us and came out with four. I plan to visit our old stomping grounds one day.

**Fort Gordon, Georgia:**

Mayumi reported to Fort Gordon in the summer of 1984, and prior to reporting to her next assignment, she began the Signal Officer Advance Course (SOAC), a mandatory course in the Officer education program. I started researching and found I could attend classes on Fort Gordon to immediately start fulfilling my requirements for a Bachelor's Degree. I started school full-time, and a degree became my mission in life. Mayumi finished SOAC, began a position with the Directorate of Combat Development Threat Division. In the meantime, I joined a local US Army Reserve unit and became a weekend warrior. The Reserve position provided a little money in addition to the stipend I received from my education benefits. We were moving on and now even had a Basset Hound named Duffy.

During late 1985 into the middle of 1986, several key events happened. Mayumi had been offered a position in Okinawa, Japan (her birthplace), a strategic Signal Battalion as a Company Commander. Obviously this was an easy decision for us. Secondly, we were expecting our third child. Marcia Ausee Cole was born on August 28, 1986 at Eisenhower Army Medical Center, Fort Gordon, Georgia. Thirdly, I finished all my requirements for my Bachelor's Degree (B.S. Business) from Paine College the summer of 1986. As I had finished my Bachelor's Degree and had time before our departure to Okinawa, I requested to go through the Signal Officers Advance Course (SOAC), and the course was approved. It also put me on Active Duty for three months, and the extra pay helped. I finished SOAC in November, and we started preparing to move to Okinawa in January of 1997. We visited our parents in the interim and then departed overseas.

**Okinawa, Japan:**

As Okinawa was Mayumi's birthplace, she had many relatives on the island. One of her aunts (Mako) and husband (Kensho) really took us in . . . they even provided us with two vehicles. My car was an Isuzu with the steering wheel on the right side of the car and was a stick shift. In Japan they drove on the left side of the road, so I really had some learning to do. Mako and Kensho fed us dinners, took us out to eat and really spoiled the kids . . ., especially the newborn Marcia. We were still getting used to the time zone—a day ahead and a thirteen-hour time difference from Georgia. Mayumi had started to work, so I had the kids on many a walk at two-three o'clock in the morning because our hours were off. One morning I was at the temporary lodge with Marcia when she was getting close to 6 months old. I was watching the Superbowl live at 8:30 a.m. on a Monday morning. This was the Super Bowl (XXII) when Doug Williams came into the game as quarterback for the Washington Redskins (changed to the Washington Football Team and now the Washington Commanders) and proceeded to orchestrate a blowout victory over the Denver Broncos. Marcia kept looking at me weirdly every time I would yell or cheer as the game progressed.

Later we moved into a temporary apartment off post. Jason and Freya started attending a Japanese school right next to the apartment, and all communication at the school was in Japanese. In the meantime, I started looking for work. Not being on active duty at the time, at the time, I was a dependent then, and American civil-service positions were in short supply. I taught English with Mayumi for a while and some substitute teaching at the American schools on base. The younger elementary classes I enjoyed but the high school substitute assignments I hated . . . enough of that.

We continued to enjoy Okinawa. Mayumi was busy with her job; the kids were happy with their school and we were enjoying the beautiful beaches. Since I had extra time on hand, I started training for the Naha Marathon, which was held every December. Naha was the Capital of Okinawa. During the summer, it was extremely hot and humid and prone to typhoons. I ran the Marathon with Mayumi's uncle and aunt. I am proud to say we all completed the Marathon, and my time was 3 hours, 34 minutes and 56 seconds.

In the interim, I asked and received permission to start a three-month, active-duty tour with the 1st Battalion, 1st Special Forces Group located in Okinawa. Serving as the Assistant Communications Officer, I had a blast, and it felt good to contribute financially. As the Communications Officer was on leave for over thirty days, I oversaw the communication section during his absence. We held exhibitions on post and did all kinds of repelling. These seasoned "Special Operators" always used me as the guy in the basket and purposely had me going down the rappelling wall headfirst or in other awkward positions. When they saw I was not going to pee in my pants, they accepted me. Since the 1st Battalion was an Airborne unit and every Airborne service member was required to jump at least every three months to maintain Jump pay, I volunteered for every jump I could. During jump school I had jumped from C-141 jets and from C-130 propeller-driven planes for a total of five jumps. In Okinawa I did my first helicopter jump from a US Marine CH 46. It took longer for the static line to deploy the parachute from helicopters as opposed to planes—this added to the pucker factor. I also made my first water jump as we jumped in the East China Sea, and I had the softest landing I ever had. I was more worried about sharks in the water until being picked up by the boats. Unfortunately, all good things must come to an end, and due to budgets, I could not be extended. 1st Battalion was willing to pay for me to stay an additional six months, but it was Active money versus Reserve and not possible.

Mayumi heard of a program from some of her peers called the Active Guard Reserve Program (AGR). The AGR program consisted of National Guard or Army Reserve officers serving full-time but not counted against the active-duty end strength. The pay and benefits were the same, and I wanted back in the Army. So, I applied and was accepted to join the Reserve Officers Training Corps (ROTC) department at the Rochester Institute of Technology (RIT) in Rochester, New York.

I was to report to RIT in August 1988. I was pumped for the job, but I was going to have to leave my family behind. Prior to leaving, I did a two-week Reserve tour at

Tom with (L-R) Jason, Marcia, Freya

Schofield Barracks, Hawaii. I remember this Hawaii tour because I called Mayumi one day in Okinawa, and she told me Freya had been playing with a neighbor's dog (a Rottweiler) and had been bitten in the face requiring several stiches. I remember crying for her, and I was frustrated because I was thousands of miles away. I also knew my imminent departure to New York was coming and this added to my frustration.

The summer before I left Okinawa, we hosted Mayumi's parents, sister and sister's husband and extended family on base for a get together and food. We probably had about fifty people there. At first some of the Japanese male relatives were very formal with me and probably not sure how to interact. Well, I had to get the grill going for the hamburgers and hot dogs, and before I went outside, I left a half gallon of Cutty Sark Scotch on the table for them. I came in about 45 minutes later, and they greeted me, "Ah Tomsan!" and everybody was all smiles.

My folks and my brother, Mike, came over about two weeks later with Aunt Norine (Mom's sister) and her husband, Roi. Roi was in the Marines in WW II and fought on several islands in the Pacific, including Okinawa. I took Roi to the beach on Okinawa where he came ashore in the US invasion and where he lost many of his fellow Marines. He showed emotion I had never seen from him before. He went through hell and ironically was called again for Korea.

I took Dad and Mike to the local Kadena AFB Exchange (BX) one day. The BX had electronics from Asia that had not been introduced to the US yet. While we were in our quarters, I showed Dad and Mike this new SONY cassette tape player that included a built-in equalizer with headphones. The sound was amazing and state-of-the-art at that time. Dad bought two immediately—one for him and one for Mike.

One special treat when my folks visited was Mayumi's relatives taking all of us out to another island by boat. They had brought food along, and we were on a private beach on an island. The water was beautiful. In some places, people paid big money for this. It was gorgeous, but it was hot. At one point, my mother got so hot she went and sat in the water with all of her clothes. My dad, Norine, Roi and I looked at each other and laughed. I joined her later. Good times.

Roi was a smoker, and Jason, at the ripe old age of 4, had been harping to Roi about smoking. One day Roi came inside from smoking and chose to partake from a bottle of Scotch when Jason stated, "If you smoke you might have to go to the hospital, but if you smoke and drink you MUST go to the hospital."

On another occasion during my folks' visit, Mom had been watching Jason and could tell he was about to do something bad. Jason noticed her watching and said, "Go cook, Granna!"

On another day during my folks' visit, I went running and stepped in a pothole, breaking my ankle. After the X-Ray, I was put in a cast. This incident was just a few weeks from departure to New York. I could not report to the AGR program with a cast on my foot and using crutches. The cast and crutches also hindered me from going with my folks on local tours. One tour was Suicide Cliffs where there are many stairs to climb. Suicide Cliffs received its name from the battle of Okinawa in WWII when many Okinawan civilians jumped off the cliffs due to Japanese propaganda stating the Americans would torture and abuse them. Many mothers jumped these cliffs, holding their babies and children.

When I was a week away from departure to my assignment in New York, I still had the cast on my ankle The cast was supposed to stay on for another three weeks. I did not want anything stopping me from getting back in the Army and employment. So, a week away from departure, I cut the cast off myself. I was not showing up for my in-processing with a cast on my foot!

Finally, my dreaded time had come, and I left Kadena Air Force Base in early August 1988 to come back on active duty. The trip from Okinawa to the US was a very long flight, the longest of my life. I would miss Okinawa, but I would miss my young family much more!

**Rochester, New York – RIT ROTC:**

I flew back to the US and took a commercial flight from the West Coast to Atlanta. My parents were still overseas. I was borrowing Dad's pickup truck for few months until I got a car of my own in Rochester. Before going to Rochester, I was to report to Fort McCoy, Wisconsin, for one week of in-processing. I had never been to Canada before, so I decided to take the northern route through Canada to Rochester as opposed to taking Interstate 90 through the northern US states. I left Fort McCoy and drove to Detroit, Michigan, where I crossed the Ambassador Bridge into Windsor, Canada, and proceeded halfway to Toronto where I spent the night. The next day I drove through Toronto to the US border, which was right along Niagara Falls and Buffalo. I arrived in Rochester a couple of hours later.

RIT was a top-notch school, and per Wikipedia, was internationally known for its science, computer, engineering and art programs, as well as for the National Technical Institute for the Deaf which was a leading deaf institution providing educational opportunities to more than one thousand deaf and hard-of-hearing students. RIT was also known for its Co-op program that gave students professional and industrial experience. Due to the academic requirements at RIT, many of our ROTC students were on full or partial scholarships with the Army. Upon graduation and commissioning, the new officers would have a mandatory period to serve in the Army. I was wondering if I was smart enough to teach these brainiacs.

Our detachment consisted of four Officers—headed by a Lieutenant Colonel (LTC), three NCOs and two civilian hires. I was a Captain at the time. My first year I oversaw our satellite ROTC campus at the State University of New York (SUNY), Geneseo. Geneseo was thirty minutes south of Rochester. We had classes once a week, and on specific weekends, all the ROTC students from RIT and Geneseo got together for training to include such skills as Infantry tactics, map reading, physical fitness and rifle marksmanship. In the summer of 1989, I was to serve as Platoon TAC Officer at Advance Camp at Fort Bragg, North Carolina. This assignment was in preparation for my taking over the training and operations of the detachment and preparing our cadets for Advance Camp the next summer. The Platoon

TAC assignment helped me train our folks because I experienced what they needed to be prepared for. This was a hard two months; I was out in the field in hot and muggy North Carolina, but I learned much. After Advance Camp, I assumed duties as the Training and Operations Officer. My two main focuses, with the assistance of SFC George Gordon, were training our juniors for their Advance Camp and overseeing and coordinating all aspects of training and operations. Advance Camp was the major barometer for the juniors because their scores at camp determined the better choices they would have: Active Duty, Choice of Branch, and other matters. SFC Gordon and I worked them hard to include physical fitness, tactics training, lessons in leadership. Our school and our cadets did very well. One year RIT won the top school in the Eastern Region for physical fitness for a medium sized ROTC detachment. I was not really surprised at our RIT ROTC's success as these bright young adults were already very disciplined and mature. Throughout my career I would run into these Officers in the US, Kuwait, Saudi Arabia and Korea.

**Other highlights of Rochester (RIT):**

Mayumi was still in Okinawa with the kids and Duffy and learned she would attend a three-month course at Fort Leavenworth, Kansas. She would bring the kids and Duffy to Rochester and leave them with me for the course and for the rest of her tour in Okinawa. I was extremely happy. I picked them up at the Rochester airport. All of them were deeply tanned, coming from sunny Okinawa. All the kids were jabbering between Japanese and English and communicating fine. Marcia was speaking about 95% Japanese while talking to me, and all I said was Hai (Yes) because I was not understanding anything. Mayumi was watching this and laughed.

I had my family back (Mayumi having left for school in Kansas). I hired a babysitter when at work. Sometimes when there was an issue with a babysitter and I had to be out of town, I asked my mother for help to watch the kids. I could not thank her enough. We got Jason and Freya in an excellent private Catholic school down the street. Marcia stayed at home. Mayumi finished her school, took some leave in Rochester and headed back to Okinawa. We later learned she was pregnant with Michaela. Later in 1989, Mayumi decided to leave Active Duty and come back to New York. She went on to serve in the New York National Guard and multiple US Army Reserve assignments before her eventual retirement.

During the summer of 1990, I was to attend the same Company grade training course at Fort Leavenworth, Kansas, as Mayumi had the previous year.

One of the perks of my assignments to RIT was that the faculty (to include ROTC personnel and spouses) could work on a Bachelor's or Master's Degree for free. Upon release from Active Duty, Mayumi took advantage of this perk and eventually graduated with a Master's Degree in Human Resource Development.

Michaela René Cole was born on January 3, 1990, at Strong Memorial Hospital in Rochester. Mick was early and breech so the doctor had to perform a Cesarean Section on Mayumi. Being premature, Mick was immediately placed in Intensive Care for several days.

It was hard to walk into that unit, seeing all kinds of tubes and needles sticking out of her and all the other babies. Mick had jaundice as well.

Mayumi was hurting in her own way. Recovering from the C-Section she was very sore and in severe pain. I did not realize how much. A few days after the birth, Jason, Freya and Marcia had been bugging me to see their mother. I took them to see her at the hospital. After about five minutes of them bouncing around her bed, she said, "Tom, please take the kids home!"

We finally got both Mayumi and Mick home.

With a bigger family and Duffy, I needed a bigger vehicle, so I bought a gray Ford E-150 conversion van with a rear seat that would fold into a bed. The van also came with a TV to watch VHS movies or watch local TV with a built-in antenna. We had the van for years, and it was perfect for my many Army relocations, vacations and just day-to-day family hauling. Years later I even had dual exhaust put on it for a sportier sound.

Our time in Rochester was coming to an end. I needed to get back to a tactical assignment for career purposes. I was assigned to the 35th Signal Battalion in Juana Diaz, Puerto Rico, as the Assistant Operations Officer. My reporting date was July 1990. I asked my mother to meet me at the San Juan Airport to watch the kids for a couple of weeks while I started work. Mayumi had to stay for two more weeks in Rochester to finalize her Master's Degree. Assignment Puerto Rican began for me, and I was loving the weather.

**Puerto Rico:**

We flew from Rochester in early July (Jason, Freya, Marcia, Mick and Duffy) and were overdressed when we arrived in San Juan. We met Mom at the San Juan Airport and took a cab to Fort Buchanan, which was in metropolitan San Juan. I could not believe all the traffic. The drivers did not treat the emergency lane for its purpose but just as another lane. We arrived at Fort Buchanan where I had a couple of rooms waiting for us at a lodge. I happened to look down from the second floor of the lodge at the cab below. The cab driver was muttering loudly in Spanish while vigorously wiping out Duffy's hair from the back seat. I do not think he was a dog lover.

My acting Battalion Commander provided me a car until our conversion van and Taurus arrived. We had shipped them via ocean transport from Bayonne, New Jersey. That was genuinely nice of him, but I think he also wanted me to get to work. The 35th Signal Battalion was an Army Reserve unit, so it did not have many full-time personnel; I was one of the few. The 35th (near Ponce) was located one and one-half hours southwest of Fort Buchanan. My next mission was to try to find a place not extremely far for me to commute and near enough for the older kids to go to the school on Fort Buchanan. I found a rental house in Caguas, roughly twenty miles from Fort Buchanan. But my commute to the 35th was more than an hour, but fortunately, the traffic south was not too bad. We had a nice little house with no AC but really did not need it. We went to sleep each night listening to the Coqui frogs, which were unique to Puerto Rico. Even though we were only twenty miles from Fort Buchanan, the kids had to be up by 5 a.m. each morning to catch the school bus—this was a definite adjustment for them. As noted before, the traffic in San Juan was unbelievable and during the day, going from Caguas into San Juan routinely took an hour or more for this short distance.

Settled in housing, I started my work in earnest and was busy as one of the few full-timers. I had some long days and then the commute. When we had drill weekends, I just slept in my office because we worked late in the night. One night I came home from work and found Mayumi was about pulling her hair out with stress. During the day around mid-morning, the school had called to say Jason was sick, and she needed to pick him up. It took an hour to get to him and another hour to get back home. She returned home, and the school called to say Freya was sick . . . same basic timeline to and from Fort Buchanan to pick up Freya. I had been feeling guilty anyway with the kids having to get up so early each morning, and at this point, I realized even if I have a longer commute, I needed to see about housing on Fort Buchanan. The housing office granted permission, and we moved into base housing with two units built as one . . . it was perfect. My commute had just increased another half hour each way, but the kids could get up at a much more reasonable time and walk to school.

Not only did I have a long commute, but the Autopista (Highway) was a toll road that went south of Caguas all the way south to Ponce. The tolls added up, especially when I had drill weekends and worked fourteen days straight. I was constantly preparing for the unit's Annual Training (annual fourteen-day training), and we were selected to send a contingent of soldiers to Panama for communications support. You cannot just send soldiers to another country without making sure they are medically ready to deploy—including required vaccinations, medical checks and other required deployment paperwork. I went to the new Battalion Commander and told him, "I have got to have some help." While higher HQ had provided additional funding to bring Reservists full-time, the new Battalion Commander brought himself, the Operations Officer and Battalion Sergeant Major on orders. Two of the above were unemployed. So, I had all three of them daily telling me what needs to be done and asking why it was taking so long.

On top of this, the Commander signed up the 35th to host the annual Military Ball for all the Reserve units on Puerto Rico, and I was responsible for not only planning the event but also to be the host. I lost it one day when the Commander threatened to relieve me because all the above was not happening fast enough for him. I replied, "If you are going to F___ me, then I quit, and second, I don't need senior officers telling me what needs to be done. I know what needs to be done. I need some working people to assist me!" This last part was true but probably not politically correct; however, at that point, I did not give a damn. I then got in my car and drove home, not sure what was going to happen next. I was physically and emotionally spent.

Normally one does not talk to a LTC in this fashion, particularly if one is Captain, but he had pushed the wrong button that day. He called me the next day and apologized and asked me what I needed. I stated I wanted SFC Jose Mendez (Full-Timer) from Delta

Company to come work for me in Juana Diaz full-time and immediately. I also asked for some other excellent Reservists to be brought on full-time for a duration of a few months to start working all the assigned missions. The Battalion Commander made it happen. I will always be grateful to SFC Mendez because he knew I was overwhelmed and he volunteered himself to me. I made sure he worked for me until I left the unit. Throughout all our Annual Trainings (ATs), the deployment to Panama and the Military Ball, I attributed the successes to him. Outstanding soldier!

We had some great friends in Puerto Rico. Two of them, Bob and Angelita Farrell, spent many weekends together with us. Because Angelita was of Filipino descent, she made Filipino egg rolls. Full of garlic, hamburger and other spices, they were simply delicious. For years on, I asked Mayumi to make them, and she did. I attribute my subsequent promotions to those egg rolls. We spent several weekends with the Farrells and their kids at the old Ramey AFB lighthouse, which had been converted to a lodge. Beneath the lighthouse was Crash Boat beach where one could swim and buy fresh fish from the fishermen. We did the same at the Roosevelt Roads Naval Station lodge.

Mom, Dad and Mike came to visit for a few days while we were still in Caguas. I remember Dad waking me up at 3:00 a.m. with the entire house flooded because the washing machine hose had burst. I remember thinking this had to happen while they were visiting. Despite the flooding, we went to the beach, ate at good restaurants and explored Old San Juan. We also explored two other interesting areas. The first was the Arecibo Observatory, which until July 2016 was the world's largest radio telescope. We also went to the El Yunque National Forest, formerly known as the Caribbean National Forest. It is the only tropical rainforest in the US Forest System/Service. There is no distinct wet or dry season at El Yunque as it rains year-round. Because the temperature never drops below freezing, El Yunque has a year-round growing season. Because it rains all year long, it surprised us when Jason famously stated, "You might know Mom would pick a day when it was raining." He did not understand why we were all laughing.

Mom also came a second time to Puerto Rico while Mayumi and I were off training at the same time, so Mom watched the kids again.

During our time in Puerto Rico, Mayumi served as well in the Army Reserve. During our time in Puerto Rico, we both had some issues with our units, and both of us were ready to move on. Moving is hard for all family members and this is the only time Mayumi said, "I don't care where we go but let's go!" When I later told her I had been approved and accepted for a position in Salt Lake City, Utah, she looked at me as if I were trying to be funny.

I left earlier from Puerto Rico while the kids were finishing the school year, except for Freya. She came with me to spend a few weeks with Mom and Dad in Georgia. Mayumi also had some requirements to complete. I had to attend a course for my new assignment in Utah. I shipped the old gray conversion van and picked it up in Orlando, Florida. Freya spent several weeks with my parents and was getting used to all the high-end receptions while Dad was President of DeKalb Community College.

At the fine age of 9, she was dining at fine receptions and drinking fine coffee until her grandma said, "No more coffee." She also enjoyed being the only kid with her grandparents to go to Florida for vacation. She had it made. Freya had always been a horror-film addict and still is to this day. So, at a dinner party, Freya connected with a Professor at DeKalb named Tina. Tina drove a convertible, and Freya was mesmerized by this open-topped vehicle. Being the nice lady Tina was, she asked, "Freya where you would like to go?

Freya replied, "I would like to go to a cemetery." Tina complied. By the way, Freya's favorite movie is *Killer Clowns from Outer Space*. After I had finished my course and rejoined Freya, we then met her mother at the airport. She saw her mom at the airport for the first time in several months and started to cry. She had missed her mom!

Mayumi got emotional as well and said to Freya, "You made *me* cry."

It was a good moment.

**Utah:**

We were excited about our assignment to Utah. We would be close to Mayumi's parents and both of her siblings, Kay and Jim. The kids would also get to spend some quality time with their other grandparents (Michiko and Mac). My assignment was with the 96th Readiness Support Command, and I was assigned as the Mobilization Officer. I had a great job—much less stress than my previous assignment—great boss and great people to work with.

Mayumi and the kids were enjoying being with her extended family, and the kids liked their new schools. In the beginning we decided to stay with her parents until we could get on base or rent something. It turned out we stayed with them until we left for my next assignment. We also had Duffy the basset hound with us. I remember this well because as winter came and the snow began, Duffy got me in trouble. One morning I heard Mac letting Duffy out on the deck to go the bathroom. What I did not realize is Duffy did not want to negotiate the steps leading down to the yard because there were several inches of snow on the steps and had been there for several days. So, Mac let Duffy out on the deck, and I heard him say, "And quit shitting on the Deck!"

About three months in Utah, I got a call from my Assignment Officer. He told me, "You are coming up on the Major's board, and you need to be in a Major's position in order to pin on the rank."

I asked him, "What about any positions here at the 96th.? I did not know my position had been downgraded from a Major to Captain. That is why we just stayed at Mayumi's parents' house until we left in February of 1994. We were there for only seven months. It was short and disappointing, but I would have taken the job in Utah again because we wanted out of Puerto Rico. We had some great times with the Utah folks as we went camping and fishing. We went to the casinos in Wendover, Nevada. Best of all for me was Michiko's excellent Japanese food, including her oven-baked Salmon and Panko Chicken.

In working with my Assignment Officer, I finally was assigned to the Third US Army

(Patton's Own) at Fort McPherson, Georgia (Atlanta), with the G6 (Communications Directorate) as a Plans officer.

**Third Army:**

Third Army is the Army component for US Central Command. Each service had their own component. Central Command was commanded by General Norman Schwarzkopf in Desert Shield/Storm. The Area of Responsibility (AOR) of course was Southwest Asia.

We left in February for Georgia with the gray van and towed a Mustang 5.0 I had bought in Utah. While in Puerto Rico, one of the mechanics in the unit had a Mustang 5.0 with a manual transmission and gave me a ride one day. After the ride, I told him, "I'm getting a Mustang when I get to Utah."

We started our cross-country trip, and I decided to take the southern route, mostly Interstate 40 (I-40) instead of Interstate 70 (I-70), which was quicker. I tried to make the new assignment travels an adventure for the kids and family. The first day we drove south from Salt Lake and spent the night in Las Vegas. The next day we headed for the Hoover Dam. I had always wanted to see it, but I do not recommend doing this while hauling a vehicle on a heavy trailer. I had to stop several times to let the brakes cool.

We reached I-40 in Arizona and started heading east. Every time we stopped for gas and bathroom breaks, I let the kids go get some snacks of their choice. Marcia—who was mainly called Boo, short for Boo Boo—took her snacks very seriously and still does to this day. Boo's particular loves were Potato Chips and Beef Jerky. She was also known as the "Chip Queen." One day when we stopped, everybody did their business and got snacks. Mayumi was going to drive for a while so I could take a nap on the fold-down bed in the back of the gray van. So, we got underway, and it was Boo, Duffy (our basset hound) and me on the bed. Boo started unraveling her beef jerky and Duffy got interested. I told Boo to give Duffy a piece. Boo, AKA Marcia, started to take off a microscopic piece of the beef jerky stick and I saw Duffy's eyes look back and forth from the microscopic piece offered to her and the remainder of the stick. Duffy lunged and devoured the whole stick, less microscopic portion, of the beef jerky. I started laughing because I could see this coming and Boo started to cry. I then handed over a bag to Boo with three more beef jerky sticks in it. Boo took it and went into the corner of the van as far as possible from Duffy.

One of our other stops was the Big Texan steakhouse right off I-40 in Amarillo, Texas. The Big Texan was famous for its 72-ounce steak challenge. If one can eat the whole steak and trimmings it was free. People came from all over the world to take the challenge. We did not try the challenge because the meat itself was as big as a small roast, but we had some good steak. The Big Texan was also a great place for kids with arcade games and souvenirs. There would be several more stops at the Big Texan in the coming years.

Over the years, we had several trips on I-40, which also covers much of the historic Route 66. Later, (in 2020), Jason proposed that we do a road trip along historic Route 66. I was all for it! Per Wikipedia, "US Route 66 or US Highway 66 is also known as the Will Rogers Highway, the Main Street of America or the Mother Road and was one of

Jason receiving Certificate of Commendation Award from Commanding Officer somewhere in Afghanistan.

Jason with his sons (L-R) Sage and Levi

the original highways in the US Highway System. US 66 was established on November 11, 1926, with road signs erected the following year. The highway, which became one of the most famous roads in the United States, originally ran from Chicago, Illinois, through Missouri, Kansas, Oklahoma, Texas, New Mexico, and Arizona before terminating in Santa Monica in Los Angeles County, California, covering a total of 2,448 miles (3,940 km). It was recognized in popular culture by both the hit song "(Get Your Kicks on Route 66)" and the Route 66 television series, which aired on CBS from 1960 to 1964. In John Steinbeck's classic American novel, The Grapes of Wrath (1939), the road "Highway 66" symbolized escape and loss.

Jason, being the world traveler he was, had been to Iceland several times and could give tours. Jason wanted to complete the original route of Route 66 from Chicago to Santa Monica. I could not quite do the whole route as I also wanted to see Boo while I was out West. Boo lived in Lehi, Utah, with her husband Tanner and sons Lincoln and Maguire. Jason flew from Denver, Colorado (where he lives), to Chicago. From Chicago he took the Amtrak train to St. Louis where I met him with my truck. We stayed at a hotel less than a quarter mile from the famous St. Louis Arch. We started the next day, and the next six days we saw so many great sights! I had two conditions on this trip because we would be on or close to I-40 for most of the trip and they both involved steak. The first condition was to stop and spend the night at the Big Texan; they have their own hotel rooms. The second condition, the following day, was to stop in Oklahoma City and eat at Cattlemen's Steakhouse. At both restaurants Jason tried out some unique appetizers, Mountain Oysters (Bull Testicles) at the Big Texan and Lamb fries at Cattleman's. If one needs to increase the cholesterol level, I highly recommend these two restaurants.

I also knocked off some items from my bucket list on the 66 trip: visiting Mickey Mantle's hometown and field where he played, and three sites in Arizona: the Petrified Forest National Park, the Meteor Crater National Park and the Grand Canyon. Jason and I parted ways in Flagstaff, Arizona. Jason completed Route 66 by taking the Amtrak train from Flagstaff to Santa Monica, California. Jason has pictures (standing by the Route 66 signs) at both his starting point in Chicago and his ending point in Santa Monica. From Flagstaff, I drove north into Utah to go visit Boo and her tribe. On the way back to North Carolina, I stopped in Denver to drop off Jason's souvenirs from our Route 66 trip and to see his boys Sage and Levi.

Back to our traveling to my assignment to Third Army. We finally reached Atlanta, and we were going to stay with my parents until we decided on a house. We also enrolled the kids in the same elementary school that Lisa, Mike and I had attended. The school had changed, and that motivated me to find a house quickly.

I started work at Third Army on Fort McPherson. I had been there about a month and a half and noticed many disgruntled officers. For Active-Duty personnel (as I was an Active Reserve Officer), the Army was going through another Reduction in Force (RIF). The Officers had two choices: volunteer to get out with a lowered pension or take a chance at not being on the RIF list. The problem was if the Officer did not volunteer to get out and did come on the RIF list he would not get a pension but a one-time payout. The deadline was approaching, and most of them had already made up their minds and really did not care anymore. I brought the RIF situation up because it had an immediate impact on me.

Prior to this assignment, the highest level I had served at was Battalion level. Third Army was a Three Star HQ commanded by a Lieutenant General. Our section (G6) was responsible for all Army Theater and Strategic communications for the Southwest Asia Area of Responsibility (AOR). During this time, Somalia was heating up with their own civil war. The timeframe on this was about a year prior to US forces fighting a raging battle in Mogadishu where several helicopters were shot down and many Soldiers were killed or wounded. The above scenario was very visibly displayed in the movie *Black Hawk Down* and the book *Black Hawk Down: A Story of Modern War* by Mark Bowden.

So, with the RIF going on and many of the Officers gone or out processing, I was selected to brief the Communications plan for the Third Army taskforce going into Somalia. The mission was later canceled. I had been on the job about two months, and now I was to brief the Deputy Commanding General (DCG – Two Star). Through intense study and much added assistance, I had told my boss I needed some help because I had never dealt with plans at this level before. I was a nervous wreck for several days. In the end, it worked out. I had to pre-brief my Colonel/G6 several times prior to the main briefing and the briefing to the DCG went well. Thank God the DCG did not ask any questions. Afterward I heard the Deputy G6 tell the G6 the following, "Cole is a good briefer; we need to use him more."

I thought, *Great*.

Well, they did use me for more briefings, and I became more comfortable as my knowledge base increased. But I remember that first briefing, and I told myself to remember this when I was in a higher leadership role to be tolerant of inexperienced subordinates in a complex situation.

**Other Reflections from Third Army (Fort McPherson):**

We finally found a house south of Atlanta and Fort McPherson. I had received many recommendations for a place called Peachtree City, Georgia, which is in Fayette County. The Fayette County school system was highly rated within the state. Peachtree City also had over sixty-five miles (now over ninety) of golf-cart paths, which were perfect for running, walking and rollerblading. Many families in Peachtree City had their own golf cart for getting around. We put the kids in the local school, and we were enjoying our new life. There was a Blockbuster movie store a quarter of a mile away, so Friday nights were movie and pizza nights. I also bought a golf cart.

One day I read about an organization called "The Basset Hound Rescue Society of Georgia." We still had Duffy, but I wanted another dog and asked Freya if she wanted to go with me to check out the event. The dogs were rescued Basset Hounds and the society was looking for homes for them. So, Freya decided (I really pushed her hard) on a dog named Quincy. He was a slow walking, slow tail wagging Basset Hound. Quincy was a male hound who peed like a female. The first time he peed like a female was right in front of Mayumi, ten minutes after we brought him into the house. The only times Quincy would really get excited was after I finished bathing him in the tub. He would run around the house like a wild man. I loved all my dogs, but Quincy and I really bonded. I still miss him.

Saddam Hussein was continuing to cause trouble around the fall of 1994 and always around our holidays. Every time he moved some scuds or troops around in Iraq, Third Army ramped up to include 24-hour operations. As one of the lower ranking Officers, I headed up the night operations. I had to do this on several occasions. On one of these episodes, the Deputy Commanding General and representatives from all sections accompanied the DCG to Kuwait in case of escalation. The G6 sent over several personnel to include the Deputy G6. They had been over there a month, and I had asked my boss if I could go there. My argument was, "If I am being asked to plan communications for that area, I would like to have a look at the facilities over there." He approved it.

This trip was the first of many trips I made to Kuwait, Saudi Arabia or Bahrain. I visited the communications areas in each of these countries and I did learn. On one trip to Saudi Arabia, I was running around a walled compound also known as Khobar Towers, and someone outside the compound yelled, "Hey, American, F___ you!" The Khobar towers complex is where American military personnel stayed if in or around the Dhahran area, whether stationed there permanently or on temporary duty. Several months later, while moving to California, the Khobar towers bombing (Truck Bomb) occurred, killing 19 US Air Force personnel, and 498 of many nationalities were wounded. It was later attributed to Iran.

One day at Fort McPherson, I went out for lunch to my favorite barbecue place in East Point, Georgia (The Only Way). On a previous occasion, I ordered pulled chicken, pinto beans, cornbread and collard greens. I was in uniform. The proprietor looked at me, and said, "Cole, white boys don't eat this kind of food."

I replied, "This white boy does!"

Another barbeque day at The Only Way, the TV was on showing a bombed building. I asked the proprietor's wife, "Where in Southwest Asia is that?" It was Oklahoma City. The Oklahoma City bombing was a domestic terrorist truck bombing of the Alfred P. Murray Federal Building on Wednesday, April 19, 1995, perpetrated by anti-government extremists Timothy McVeigh and Terry Nichols.

On one of the trips to Kuwait, I learned on my shortwave radio (British Broadcasting Corporation) that the Atlanta Braves had won the World Series. I did a quiet cheer while eating breakfast in a Kuwait City hotel.

Years later I come back to Fort McPherson, and I went to the The Only Way for some barbeque, and the proprietor said, "Hey, Cole, not seen you in a while."

During my time at Third Army, I was promoted to Major. One of my fellow Officers was also promoted to Lieutenant Colonel (LTC) and selected for Battalion Command. LTC Bob Koester was to command the 319th Signal Battalion in Sacramento,

California. I learned the Executive Officer (XO) position was full-time and would be vacant shortly. I asked LTC Koester if he would take me as his XO, and he quickly agreed. Based upon our time and experiences at Third Army, there was a mutual respect between us. Because the 319th was a Reserve unit, normally the Battalion Commander was not a full-time position. The 319th priority status had recently been upgraded, and Army Reserve leadership decided they wanted a one-time, full-time Commander while upgrading the unit.

We left for Sacramento the summer of 1996. This was also the summer Atlanta hosted the Olympics.

**319th Signal Battalion. Sacramento, California:**

As stated previously, normally on assignment changes, I like to spend some time and go see exciting places with the family. I had to ask a friend (John) to help drive me across the country since Mayumi was in training. I offered to pay his meals and gas, and I gave him some money and paid for his air travel back from Salt Lake City. John also wanted to see some sites like the Grand Canyon and others. I needed to leave the kids and dogs with Michiko and Mac in Salt Lake while I went on to Sacramento to acquire housing. I left the gray van there as well. By this time, I had traded in the Mustang for a pickup truck, which was much more practical with four kids and two dogs.

We left Georgia and about a day out, John informed me that he needed to be back in three days. So, John was driving the gray van and I was driving the truck. I had installed mobile Citizen Band (CB) radios in each so that we could communicate between vehicles. John informed me of this new timeline on the CB, and I was about to blow a gasket. I was sure the truck drivers on Channel 19 were enjoying this. I had to get four kids, two dogs, our interim personnel assets and two vehicles across country! After a minute, I responded, "John, there is no way in hell we can travel across country, see the sights you want to see and get you back in that timeframe!" He had not traveled across country before. John later gave on a few more days when he realized how big this country is... but the first two nights we slept in our vehicles for a few hours at truck stops and kept heading west. After he told me he had a few more days, I told him, "We are getting a hotel room tonight." I wanted some solid sleep, a good hot shower and not truck stop food.

The fourth day we stopped at Meza Verde National Park. Mesa Verde is an American national park and UNESCO World Heritage Site located in Montezuma County, Colorado. The park protects some of the best-preserved Ancestral Puebloan archaeological sites in the United States. The following day, we made it to Mac and Michiko's house in Layton, Utah, and John flew back to Atlanta the following day.

I spent a few days in Utah getting the kids settled and telling them all they needed to do to take care of the dogs, to include feeding, watering, walking and getting rid of Shoo Shoo in the yard. In the Cole house, if there was any discussion about poop or needing to defecate it was called Shoo Shoo! I also did not want any more deck incidents although it was summer.

I reported in to the 319th and LTC Koester had been there about a month. I walked in to in-process and he stated, "What took you long?" This, coming from a bachelor with no kids or dogs. He said he was just kidding, but I was not so sure. He also knew my report date because he had a copy of my orders.

My priority was to find housing. There were two Air Force Bases in Sacramento at the time, McClellan and Mather. McClellan was the only one with housing. It was a good day in that I had a house within hours of meeting with the housing office. The McClellan housing area was an enclosed community with a little convenience store, sport fields, a swimming pool and an elementary school right next to the housing area. Jason was in high school now, and the high school was two blocks away. Within two weeks, I had the family settled in. I had already begun work as the XO.

It was busy the whole two years that I was assigned as the XO of the 319th. We were so busy we received funding to bring on some Reservists to work full-time for several months. One of the Reservists was Mayumi, who served as the Operations Officer. Because of the 319th's increased Readiness priority and the unit conversion to a more modern communication unit, we were constantly receiving equipment. The communications equipment were millions of dollars in value. My priority mission as the XO was to coordinate the timing and receiving of the equipment, and with the assistance of Operations, the training of the equipment for all our Soldiers. We received the new communications equipment, new weapons and new support vehicles. In addition, we had to turn in all the old equipment. As a Reserve unit, we had to work with our Reservists on all the aforementioned requirements because they were not on full-time duty. We also had our Annual Training (AT) requirements, inspections and day-to-day issues. We were busy!

## Other Reflections from Sacramento/319th Signal Battalion:

Jason, Freya, Boo and Mick loved the McClellan housing area. Everything was so convenient and nearby. Here are some reflections on some of their experience there:
The Infamous Shoo Shoo Incident.

One day I came home from the 319th and Freya had something to tell me. I asked Mick to provide a synopsis of the incident, and these are Mick's words.

> "We were living in Sacramento, California, on McClellan Air Force Base. We were always wanting to play with all the neighborhood kids. There was one new girl from the get-go who rubbed us the wrong way. She was a very obnoxious and entitled little girl. Her name I had forgotten, but I remember one day this little girl was hanging out with Freya and I. She was bragging that her daddy was a higher rank than ours, so that made her daddy better. I'd like to think that I was not usually quick to get mad, but growing up, I always remember being very protective of my parents. Well, I had the bright idea and told Freya that we should go get a piece of candy and dip it in dog poop and give it to her. Freya was not really the type to ever want to do something bad or get in trouble, but in this case, she was willing. I was pretty sure the fumes from what the girl was saying about our dad got to her too. Well, we grabbed a piece of white taffy and went and found a dry pile of dog poop, dipped it, and re-wrapped the taffy. We walked over to the girl and gave it to her. She immediately

opened it up and threw it in her mouth. Seconds later she spit it out and said, 'Ew, it tastes like dog poop.' "Freya and I were dying inside because we both knew what we had done. Well, leave it to guilt-ridden Freya to rat us out. That night, after Freya told our dad what happened, he wanted to teach us a lesson. "Go grab a piece of candy," he said. We both did. I grabbed a pink starburst, and Freya grabbed a Hershey's Chocolate Kiss. He led us outside and dipped both pieces in dog poop and handed it back to us and said, "Now, eat it." Crying, we did as we were told, and after a couple seconds he told us we could spit it out. We did. Unfortunately for Freya the Hershey's kiss had mostly melted in her mouth. I, on the other hand, was grateful I chose a starburst, a candy that would not melt. It was a lesson learned that I will forever remember and be humbled by."

Mick told the story and what I did as part of the lesson, although while they both were getting their candy I turned away and was quietly laughing hard inside. I then walked over to the LTC's house and told him I was sorry my girls had given his daughter candy that had been dipped in dog poop, I would have said Shoo Shoo, but he would not have understood it. He was torqued! I then added, "But don't worry, sir, I made my girls eat candy in dog poop as well." The look on his face I will always remember. The LTC probably was thinking, *Friggin Army Major, no wonder that whole family is messed up!*

Marcia (Boo) was a real tomboy during this stage in her life. Marcia, as well as my other daughters are beautiful, very ladylike and are beautiful women today. Marcia mainly played with boys in everything they did. In addition, Marcia dressed like a boy to include a University of Georgia football hat. Boo wore one of Jason's underpants to complete the mission one day or maybe many more. Her friends, the boys, just accepted her for who she was. Well one day, one of the friends had really been convinced. The doorbell rang and Jason answered the door. Marcia's friend asked, "Is your Brother Marcia here?"

Jason had been bugging me for weeks to allow him to jump off the roof of our quarters. Our quarters were of the Capehart housing designs that came in legislation in the 1950s and were on many military bases. I did not know why he wanted to, but he was persistent. I finally realized he was going to do it whether I gave permission or not. This section of the roof was not that tall, and his fall would be in the grass, so I said, "If I let you do this, will you not do it again?"

He said yes. So, for the next ten minutes, I gave him lessons I learned during Airborne (Parachute/Jump School)—Parachute Landing Falls (PLFs). A PLF was a safety technique that allowed a parachutist to land safely and without injury. When executed properly, a PLF was capable of allowing a parachutist to survive uninjured during landing speeds that would otherwise cause severe injury or even death. I also instructed him to not to look at the ground while falling because one tended to lock knees and would have serious consequences for the knees, back and everything else. So, Jason jumped, performed a perfect PLF, and for his own reason, had accomplished the roof fall. Jason later in life went parachuting with a girlfriend one day. Mick also jumped but with no girlfriend.

My father is my mentor and main confidant, and I have the utmost respect for him. When younger I would be stressed on something, and he would calmly say, "Sleep on it, and it will work out." Dad also performed Mark Twain. I am talking about rehearsing hours of Mark Twain (Samuel Clemons material) and performing for live audiences. For further proof, look at "Marvin M. Cole, Mark Twain" on You Tube. Needless to say, I am proud of my dad and of course, my mom. The last year at the 319th, I guess I was a "glutton for punishment." I went to LTC Koester and said, "Lets host a Military Ball and invite our higher HQ leadership." LTC Koester, being the succinct man he was, said, "Sounds good, handle it." Bob was as ambitious as me but preferred I do the details. So, we arranged the 319th Military Ball; well really the S-1, Peggy, the Personnel Officer, and I did. Peggy should be credited for most of the work, and I will always be grateful. She worked tirelessly! I asked Dad to come to Sacramento and do Mark Twain for the Military Ball. Based on Dad's acceptance, we decided to host the event on the Delta Queen steamboat on the Sacramento river. Mark Twain had several years in California and many of his reflections were based on his time in the state. Dad performed Mark Twain after dinner to include a white suit with bow tie, and I was exceptionally proud seeing him doing it. At one point in his performance, some of the unit's participants were a little loud, probably something to do with beer, and I glanced back to give them a dead eye stare and the noise quieted down. After this, Mom and Dad spent the night in a room on the Delta Queen. Later, I had many people tell me how much they enjoyed his performance.

I had been at the 319th for two busy years. LTC Koester's full-time tour as the 319th Battalion Commander was ending, and he had orders for Korea. When I found out he was leaving, I went to him and said, "We made a great team here, and I don't want to have to work for another Battalion Commander when I had the best." I was not buttering him up; I meant it and he knew what I meant. I was also a little concerned my kids were growing up a little too fast in California, and I wanted a change to their surroundings.

I worked with my Assignment Officer and secured a position with the Information Management Directorate of the 96th Regional Support Command (RSC) as the Telecommunications Branch Chief. Back to Salt Lake City, Utah.

## 96th Regional Support Command (RSC). Salt Lake City, Utah:

I left early in late spring of 1998 for Layton, Utah, to stay with Mac and Michiko. The kids were still in school, and we wanted them to finish the school year in California. I also worked on housing, and I was able to obtain quarters on Hill AFB. The base was only about four miles from Mac and Michiko's house and where Mac retired from the Air Force.

I started work at the 96th RSC as the Telecommunication Branch Chief and provided telecommunications support for all Reserve units in the 96th. The 96th included the units within the following states: Utah, Colorado, Idaho, Wyoming, Montana, North Dakota and South Dakota. The major issue at the time was replacing all the antiquated phone systems in our Reserve Centers across the aforementioned states because of the Year 2000 (Y2K) problem. The Year 2000 problem did not really morph into such a problem as predicted, but these phone systems needed replacing anyway. I had a fantastic NCO in Master Sergeant James Stover who came up with a brilliant plan. We contracted with a local telecommunications company (GSL) to prebuild the new phone systems on plyboard (we had standard designs based upon the size and requirements of the Reserve Centers). Once the systems were built, GSL sent teams to the Reserve Centers, deinstalled the old phone systems and installed the new systems. The whole plan worked great.

I had been working several months at the 96th, and one day I got a call from my Assignment Officer. He informed me that I was being considered for a position at the Office, Chief Army Reserve (OCAR) as the Signal Force Integrator. At the time, OCAR was located at the Pentagon and in Crystal City, Virginia, about a block and a half away from the Pentagon. At first, I was thinking, *Great, our time in Utah is cut short again.* But the Assignment Officer also stated it was a LTC's position, and I would be going before board in a little less than two years. It was also a highly visible position at a Three Star HQ, and they were looking at my file strongly. It ended up that I was selected for the position. I was to report next summer (1999) after my predecessor retired. I would have to complete a three-week Force Development course at Fort Belvoir, Virginia, prior to my reporting in.

Duffy was 14 years old and had been showing her age. Lately she began peeing all over the house and drinking constantly. Something was wrong because Duffy was housebroken and rarely had accidents. I took her to the Veterinarian one morning after I noticed both her cheeks were swollen. The Veterinarian said her kidneys were shutting down and toxins were backing up into her body. He said it would only get worse and more painful. I had a decision to make as we are a few weeks out from leaving cross country for my new assignment to OCAR. There really was no decision to make. The next morning, I took her to the Veterinarian to put her to sleep. I held her as she was injected and watched her peacefully lower her head and pass away. I unashamedly wept for my sweet Duffy as she had been with us for fourteen years. When the kids came home that day from school, I told them what I had to do. They were upset that I did not tell them that morning, and I replied, "How could I tell you what I was going to do and then say have a good day at school." We had wonderful memories with Duffy, and we still had Quincy.

I asked Dad for help driving (I was not going to ask John again) from Utah to North Carolina as Mayumi had Reserve requirements to meet. The kids were going to stay with Mom and Dad until I had housing and could bring everyone together.

When we were getting ready to leave Utah, it was time to trade in the gray van. It had nearly two hundred thousand miles on it and was starting to have issues. I purchased a Dodge Durango and a used Subaru. With a trailer, I hauled the Subaru behind us so we could trade off driving with one vehicle.

One of the highlights of the trip back with Dad, the kids and Quincy was stopping at Four Corners. It was way out of the way but very well worth it. The Four Corners Monument marks the quadripoint in the Southwestern United States where the states of Arizona, Colorado, New Mexico, and Utah meet. It is the only point in the United States

shared by four states, leading to the area being named the Four Corners region. So, one could go in this circle where the four states meet put each foot into one section and the same with your hands into their respective sections . . . and you were in four states at one time. We all did this.

## Office, Chief Army Reserve (OCAR), Arlington, Virginia:

As the United States Army Reserve (USAR) Signal Force Integrator, I was responsible for all USAR Signal Corps (communications) units, coordinating the unit force structure of personnel, equipment fielding, new unit designs and working with HQ, Department of the Army (HQDA) on getting Reserve units on the new equipment fielding lists including the latest Satellite technology. At this point I had served with all levels of USAR Signal Corps force structure to include Theater level Signal Commands, Brigades, Battalions, Companies and Detachments. I came into this position confident and ready to work. I had gone to conferences in the past at Fort Gordon and listened as my predecessors in this position provided updates on all the force structure actions, which were currently taking place. I knew what I had ahead of me.

## Other Reflections at OCAR, Virginia:

I reported in to work and learned to use the Metro. The Washington Metro (or simply Metro) is the rapid transit system serving the Washington metropolitan area. The traffic was terrible all around the Washington area, and if possible, the Metro was the way to go. I had been working with a realtor, and it came down to two townhome choices. One townhome was in Springfield, Virginia, and the other townhome was in Chantilly, Virginia. The Springfield location would have been closer and quicker to work as the location was right next to a Metro station, but it was too built up and busy. I chose the Chantilly location because it had three floors and four bedrooms to include the master. Freya and Mick had two of the rooms on the top floor. The master bedroom was also on the top floor. Jason had the room on the bottom floor and Boo had the living area all to herself so she could have her drum set, desk and bed all in one location. We had a bathroom on each floor. It was nice and in a nice area of Fairfax County, convenient to about everything except my work. My commute was well over an hour each way.

Fairfax County had an excellent school system and the kids learned quickly how tough it was. One day Freya came home crying because she was frustrated with some courses. Mayumi and Freya met with some teachers and Freya soldiered on! We also got the kids into Soccer and other sports, and they were busy. Boo also played basketball and Mick was into cheerleading and gymnastics.

I had come to know and respect a Colonel on the Joint Staff who was the National Guard Liaison Officer (LNO), and he represented the USAR as well. His name was Colonel Roy Pansey . . . do not let the name fool you. He called me one day and said the Air Force was upgrading a mobile satellite assemblage and did not have a need for the current assemblage in stock. Would the USAR be interested in having it? I called the 335th Theater Signal Command Operations, and they jumped on it. Through Colonel Pansey's offer, I was able to acquire the Army Reserve's first satellite assemblage. I later arranged for Colonel Pansey to receive a Chief Army Reserve challenge coin and thank you note from the Chief himself. Of course, I wrote the note.

I had a second satellite success shortly thereafter. In coordination with HQDA and some political help, the 804th Signal Company at Fort Shafter, Hawaii, was fielded a brand-new, state-of-art mobile satellite. The 804th routinely supported the US Army Pacific (USARPAC) in communications so this was a win for all. I was able to go to the unveiling of the satellite on Fort Shafter and Senator Daniel Inouye was the keynote speaker. Senator Inouye fought in World War II as part of the 442nd Infantry Regiment. He lost his right arm to a grenade wound and received several military decorations, including the Medal of Honor (the nation's highest military award). When the Senator got out of his car, he asked me, "Major Cole, where is the pisser? I've got to go!" He was definitely a prior soldier and a man I had the utmost respect for.

During our time in Virginia, Mayumi found a Reserve position that ended up with her being brought on full-time duty for most of the three years we lived there. She was promoted to LTC during this timeframe.

I was promoted to LTC during my tenure at OCAR. My goal upon coming back into the Army was to achieve the rank of LTC, and I was very humbled and proud the day those silver oak leaves were pinned on me.

It was September 10, 2001, and I left Dulles Airport in Virginia to fly to Augusta, Georgia, and Fort Gordon. Upon arrival in Georgia, I retrieved my rental car and proceeded to my hotel. The next morning, September 11, 2001, I met my counterpart from the United States Army Reserve Command (USARC – Major Lynette Minnick, a superb Officer) and we were briefing the USAR LNO on the 7th floor of the Signal Center. Suddenly the door opened and the National Guard LNO Colonel stated a plane flew into one of the Twin Towers in New York. I remembered thinking, *What a tragedy!* A few minutes later he came in stating a second plane just flew into the other tower . . . the briefing was over.

We all know what happened next, all planes were immediately grounded or told to land. People were stuck all over the country and other countries. I tried calling Mayumi at her location somewhat close to the Pentagon, because the Pentagon was hit as well. I could not reach her . . . "All circuits are busy" was the message that I heard. This was throughout the Washington metropolitan area. I could not reach the kids, Mayumi, my work! This went on for hours. Finally, later that day, I did reach my boss and she wanted me to stay put . . . I didn't really have a choice. I finally reached Boo that night on a chat forum and she was terribly upset. Mayumi was still not home, I was gone, and she told me, "They keep showing the images of the planes going into the towers!"

I told her, "Turn the TV off, and do not watch it, or put on a movie." I made my decision right there! I was headed back. I called the rental car company, and they had no issue with me taking the car to Dulles Airport, even though I rented it in Augusta, Ga. I was up early the next morning and hit the road listening to the news all the way to Dulles. I finally reached the airport and it was eerily quiet and empty. I was not charged for the rental vehicle and not charged with parking. Something was not right, and I realized I did not hear any planes flying, and I was at a normally extremely busy airport. I made it home, and we were all glad to see each other.

The Operational Tempo (OPTEMPO) increased dramatically for everyone in the Department of Defense and other agencies as the country geared up for war.

Unfortunately, we lost James "Mac" Maguire during our time in Virginia, but we all went to see just him prior to his passing.

\*\*\*

Life moved on. We now had several of the kids getting close to college and Virginia did not offer in-state military tuition waivers as many states do, such as Georgia. Georgia also had the Hope Scholarship where if one maintained a certain grade average, the tuition was much cheaper. We still had our house in Peachtree City, and I knew of a position coming open at the United States Army Reserve Command (USARC) at Fort McPherson, Georgia. I was in the Force Programs Directorate and the Colonel in charge of both Force Programs Directorates at OCAR and USARC was the approver. I lobbied the Colonel for the position, and it was approved.

The USARC Organization Integration (OI) Team Chief position was fast approaching as I had an August 2002 report date. Jason decided to stay in Virginia to work. He has met a girl . . . our kids were growing up. Mayumi and Freya would come down later. Boo, Mick and Quincy would go down with me.

## USARC/Fort McPherson, Georgia, Organization Integration Team Chief:

As the Organization Integration (OI) Team Chief, I oversaw all force structure actions for all branches within the Army Reserve and subsequently served as the Division Chief for the Organizational Integration Division upon my predecessor's retirement.

USARC commanded the USAR intermediate commands and units throughout the Unit States Army Reserve (USAR). All the USARC directorates were busy—getting personnel and equipment to units deploying, setting up training for deploying personnel, acquiring more training equipment and resources—and it was non-stop. My Organization Integrators (OIs) consisted of every branch in the US Army Reserve (USAR). As Team Chief and later Division Chief, I had to learn specific aspects of other branches when briefing higher leadership if my OI branch subject matter experts were not around. These branches included: Aviation, Medical, Quartermaster, Transportation, Civil Affairs, Signal Corps, Military Police, Adjutant General. We were also changing the way units were organized, manned and equipped. There were no front lines anymore; the enemy was everywhere and we could not have units that took months to deploy to execute assigned doctrinal missions.

## Other Reflections at USARC, Fort McPherson, Ga. Organizational Integration Division, Force Programs:

We had purchased the house in Peachtree City in 1994. During all my assignment changes, I used a Property Manager to bring in the renters, take care of the house maintenance issues and tell the renters to move on when we were coming back. I was not done at the USARC yet even after this assignment and kept the house in Georgia, hoping to return.

Boo, Mick, the Quince and I returned to Georgia in August 2002, and I could see the renters were not big on yard maintenance or trimming. It was August in Georgia and incredibly humid and hot. We were living with just the basics while I was still waiting for our household goods to arrive. The girls had air mattresses, and I slept on my Army cot with a sleeping bag. The AC was on in my name, and we were comfortable inside the house. I had the girls work with me every morning for three–four hours cleaning up the yard, trimming and dumping rubbish. We came in drenched, dirty and tired. I let the girls do what they wanted to do the rest of the day. Life improved tremendously when the cable man arrived.

All the moves were hard, but I knew this one might be harder because all the children, now becoming young adults, loved Chantilly, Virginia, their friends and activities. This time I had promised Boo and Mick if they read a book entirely and had a discussion with me upon completion, I would pay them $50.00 each. Besides, the yard work was rough ... they earned it. The book was titled *Who Moved My Cheese? An Amazing Way to Deal with Change in Your Work and in Your Life.*[1] The author was Dr. Spencer Johnson. Per Wikipedia, the book described change in one's work and life, and four typical reactions to those changes by two mice and two "Littlepeople," during their hunt for cheese. It had sold more than twenty-six million copies worldwide in thirty-seven languages and remained one of the best-selling business books. They both read it, we discussed it, and they each received a new $50.00 bill. They still had some post-move adjustments coming.

One night we had pizza, and I left the container near the stove by the dining room window. The next morning, I noticed literally an Army of ants coming in the window and not going for the pizza. A few did, but most went under the stove. I pulled back the stove and found a literal grease pit underneath it. It had half-cooked bacon, other meats and a whole lot of grease. This took us about an hour and a half to clean it up. We had had better tenants before. I started thinking maybe I was not charging enough rent.

The household goods arrived, and we got our furniture and some new furniture Mayumi bought in Virginia to include a new King-sized bed.

I started work at USARC, and Boo and Mick started school. One night I got home from work, and Boo was crying because she did not make the Starrs Mill high school's basketball team in Peachtree City. She had been on the basketball team at Chantilly high

---

[1] Johnson, Spencer, MD. *Who Moved My Cheese? An Amazing Way to Deal with Change in Your Work and in Your Life.* 1998.

school. This was one of those times any father wishes he could fix the problem, but I could not . . . Boo later made the team. I called Mayumi that night and Mayumi talked with her boss to come down and see Boo for a few days. We were all sad.

Mayumi and Freya were back in Peachtree City, and we started to settle in. Freya graduated high school in Virginia, and we started looking for college for her. After some initial struggles in Virginia, she had done very well academically.

Initially we finally decide on Gordon College for Freya. Gordon College was roughly an hour south of Peachtree City. We just wanted to get her started. After a quarter, she would transfer to the University of West Georgia (UWG) in Carrollton, Ga. Eventually Boo would join her there.

In 2004, Boo graduated Starr's Mill School and joined Freya at UWG in the fall.

At USARC I had a good buddy (LTC Ralph Sparks) who worked in the Full-Time Support (Personnel) Directorate. We had worked at OCAR together and came to the USARC about the same time. We bugged each other constantly. One day I had to go to the restroom to take care of some business. Ralph had watched me go in the bathroom and waited a minute to let me get settled on the throne and purposely spoke like there were other people in the bathroom and stated, "Has anyone seen that Son of a Bitch Cole? What a jerk!" I knew he was messing with me, so I replied, "Leave me alone, I'm taking a Ralph."

Later in 2004, I started putting my packet together for the Colonel's Promotion Board with the results to be released at the end of the first quarter of 2005. By this stage of my career, to my mind, I had far exceeded the expectations of my parents. I had some good assignments under my belt with very good efficiency reports, but I was not holding my breath on making Colonel. Percentage wise, Colonel was a much tougher promotion to make. It was also a satisfying feeling that I had qualified for retirement because I had roughly twenty-five years of service by late 2004. Nonetheless, I put a very diligent effort in my promotion packet and had several people review the packet to include my leadership.

The year 2004 turned into 2005, and I continue to work. Ralph and I talked about the pending release date because Ralph was being considered as well. In the back of my mind, I was starting to plan for what I was going to do after the Army if not selected. The Mandatory Retirement Date (MRD) for a LTC was twenty-eight years of service.

It was the night before the promotion list was to be released and I got a call from Ralph on the home phone. Ralph said, "Guess what I'm doing?"

I replied, "Not sure."

Ralph then replied, "I'm having a cigar and a bourbon celebrating because we both made it, Bitch!" Because Ralph worked in Full Time Support (FTS) Directorate, the FTS Director was given an early release of the Colonel's board selectees. The FTS Director let Ralph look at the list prior to Ralph leaving work that day. I did not say anything to anybody because I still wanted to see it in black and white.

Shortly thereafter, all the new Colonel selectees were to turn in their assignment preferences. For the last six years I had been in Force Structure positions and not my basic branch, Signal Corps (communications). I called the Colonel's assignment officer and stated, "I am not sure what to list for assignments, Force Structure or Signal Corps positions?"

She replied, "Oh it's Signal, both Theater Signal Commands (TSCs) want you, so you need to decide your preference." Senior USAR leadership also had a say in assignments.

It turned out the decision was made for me. The Commanding General (CG) of the 311th TSC, currently based at Fort Meade, Maryland, was shortly beginning the process of moving the 311th from Maryland to Fort Shafter, Hawaii, and they wanted a Colonel in Hawaii to establish the command. This was a high priority event as the 311th was the Theater Signal Command for the US Army Pacific (USARPAC) and eventually US Forces Korea (USFK) would also fall under USARPAC chain of Command. My Signal Corps OI (LTC Donald Greenlee) and I were working the 311th transition plan for months and this pretty much sealed my future assignment. An outstanding Officer, LTC Greenlee, deserved most of the credit for the 311th's transition plan. The 311th also had a Colonel's position in Korea, and this is where I originally thought I was going, but the CG of the 311th chose differently.

**311th Theater Signal Command (TSC), Fort Shafter, Hawaii:**

My mission was to immediately establish the 311th TSC from on Fort Shafter, Hawaii (outside of Honolulu). The move entailed all inherent force structure—logistical, obtaining facilities, maintenance, and personnel responsibilities—in establishing the unit. The 311th TSC already had a detachment at Fort Shafter who worked in coordination with the USARPAC G6 (Communications Officer/Directorate). With three LTCs and several NCOs in position, I had some immediate help, but they also had their responsibilities with the USARPAC G6. I had one of the LTCs (LTC Frank Skirlo) work directly for me, and we started working all the aforementioned requirements in establishing the 311th in Hawaii.

I was on the phone daily with the 311th Chief of Staff (COS) at Fort Meade and weekly telephonic meetings with the 311th CG and staff. About a month later, a miracle reported to duty in the name of Sergeant Major Mark Pappenfuss. He was a godsend. With almost thirty-three plus years of experience, he had knowledge about everything and was previously assigned to the 311th in Korea. He had established units from scratch previously and started making things happen immediately. We soon had our own facilities, furniture and telephone systems. While I was primarily coordinating with the 311th staff, USARPAC and TSC leadership, Sergeant Major Pappenfuss was the main orchestrator of establishing the 311th on the island of Oahu.

As we received more and more staff, establishing the command continued to accelerate in motion. The 311th was a subordinate unit of USARC, and I was continually flying back to Atlanta and Fort Meade to brief Army Reserve leadership on our requirements. We were asking for substantial amounts of funding, equipment, and more full-time support personnel. I was continually meeting with the CG of the 311th and the COS at USARC. I also had briefing requirements at the Network Enterprise Technology Command (NETCOM) at Fort Huachuca, Arizona. NETCOM had overall responsibility for all US Army strategic communications to include overall security. This entailed TSC reporting responsibilities to NETCOM in meeting overall security and communications protocols.

The assignment to the 311th TSC ended up being only a year long as the USARPAC CG wanted a more seasoned Colonel for the COS position. I was still a very junior Colonel with not even a year in the rank. The 311th CG offered me another position on Hawaii, but I was not thrilled at being a geo-bachelor (living in a different location from the family members) for another two years out in the Pacific.

## Other Reflections from 311th TSC, Fort Shafter, Hawaii:

Prior to departing for Hawaii, I had my Colonel promotion ceremony at the Fort McPherson Officer's Club. I had my whole family, to include Jason who had arrived the previous day from Virginia. I also had Mom, Dad, Lisa and Mike in attendance. I had my soon-to-be COS from the 311th and Mayumi pin on the Eagles on my dress jacket. I took off my dress jacket and each kid put a rank on my collar epaulettes and hat, and then we had a group hug.

The first day I went into the Army, September 4, 1980, and was picked up at the crack of dawn by my recruiter, Dad gave me a sealed letter and told me not to open it until I arrived at Basic Training. I had been promoted to Colonel, and it was my turn to speak. I pulled the letter out of my jacket pocket and began my talk by saying "On 4 September 1980, leaving for my first day in the Army, my father gave me this letter with instructions not to open it up until I was at Basic." I then read some excerpts from the letter on his recommendations, his thoughts and Mom and Dad's love for me. I think he was touched that I still had the letter twenty-five years later. The year of this writing is 2021, and I still have the letter.

Because Mick was still in high school and Mayumi was on full time duty at the USARC, I went to Hawaii as a geo bachelor. While all the Temporary Duty (TDY) away from Hawaii was getting old, I did not complain about my trips to the USARC because I could see my family in Peachtree City.

I had shipped my car two months earlier from Atlanta to Hawaii. I wanted immediate transportation, and I had it when I arrived at Honolulu.

Two of my Soldiers had been dating for quite a while. MSG Cox was with me at the 319th Signal Battalion in Sacramento. They decided to get married, and the ceremony was held on a private beach in Hawaii. As the Commanding Officer, I declared the day off.

I had rented a basic apartment in Mililani, Hawaii, right next to a golf course. The Army provided a housing allowance and the amount provided depended on one's location. Hawaii was expensive, particularly the housing; thus I had a barebones apartment as I still had a mortgage in Peachtree City. It worked out because my housing allowance provided for me to pay both the apartment and the house without any extra money coming out of pocket.

On one trip to Fort Huachuca, Arizona (Sierra Vista), LTC Frank Skirlo and I stayed over a Super Bowl weekend prior to continued working with the NETCOM staff the following week. Our hotel was next to a particularly good Mexican restaurant. On Super Bowl Sunday, Frank and I went to the restaurant late in the afternoon to have a beer. After a short time, the restaurant was closed because the staff was going to have their own Super Bowl party. We asked the Manager if he wanted us to leave, and he said no. He asked us to stay with them for a meal and all the beer we wanted at no charge while watching the Super Bowl. We had a great time and thanked him profusely.

I had two sessions of visitors while in Hawaii. Mayumi brought Michiko over for a couple of days, and we explored the island. The second visitor was Marcia the Boo. When I found out Boo was coming, I decided to do her visit right. So, I booked a room at the Sheraton Waikiki, which is right on the beach. When I booked the hotel, I explained I lived on Oahu and did not need an ocean view. This cut down the cost considerably. One afternoon Boo and I were on the Sheraton's patio and bar on the beach, and the sun was going down. When the sun starts to set in Hawaii it is fast. Boo wanted me to take a picture of her with the sun in the background. She wanted me to take the picture when the sun looks as if it is sitting on the ocean before its final descent. I got distracted and the next thing I knew was the sun wss gone. Boo was torqued and came stamping over since this was her last night on the island. I was feeling bad about not getting the picture, and a few minutes later, a pompous guy and his equally pompous wife, who had probably egged him on, said to me, "You ought to be ashamed of yourself for being with a girl her age." Well, that tore it! I just looked at him and said, "She's my daughter, Asshole." He quickly walked away.

I finally found out I was being reassigned back to the USARC but in the G-2/6 Directorate. I was thrilled to be back at the USARC and home to Peachtree City, Georgia.

## USARC G-2/6 Enterprise Operations Officer. Fort McPherson and Peachtree City, Georgia:

The G-2/6 consisted of two functional areas in one directorate. G2 was Intelligence and G6 was Communications. So, my boss Colonel Phillips wore two hats.

My new position was the Enterprise Operations Officer for the Army Reserve Network (ARNET). I was responsible for all Enterprise Operations for the ARNET including the associated Command, Control, Communications and Computers (C4) requirements. ARNET responsibilities covered a virtual installation, within the contiguous United States, consisting of 3.7 million square miles, 900 plus reserve centers, over 3,000 buildings, over 50,000 full-time users and an authorized component end strength of 205,000 Soldiers.

The USAR G-2/6 was in three locations in 2006: USARC Headquarters at Fort McPherson, G-2/6 North in Chrystal City, Virginia, servicing OCAR, and the USAR Data Center and associated functions located in Peachtree City, Georgia.

The primary Data Center was in Peachtree City (in 2006) and this is where my office was. Home was less than five miles from work unless I had other responsibilities at HQ, USARC on Fort McPherson.

**Other Reflections as the Enterprise Operations Officer. G-2/6, Peachtree City and Fort McPherson:**

Mayumi also worked in the G-2/6 directorate and was the full-time Administrative Assistant for Colonel Phillips while on full-time orders. So, before I even arrived, I had good information on how my new boss was, current issues at the time and what some of my new responsibilities would be.

I reported in early August 2006 and realized very soon how much I needed to learn. When I first arrived in the position, I felt as if I were drinking water from a fire hose. The Data Center in Peachtree City had approximately thirty Soldiers and Officers, about the same amount of Army Civilian employees and over two hundred contractors. This was a big budget operation in maintenance and support of the ARNET and other Information Technology (IT) functions.

A few months into my new position, Colonel Phillips called me one night at home and told me he would be out the next day to take his wife to the Doctor for stomach issues. It ended up she had to have emergency surgery, and Colonel Phillips was out for several weeks. We were going through some major contract changes, and it was a tense time while I was still learning my new position. I hated to bother him during this timeframe as his wife had major surgery and needed a good amount of recovery time and his support.

While Colonel Phillips was out, I had to continually update the USARC COS daily of the major contract negotiations. If we did not get this right, the ARNET could have shut down for all USAR personnel. Eventually, all the issues worked out but not without a few restless nights.

I was happy with the Enterprise Operations position, the location of the job and my boss. But then I received a phone call from my old boss, Major General (MG) Donna Dacier, CG of the 311th TSC. MG Dacier was full time in Hawaii now while the 311th TSC was fully performing its mission in Hawaii and for the US Army Pacific (USARPAC). The 311th still maintained a detachment in Korea and MG Dacier wanted me to come to Korea to be the Eighth Army G6. This was a hard choice because I loved my current position, but I had always wanted to go to Korea, and this was the opportunity to be the G6. I also knew my timeclock was ticking on how much time I had left in the Army. My Mandatory Retirement Date (MRD) was approaching, and this was possibly my last opportunity to go overseas. I talked to Colonel Phillips, and he agreed to let me go.

Mick was still in high school so Mayumi stayed in Peachtree City until Mick graduated. Mick would join Boo at the University of West Georgia in the fall of 2008.

In May of 2007, Freya graduated from the University of West Georgia, and we all attended the ceremony to include my parents and siblings. Freya worked around Atlanta for about six months and finally took a position at AccuWeather in State College, Pennsylvania, in December of 2007. Freya still lives in State College today (2022) with her husband Cobb and new baby girl, Kai.

My report date to Korea was early September 2007. It was a long flight from Atlanta to Inchon International Airport in Korea (thirteen to fourteen hours) and I arrived a day later.

**Eighth U.S. Army, Yongsan base, Seoul, Korea:**

I arrived at Inchon Airport, and I was met by my soon-to-be temporary predecessor and we drove to Yongsan Army Base in Seoul.

I would serve as the Eighth US Army (EUSA) G6. Eighth Army is the Army Component of the United States Forces Korea (USFK). In 2007, Eighth Army was a US Field Army and the commanding formation of all United States Army forces in South Korea. It commanded US and South Korean units and Headquartered at Yongsan, Korea, in metropolitan Seoul.

There were four major transformation efforts on-going in the Korean Theater of Operations (KTO) in 2007:

– Yongsan Relocation Plan (YRP).
  – Relocates US Forces out of Seoul to US Army Garrison (USAG) Humphreys outside Pyeongtaek, Korea. South of Seoul.
– Land Partnership Plan (LPP) agreement.
  – Reduces major installations within the KTO; 2ID relocation to USAG Humphreys. South of Seoul.
– Strategic Transition Plan (STP): Involving Command and Control (C2) of Korean forces with USFK.
– Combined Forces Command (CFC)
  – Transforms into two national commands: US KORCOM and ROK Joint Forces Command, in doctrinally "supporting to supported" roles.
– Eighth USA (EUSA)/Pacific Integration
  – Reorganizes Army forces all over the Pacific.

Of the four major Transformation efforts above, the Yongsan Relocation plan and the EUSA Pacific Integration were the main efforts in my lane. The other efforts were at the USFK level.

**Other Reflections from Eighth US Army, Yongsan base. Seoul, Korea:**

When having meetings with other units/personnel on the Korean Peninsula and throughout the world, this was accomplished by Video-Teleconference (VTC). Which is today's world. More people would understand this technology as a Zoom meeting. Our VTCs were secure for classification reasons, and we were communicating primarily on the Peninsula; at the US, mainly the Pentagon; and throughout the world. The VTC sessions occurred at all hours of the day or night (depending on what time zones were involved), seven days a week.

The G6 was responsible for all VTC sessions to include providing the operators, scheduling the sessions and maintenance of the equipment. With my short time on station,

I had noticed many outages where the VTC lost connection with the other party/parties. I was tired of getting these looks from the CG and COS and needed to come up with some solutions quickly. I then realized USFK did not have these issues and later found out in recent years they spent thousands of dollars on buying top quality VTC equipment and upgrading their IT infrastructure. They also had a staff of nicely paid contractors and a much bigger budget. I had lower enlisted personnel with some NCO and Officer leadership who were not the sharpest knives in the drawer.

I had a meeting with my Deputy (LTC John Jordon) and my Information Assurance/Network Planner (Major Chris Heath) and gave the following directives: "Come up with a plan and budget to upgrade both of the EUSA Command conference rooms to include all the VTC equipment and IT infrastructure and to include more bandwidth for better quality video." With this plan, I was going to brief the COS for all the above upgrades and the money required to make it happen. Part of the plan eventually included the upgrading of the EUSA exercise facilities in Daegu, Korea.

I also made some personnel moves to get some leadership in the VTC section. I had recently been assigned a new Major (Kim Bivin) from the states who was of Korean American descent (he spoke Korean), which helped the G6 tremendously on multiple future occasions. One day I came back from another VTC meltdown and had a meeting with the aforementioned officers including Kim and stated, "I need the VTC upgrade plan yesterday," and then I looked at Kim and said, "You are now in charge of the VTC section. Pick who you want as operators, train them to include running drills and fix this." I was losing sleep over these VTC issues.

The plan was developed. I briefed the COS on the VTC upgrade plans for the EUSA HQ and exercise facilities in Daegu. I also briefed the COS on my new head of the VTC section and training plans for the operators. I further stated I needed the conference rooms closed for a month to make this happen. The COS approved the plan with the requested budget, and the next month we initiated the improvements with our chosen contractors. Major Kim Bivin did pick his preferred operators and immediately started training and running drills for the new VTC section. When the improvements were completed and the operators were trained and having fantastic leadership of the VTC section, my sleeping improved immensely. I had three outstanding Officers in Korea (LTC John Jordon, Major Chris Heath and Major Kim Bivin). LTC Bivin went on to become the G6 of the 2nd Infantry Division, which, at the time, was located along the DMZ.

One other story on Major Kim Bivin: We were having one of our quarterly Hail and Farewell luncheons. Hail to the new arrivals and farewell for those Soldiers soon departing. Major Kim Bivin had a sense of humor. One of our Soldiers soon to depart had made some very weird and goofy choices. As this Soldier was in Kim's section, he told him one day, "Get your head out of your ass." Well, as part of this Soldier's departure, Major Bivin gave a little speech and handed the departing Soldier a gift. It was a wooden hand-carved man bending forward with his head up his ass.

The whole room broke up, and later I told Kim, "I want one of those when I leave." I still have it.

In September 2008, Mayumi finally arrived in Korea and eventually began a Reserve position at USFK and came on full-time orders.

Mayumi and I went on many tours, but the tour I remember the most (I did it twice) was The Joint Security Area, (JSA), often referred to as the Truce Village of Panmunjom. It is the only portion of the Korean Demilitarized Zone (DMZ) where North and South Korean forces stand face-to-face. You have probably seen the famous UN blue colored buildings in the news, and it is used by the two Koreas for diplomatic engagements. In the middle of the building is a line that indicates the border and whether you are in North Korea or South Korea. Tourists go in the building and the tour guide gives them an historical briefing about the building and other events. During both briefings, I stood on the North Korean side and listened. Upon completion of both briefings, I hurried back into South Korea!

In 2008, Boo graduated from the University of West Georgia with her Bachelor's Degree and also obtained a grant to start her Master's. Boo graduated in 2009 from the University of West Georgia with a Master's in Business Administration (MBA).

Through an Army program, Mayumi arranged for Boo and Mick to come visit us in Korea. We paid for Freya. Jason could not make it. For two weeks we had the pleasure of our girls in Korea. We visited many sites, went shopping and took several more tours. We also had Kay and Dusty's daughter, Charlotte, visit us with her husband Adam. One of Mayumi's friends also came to visit unannounced since she had lived in Korea previously. The security precautions were a little tighter now and we, mainly Mayumi, had to jump through hoops to get her a visitor's pass on base. I did not appreciate it when, upon her departure, I saw in the rearview mirror her flossing her teeth in my new Pontiac G8 . . . she even left the floss on the floor.

My two-year tour in Korea came to an end in September 2009, and I was tired of Kimchi. I had two years remaining until I hit my mandatory retirement mark. I emailed my old boss Colonel Phillips at the USARC—he was now the acting COS—and asked if he could use me again in the G-2/6. He readily agreed but stated I would be serving in a different capacity.

## USARC G-2/6. Base Realignment and Closure (BRAC) Team Chief and G-2/6. Fort McPherson and Peachtree City, Georgia:

My new position was to serve as the G-2/6 BRAC Team Chief for the movement of the G-2/6 to include both elements of the Directorate on Fort McPherson and our Data Center and other G-2/6 elements from Peachtree City, Georgia, location. A G-2/6 BRAC team had been working the relocation since I had left for Korea, and the plan was in motion. Becaiuse the G-2/6 was responsible for the operation and maintenance of the Army Reserve Network (ARNET), hosted by our Data Center, we would have to build a new Data Center at Fort Bragg, North Carolina, to transfer ARNET operations. The plan was to build the USARC Data Center in the same building as the Forces Command (FORCOM) Data Center. The building of both Data Centers was in progress when I returned from Korea.

The 2005 Base Realignment and Closure Commission (BRAC) preliminary list was released by the United States Department of Defense on May 13, 2005. It was the fifth

Base Realignment and Closure proposal generated since the process was created in 1988. It recommended closing twenty-two major United States military bases and the "realignment" (either enlarging or shrinking) of thiry-three others. Fort McPherson and Fort Gillam (both in the metropolitan Atlanta area) were on the BRAC list for closing. Fort McPherson itself had three major commands on the installation, and all would move to a new installation. FORSCOM and the USARC would move to Fort Bragg, North Carolina, and Third Army would move to Shaw AFB in South Carolina. All the above HQ's moves were to be completed by 2011.

Many people, in all the aforementioned HQs, were not happy moving from Atlanta to Fort Bragg (Fayetteville, North Carolina). For military personnel there was no choice unless one retired or left the service. For Army civilian personnel, their choice was to find another local or other civilian position or retire. The contractors had much more of a choice. Of the more than two hundred contractors working the Data Center, Information Assurance (IA) and other ARNET functions, these skilled contractors had more options. Many of the contractors were highly trained, holding IT certified credentials, and in-demand specialties with a multitude of opportunities around the metropolitan Atlanta area. Fayetteville (Fort Bragg), as opposed to Atlanta, was no contest. By far the biggest issue the G-2/6 (other Directorates as well) had—and I would work until I retired in 2011—was losing highly skilled contractors.

In the summer of 2010, Colonel Chip Phillips retired from the Army. The Deputy G-2/6 was Terry Brown (a retired Colonel and the G6 when I was at Third Army). Terry asked me to act as the interim G-2/6 until the new G-2/6 was assigned. To be frank, I really did not want the position since I was preparing for retirement and post Army. Terry further explained, "I need you to be the interim G-2/6 so I can deal with the day-to-day issues to keep our BRAC plan moving and working the contractor issues. Terry further stated if he were the G-2/6, he would have to spend most of his time in meetings with the leadership . . . he was right. I took one for the team and became the interim G-2/6 in July of 2010. The other major issue I had, besides the contractors, was senior leadership continually coming up with these great ideas involving the network or other IT initiatives. I was continually having to tell the senior leadership we did not have resources to do it, and it was not my priority. I reiterated BRAC was the priority and had a Congressional mandate with a fixed date for completion. The G-2/6 was barely making it with the continued loss of contractors and transferring personnel. Some of these General Officers and Senior Civilian personnel did not like being told no or their initiatives were not my priority.

In the beginning of 2011, the next G-2/6 was selected, and I could not wait for him to take over. The last year and half had been highly stressful (I was used to stress but not stupid stress) and for the first time in my Army career, I was ready to retire. The new G-2/6 took over in February 2011, and I soon began my terminal leave. I had over 120 days of leave. The COS hosted my retirement ceremony at USARC in the early spring and Mayumi, Boo, Mom, Dad, Lisa and Mike were able to attend. I wished Jason, Freya and Mick could have attended, but we could not make it happen. I retired from the US Army on May, 31 2011, comprising a time period of thirty-one years and three days.

**Final Thoughts:**

When my father asked me to contribute to this book, I had no idea how much I would get into it. In the process of writing, the memories just kept coming. At first, I was going to write just about my experiences in Pakistan and Afghanistan, but I realized these initial overseas tours later influenced my decision to join the Army. My own family had many wonderful times in our travels and some hard times too. I wanted them in this book because they were part of the grand adventure. All in all, I have been extremely fortunate to have had the experiences in my life, and this writing was very enjoyable for me. I also wanted to let my children know some of my thoughts, concerns and trials during my assignments and why I made some decisions. I also wanted to share some special memories of the children so my grandkids can read about it one day. I hope this writing brings some smiles and laughs, but some of the grandchildren may need to wait a few years before reading it. Hooah!

Kimonoed Boo Boo, Michaela and Sherry.
Jason, Levi, Sage and Michaela.
The "Girl's" visiting Tom and Mayumi in Korea.

Freya with Cobb and Kai dressed ready for the unicorn race.

Marcia The Boo Boo and Tanner, with Lincoln and Mac.

Levi in what looks like heavenly milkshakeland.
Michaela on Graduation Day with Sage, Freya and Jason.
Tom with friend Quincy. Levi supporting Peace.

Quincy

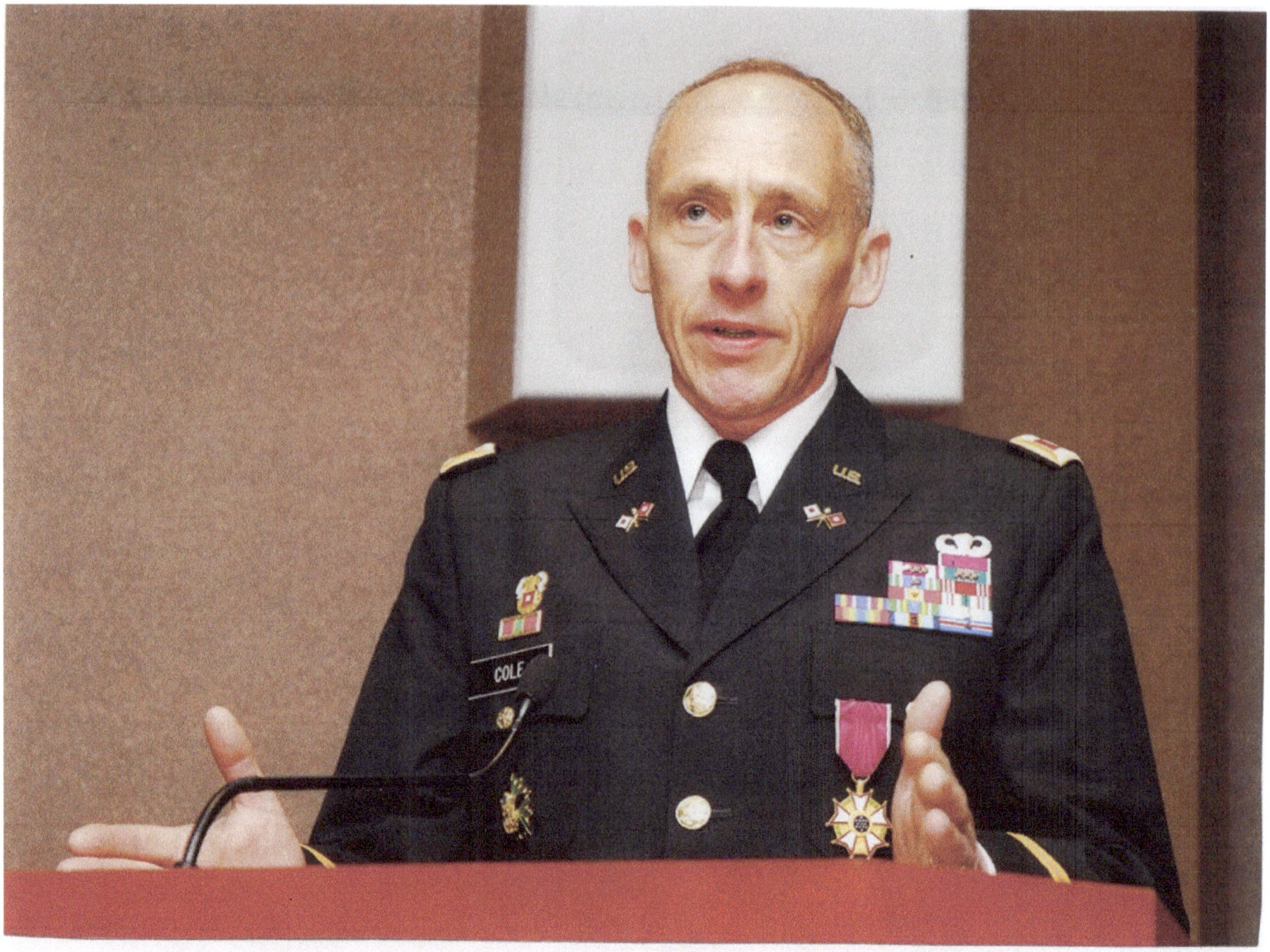
COLE

Congratulations
Colonel Cole!

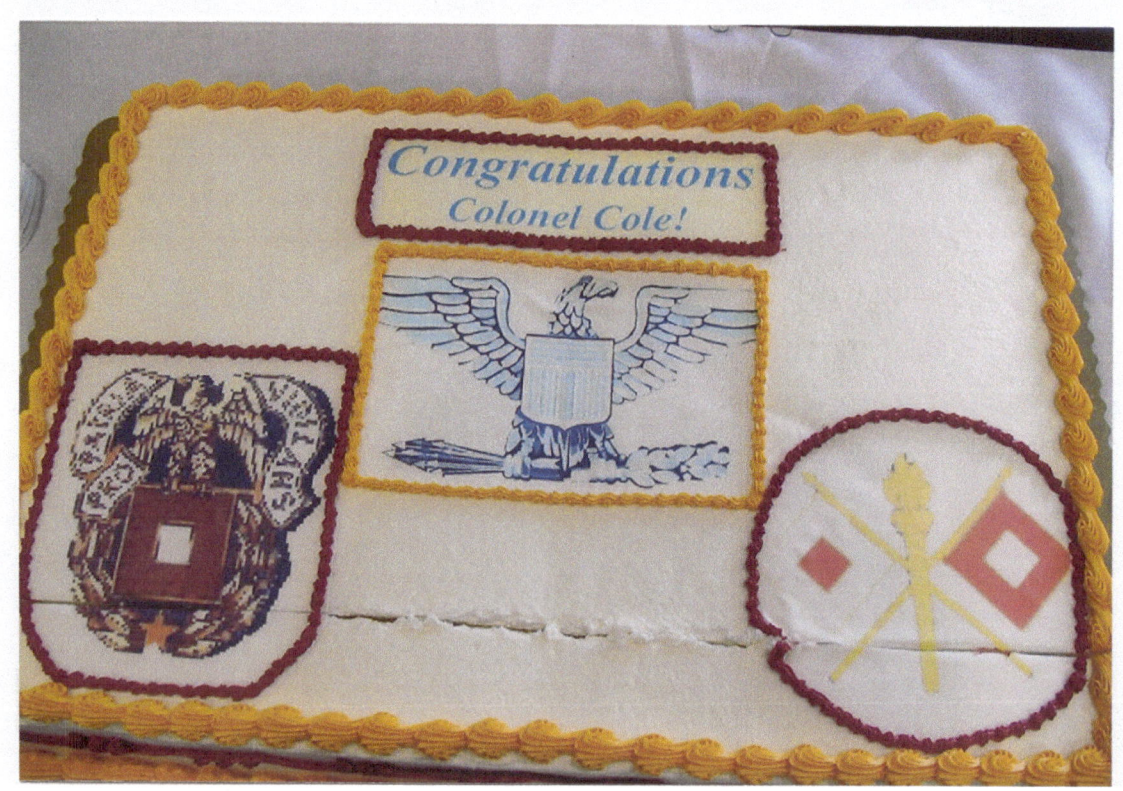

Tom in his element

# 4

# A Snapshot of Memories
# Marcia Elizabeth (Lisa) Cole Slocum

Put me in Coach...

The Volvo Construction Legal duo.

Slocum's at Christmas

**Moore trouble!!!**

On this our wedding day…

Celebrating at the Ridge Road Bad Girl Festival

# A Snapshot of Memories
# Marcia Elizabeth (Lisa) Cole Slocum

When Grandpa Marvin (Dad to me) asked us to write a chapter in his book to grandkids, I had to think a little about what I would write. What's it like to grow up with Mimi and Marvin? "Grow up" is a relative term. I often say, "When I grow up, I want to be . . . or I want to do . . . But really when do we grow up? As I've told many people, "I don't have to worry about growing up because my father still hasn't grown up at the young age of 90."

What did our parents teach us and continue to teach us? They taught us many things—morals, ethics, humor, kindness, decency, but the most significant in my book is diversity and open-mindedness. When I applied for a position with Volvo Construction Equipment (we'll call it VCE) fifteen years ago, they did a detailed background check. The gentleman that performed the background check was a former Scotland Yard Agent in the UK, so believe me when I say it was thorough. He called previous employers and my references. When he called one of my former bosses, Rosario, from the Street Department of the City of Aurora, Illinois, he asked if I was open to diversity and working with people from different countries. Rosario replied, "I'd definitely say so because I'm Mexican and we got along just fine." Rosario, also known as Butch, contacted me immediately after that call because he thought it was really funny.

Living in Pakistan and Afghanistan as children taught us how to appreciate different cultures. We learned from the people we met and we taught them some things too. For instance—apparently, I have no memory of it since I was only 2-3 years old—I taught one of our household helpers the word Shoo Shoo (our family nickname for Number 2). I probably told him it was our secret word because when he greeted my parents with hello, he greeted me with . . . Lisa, Shoo Shoo! I was simply trying to help him out with his knowledge of the English language. There apparently is another story that Brother Tom and I wrapped towels around our heads, sat outside our house in Pakistan and told the passersby the English equivalent of "Go to Hell!" Yikes! That was all Tom—he made me do it!

There is another story, which I have no memory of but is told often with giggles. When I was around 3 years old, we visited the Taj Mahal in India. There is a picture of me in front of that majestic mosque, wearing a cute red and white dress, red tights and a blue sweater. I was stylish back then as well. That was a very traumatic day. Mom told us to stay close to them because there were wild monkeys roaming around. Sure! Like there are really monkeys roaming around. They were busy talking and taking pictures, so off I went to explore. The next thing that happened was that Mom heard me screaming and saw me running, crying hysterically with a monkey attached to my back! I can literally say I had a monkey on my back. Later that night, we went out to eat at a fancy restaurant. The waiters were very formal with turbans on their heads and white gloves—think of the Disney movie Aladdin. They brought a beautiful red velvet pillow for me to sit on. Now remember, I had a traumatic day. Apparently, my tummy wasn't feeling so well, and I proceeded to go "shoo shoo" all over that beautiful, red velvet pillow. As my parents rushed us out of the restaurant, they turned around to see that formal waiter walking quickly away wearing a very disgusted face holding that beautiful red velvet pillow in his white gloved hands. Wow, I know how to clear a room.

I don't have any memories of Pakistan because I was so young, but I do have fond memories from Afghanistan. I was in 4th, 5th and 6th grades. Tom is twenty-one months older and Mike is seven years younger. Mike was very little in Afghanistan. To me the best part of Afghanistan was all the sports we played. There wasn't any television or radio, so we read a lot and played any type of sport we could. We played softball, football, field hockey, basketball and tennis, and we swam. I remember taking tennis lessons at the American International Development (A.I.D.) complex. Our house helper, Ali Baba, would take me to my lessons on the back of his bike. I bet that was a sight to see. To this day, I am a lousy tennis player. We also listened to some wonderful music.

It was very common in Afghanistan to have help around the house. We had a house helper, a cook and a gardener; we had different gardeners and cooks, but Ali-Baba was our consistent house helper through our stay in Afghanistan. We were very fond of him.

As families would leave Afghanistan, they would leave various items with their friends. Some of those items were record albums—I wish I had those records to this day—wonderful music from the Beatles to the Rolling Stones. Tom and I loved to listen to those records. One of the albums was psychedelic—it was really neat to watch it play on the turntable. We also were given two beautiful dogs, Doingla and Princess. Doingla was a large, weenie dog and Princess, a German Shepherd. We loved those dogs very much. We were able to bring Doingla back with us when we moved from Afghanistan. Tom saved his money to pay for her ticket back to the States. We made sure Princess had a good home since we couldn't bring both dogs.

One of my favorite memories of Mike in Afghanistan was that Mom and Dad had purchased several toys for Mike for Christmas. I believe there was a wagon and a tricycle. They hid the toys from Mike in the little house on the property of the gardener (Baba) and explained that these were for Mike. Baba didn't speak much English. Well apparently, there was some confusion in the translation because Baba got really excited and brought all the toys out into the yard when Mike woke from his nap. There goes the Christmas surprise! Mom and Dad came up with the brilliant idea to paint the items so Mike wasn't aware on Christmas day that what he played with earlier wasn't one and the same. Crisis diverted!

Along with learning diversity from our parents and the many different ethnicities we met in Afghanistan, my love of reading and softball started in Afghanistan. I read the complete Nancy Drew series and when I was done with Nancy Drew, I read the entire Hardy Boy series. There is no telling how many more books I read in Afghanistan. To this day, I read at least three books a month.

There were large walls around the houses in the area of Kabul, Afghanistan, that we lived in. One of our pastimes was to climb the walls and go from house to house. Kind of dangerous now that I think about it. The walls were about ten feet tall. The beauty is we got to do some eavesdropping on the neighbors. One of our neighbors, Bob Greenberg (also dubbed Kabob by Mike), lived diagonally from us. We had a ladder up on our wall and he had a ladder on his side so we could easily go visit each other. We once had a dog named Myert (not sure about the spelling but it means My Heart); he would climb up the ladder on our side and go down the ladder on Bob's side. It was pretty wild to watch. I never knew dogs could climb ladders. I think Bob had a deer at that time and Myert liked to visit the deer. We also caught Myert jumping on the dining room table and lifting his leg to water the flowers on the center of the table. Mom wasn't too pleased about that! But seriously, it was one less thing she had to do ... water the plants.

One year while in Afghanistan, Tom gave me a pair of boxing gloves for Christmas. It was an interesting gift—now that I think about it, I'm pretty sure he had ulterior motives. One night he said, "Let's box. I'll have one boxing glove, and you'll have one boxing glove. To make it fair, I'll turn off the lights." So, here we were in his room, standing on top of the bed, each with one boxing glove on. The lights were out, but the door was left open a tiny crack ... the second my face showed in the crack of light, boom—right in in the kisser! Off the bed I flew and onto the floor. Yeah! I didn't put those boxing gloves on again. In fact, I think Mike was soon thereafter the owner of a slightly used pair of boxing gloves.

***

After Afghanistan we moved back to Atlanta. I was in 7th grade. I made some great friends that year who I keep in touch with to this day. One of those friends was Becky Dailey. One afternoon after school, we were walking home, and she said. "I have to go because I have softball practice."

I said, "Oh! Can I go with you? I love softball!"

She said, "Sure, maybe they could add you to the team."

Signups were over, but hoped they would let me play.

We got to the practice field. Becky introduced me to the Coach. The Coach said, "It's too late to join the team, but you can practice with them. You can bat first."

I went up to the plate to hit. The pitcher looked at me and motioned me to move off the plate a bit. I did as she asked after rolling my eyes. She pitched the ball. I swung and hit the ball over the fence. I ran the bases, and when I ran over home plate, I noticed everyone was staring at me—including the Coach. The Coach said to me, "Let me see what I can do." Somehow she made it happen, and I was then a member of the team, and I played for that same team all through high school. We were undefeated for five years.

Thinking about high school, I remember a time after I graduated when I was walking through a store at the Mall with my mom. I saw one of my teachers from school. I was so excited that I ran up and said, "Hi, Ms. So and So." I could see some confusion in her eyes as she tried to remember me. I was such a nice and quiet good girl that apparently I didn't stand out.

She said, "Oh, Hi! And, how is your brother Mike?"

*What the heck!* I thought. *You don't remember me but you remember my brother, Mike?* He was obviously the more studious sibling.

After high school, I continued to play softball for various Church and company leagues. When we moved to Chicagoland, I played for the Hair Balls. Yep! The HairBalls! It was a Hair Salon's team that Karen Guither worked for—more about Karen later. Our t-shirts had a picture of a ball with hair spouting out of it. Haha! I'll have to find one of those famous t-shirts. I played for the HairBalls for many years. It took some getting used to though because in Chicago, they play sixteen-inch softball and not the normal twelve-inch. It was a co-ed league; the guys didn't use gloves but the girls did. It took some practice to learn how to hit that huge ball, but eventually I got the hang of it. Tom came to visit one year, and I got him to play in a game—he was shocked about the strange size of the ball. I explained to him that you have to "pop" the ball, not swing all the way through. He didn't like it. Haha! I played for softball teams until in my 40s when I retired from the Hairballs. They asked me to substitute when they didn't have enough female players, and I agreed. Well, even though I was supposed to be a substitute, I still pretty much played every game. I broke a few fingers playing softball—one finger was broken really badly, and the Orthopedic doctor told me I needed surgery. I begged him not to do surgery because then my husband wouldn't let me play softball anymore.

He said, "Okay, but keep it wrapped up in this splint, and I'll see you in two weeks. I kept that finger wrapped up and never used it. Thankfully, it started healing nicely, and I didn't require surgery after all. Crisis was diverted and I continued to play softball.

After we moved to Candler/Asheville and I started working for VCE, I was asked if I would be interested in playing for the VCE softball co-ed team. I signed up and had a ton of fun. I played third base and got quite a few bruises on my shins from blocking line drives from the male players. Tom came to visit, and he subbed in because we were short of players. He had a lot of fun—so much fun that he ended up breaking a bone sliding into 2nd. But he was safe!

Back to my high school friend, Becky Dailey. The Daileys had a huge backyard, and we spent our summers playing sports in their backyard. Baseball, tag football, softball—it was awesome. We spent a lot of time in that backyard and have many fond memories. Especially brother Tom and John Marchetti arguing about who was safe and who was out!

How did we end up in Chicago? Well, to tell that story, I must begin with meeting Greg. My good friend at the time was named Jenny. Jenny was an interesting bird. She could be kind of crass and had a tendency to turn people off. Anyway, she wanted me to go to a party with her to meet a guy she had a crush on. So, I went with her and met the guy. His name was Greg. Well, Greg apparently didn't have a fondness for Jenny, but it was love at first sight when he saw me. Shy Greg planted a kiss on my cheek that night, and he got my phone number. We went on a date a few days later, and after that we saw each other every night—it was just over a year when he begged me to marry him (he might tell the story a little differently). The year was 1984 when we were engaged on Valentine's Day, married March 31 and moved to Chicago May 1. Those were crazy times. I remember we got in several fights or discussions during that stressful time. I asked him what his problem was, and he said, "I am under a lot of stress. I'm moving, starting a new job and getting married!"

I said, "Well I am too."

He stopped, thought about it and said, "You're right!"

After that the "discussions" ended.

We moved to Woodridge, Illinois, a suburb of Chicago. Because Chicago and the surrounding suburbs were all a part of Chicago, the locals called the whole area Chicagoland. Greg worked for Griffith Labs as a Food Scientist in Lithonia, Georgia. He was given a promotion and an offer to work for Griffith Labs in Alsip, Illinois, one of those suburbs in Chicago. He worked in Product Development and developed new food products for many years, and for restaurants many of us are familiar with, including McDonalds, Hardees, Red Lobster, KFC, to name a few. I became very familiar with McDonalds. It is always a little intimidating cooking for Greg because I know he is analyzing the food as well as enjoying the tastiness of it. He learned rather quickly that sometimes we don't want to learn what would make it just a little bit better or "you know so and so spice is really not needed in this dish."

It was at the Griffith Labs Company picnic after we first moved to Chicagoland that we met the Guithers, Glenn and Karen, for the first time. Glenn and Greg were both Food Chemists and worked together in the Lab. Little did they know that their wives would become inseparable.

About a month later, we were both at a company party, and Karen and I really hit it off. I found out she had a weenie dog, and I had to meet him. His name was Sam. Karen and I became the best of friends and are to this day!

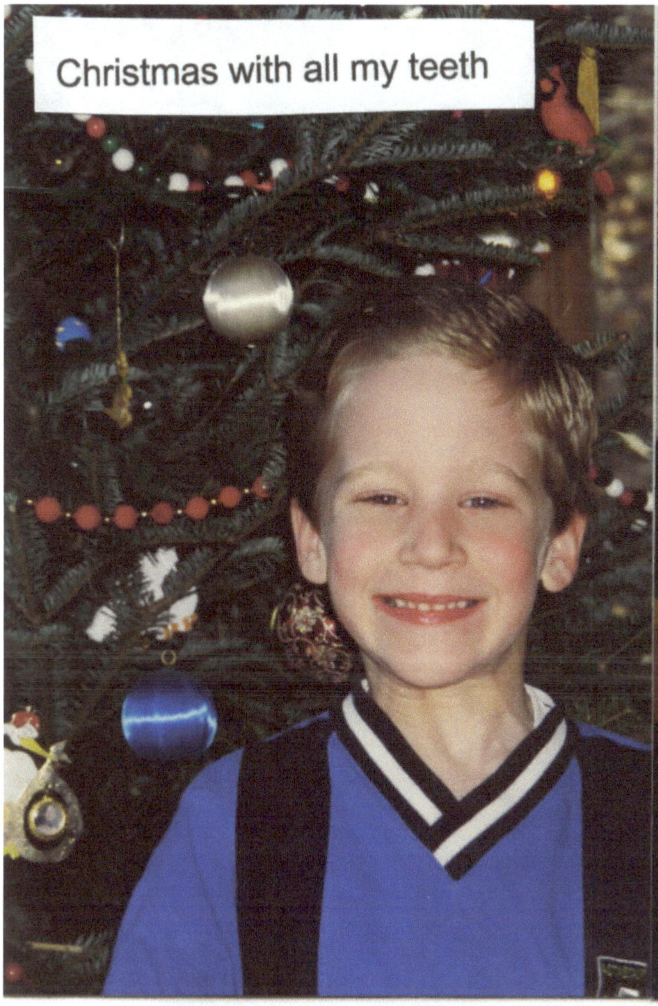
Christmas with all my teeth

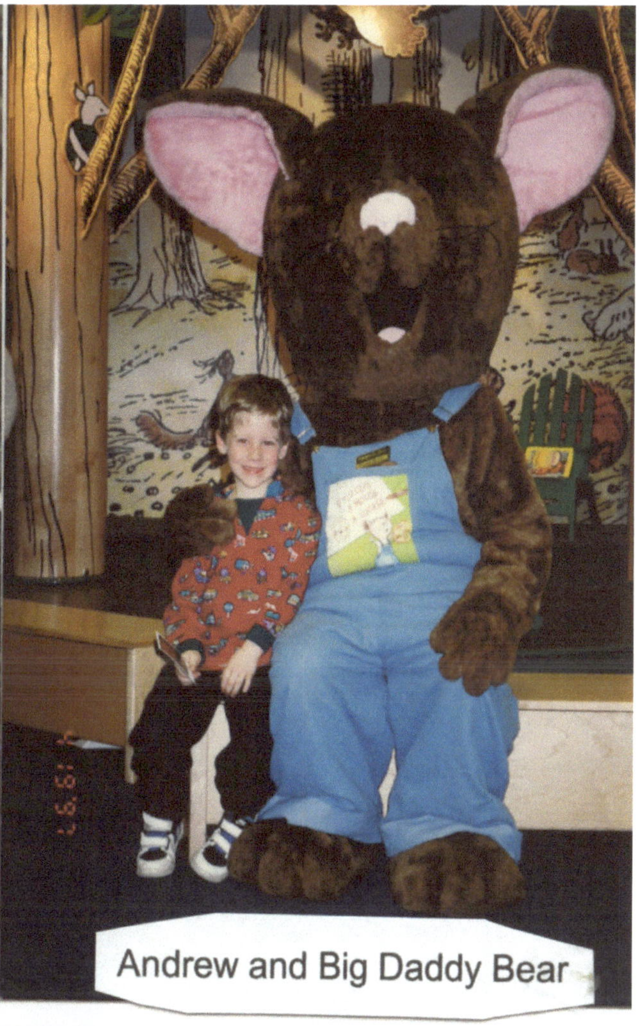
Andrew and Big Daddy Bear

Revealed

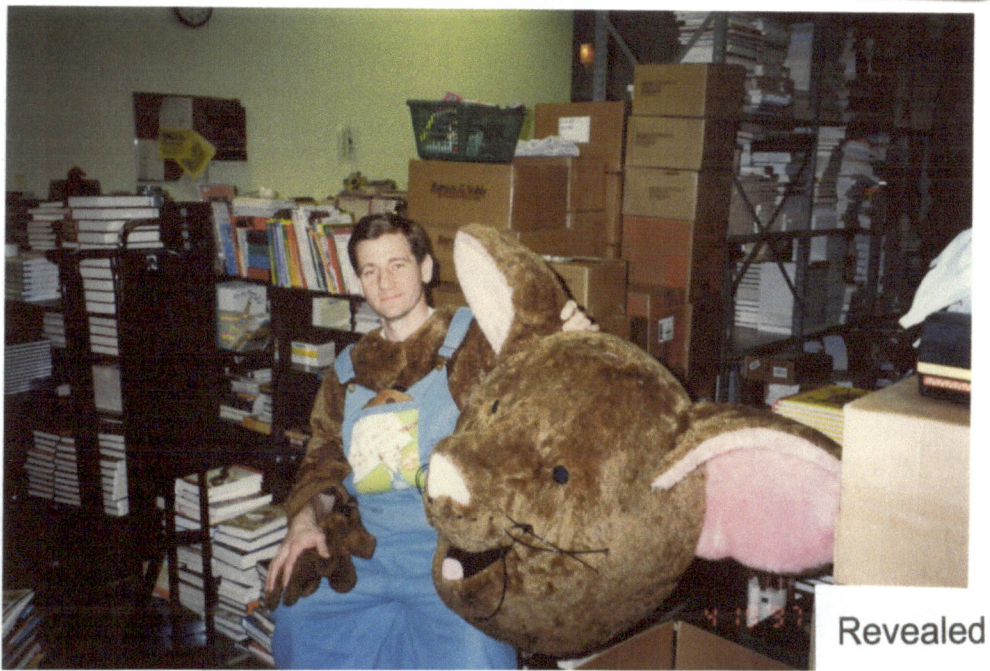

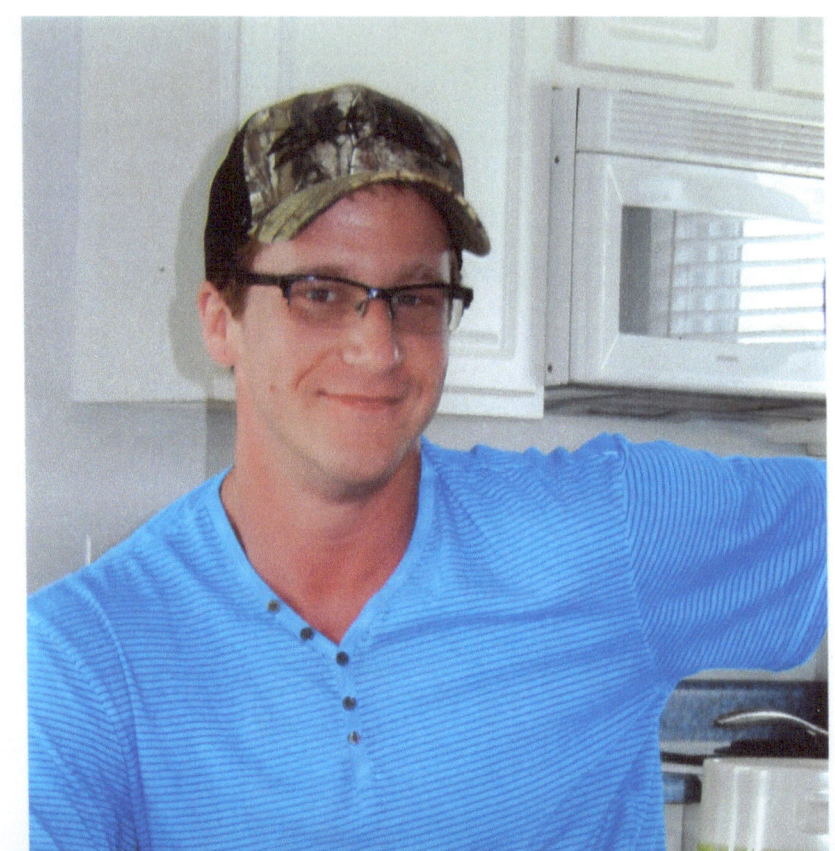

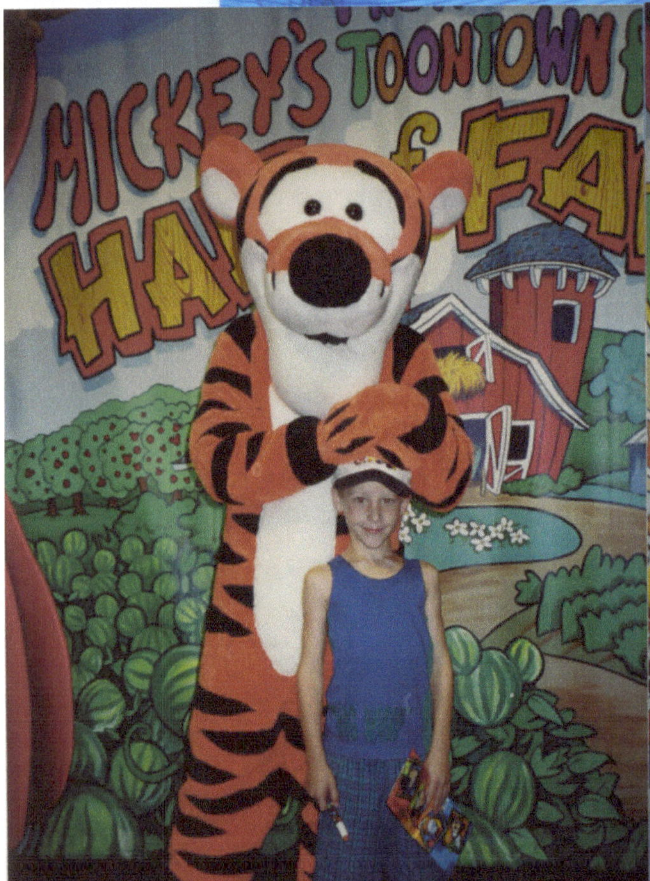
MICKEY'S TOONTOWN

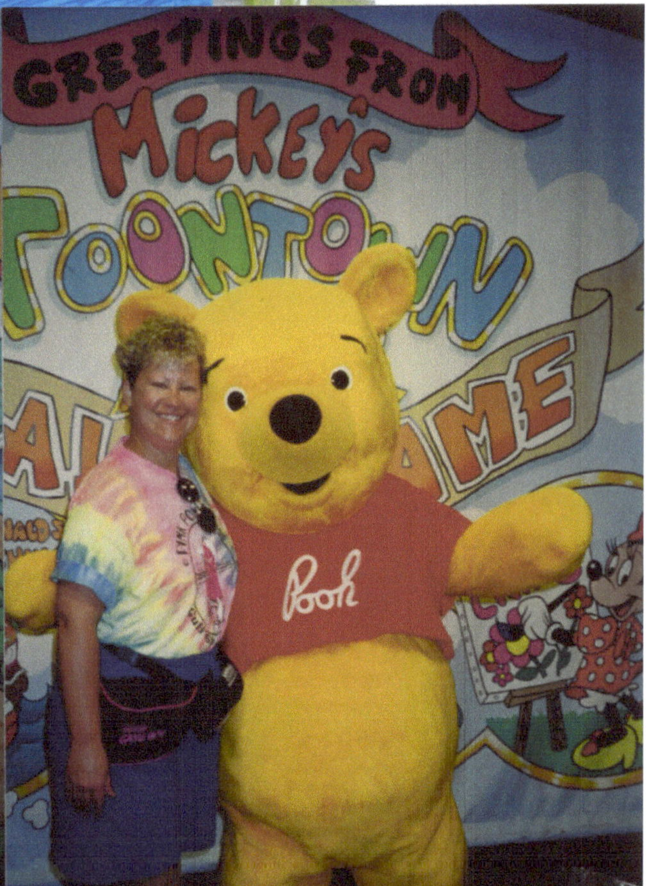
GREETINGS FROM
Mickey's
Pooh

Sam would come visit us at our house. We lived about two miles apart from each other. We didn't have a dog at the time, and I adored Sam—we had a special bond. I kept dog treats at all times for his visits. When he came running in the door, he would immediately walk right up to the Kitchen cabinet that I kept the treats in and start begging. He was a sweetie.

One night, Karen and I had a heart to heart. She said Glenn wanted to have kids really badly, but she was nervous about it. I said, "I want to have kids too, so we'll do it together. We made a pact that night that we would get pregnant at the same time and go through it together. Well, life happens and jobs change, and we both moved away from Chicagoland. She had the beautiful Lauren, and she went through it without me. But! A few years later, I called her to tell her I was pregnant. Within a few weeks, she called me with the same news. Andrew and Kyle were born three months apart. And, guess what, we moved back to Chicagoland around the same time frame as the Guithers, and again lived about three miles from each other. Andrew and Kyle first met when they were 9 months and 6 months old, respectively. The Guither family had moved back to Chicagoland from California, and we were living in Rome, Georgia. Andrew and I flew to Chicago for Kyle's Christening. But Andrew got very sick and we weren't able to attend the Christening. However, Sam slept outside our bedroom door all night to protect us. He knew Andrew was sick. Little did Kyle and Andrew know that a few months later we would move back to Chicagoland and they would develop a wonderful friendship as they became the best friends like their mothers. One day Karen and I were riding around in the car and Andrew and Kyle were jabbering in the backseat. Karen looked at me and said, "I bet they will be best men at each other's wedding." And, it happened, Andrew was Kyle's best man when he married Kaitlyn. Now we are just waiting on Andrew.

The Guither family now lives on the outskirts of Savannah in Richmond Hill, and we visit each other often. Kyle and Kaitlyn have a daughter, Winnie Blake Guither, who calls me Weesa or G3 (for grandmother number three). Karen and Glenn own a very successful Aveda spa in Richmond Hill, which Lauren manages. Kaitlyn is in real estate and Kyle is a recruiter.

Greg and I moved to Chicagoland three times. In fact, we moved quite a bit in our history. We moved to Woodridge, IL (Chicagoland) right after we got married for a year and a half; moved to Columbus, Mississippi, for four years (I got my Bachelor of Science in Paralegal Studies from the Mississippi University for Women while there); moved to Fayetteville, Arkansas, for a little over a year (Andrew Cole Slocum was born there at 4:41 a.m. on May 4, 1991). Next was Rome, Georgia—that was awesome! We had an inground pool and were an hour and twenty minutes away from Mom and Dad in Atlanta. We were very happy in Rome. We loved our house, the location and our neighbors, but staying in Rome wasn't meant to be. A little over a year later, back to Chicagoland we went, found a house in Woodridge (about three miles from the Guither family) and lived there for nine and one-half years. Next, Greg was offered a position in Milwaukee, Wisconsin. We sold our house and moved. Three months later the rumors started that the company was moving to Chicagoland. I quit unpacking and just organized the boxes in the basement. We were in Milwaukee a little over a year when we sold our house and moved back to the suburbs of Chicago. This time it was to Batavia, IL (Chicagoland). The funny thing is Greg's new location was five miles away from our old house in Woodridge. We lived in Batavia for almost four years. All of these moves were in the timespan of twenty-two years, and we always wanted and looked for jobs closer to home. Depending on the timeframe, home was either Atlanta or Asheville after Mom and Dad retired in Asheville. Greg's parents retired in Martin, Georgia, which is two and one-half hours from Asheville.

Greg's career started after he graduated from the University of Georgia with a Bachelor of Science degree in Food Science. He was very successful in Food Product Development and worked for a number of companies including Griffith Laboratories, Precision Foods, and Unilever, to name a few. All of our moves throughout the years were due to Greg being offered a new position in another city, a promotion or better opportunity. At one point, Precision Foods made some organizational changes, and Greg was laid off after working there for nine and one-half years. We were in shock. Andrew was young at the time, and it was Halloween. I took Andrew out trick-or-treating and Greg gave out candy at the door. I remember being angry at the upper management at Precision Foods, but Greg just took it in stride. He reminded me that things would work out to the better and to remember it was not personal. This lesson helped me later in my career—a lot of decisions made in business aren't personal, they are just business decisions. He was offered a job six months later in Milwaukee, Wisconsin, and we moved once again. Luckily, it was only a little over an hour away so we could still visit our friends, and we were only there a year before we moved back to Chicagoland.

Years later when we made the decision to move to Asheville, Greg was a Director of Product Development at Unilever—the same company he worked for in Milwaukee, and then we returned back to Chicagoland the third time. After we moved to Asheville, Greg started working for the State of North Carolina as a Food Inspector. His degree and background in product development were a plus when inspecting breweries, goat dairies, juice processors and larger food production businesses. He worked for the State for ten years and then retired. Greg has really enjoyed retirement and keeps busy with The Lion's Club, Lisa's Honey-do List and work around the property.

Both Greg and I had stressful jobs when we lived in Batavia. He worked for Unilever and I worked for the Mayor of Aurora. We both weren't sleeping well and woke up about 3:00 a.m. every morning. One night during our early morning wakeup, Greg said, "Well, if we are going to be working all the time and stressed out, we might as well live where we want." We started planning, discussing and researching how to quit our jobs and move to Asheville. It was a very risky move, and we weren't sure how it would work out. We sat down one night and talked to Andrew. He was in 9th grade. We told him what we were thinking to see what his thoughts were if we decided to move. Greg and I had already decided if Andrew was totally against it, we would wait to move until he after graduated high school. Andrew said … let's do it. So about a year and a half later, after saving money, getting rid of a lot of "stuff," planning and preparing, we quit our jobs, sold our house and moved to Asheville.

A lot of people helped us with the move. Our friends, the Townleys who owned a restoration business, donated boxes and packing paper. Their sons loaded the storage units. Once we got to Asheville, a lot of our boxes and furniture were stored in Jim and Karen Moore's (our cousins) basement and in Mom and Dad's garage. We lived in Mom and Dad's house for about six months before moving into the log cabin on their property. A lot of family lived in the cabin during transition times in their lives, Steve and MaryAnn Swayngium, Janie Moore, Jim and Karen Moore with Clint and Tanner, Kellie and Jon Deel, Mimi and Marvin—just to name a few.

We had a lot of fun living in the cabin and have some great stories. The cabin is approximately eight hundred square feet. The only source of heat is a wood burning stove. I swore my core temperature would never be the same. The living room was warm, but it got quite chilly in the bedroom. I remember one night I was almost asleep when Greg held my hand and said, "Wow, your hands are really rough." I pulled my hand out from under the covers and showed him I had gloves on. Living in the cabin was a reminder of how good we have it now, a thermostat on the wall to heat or cool our houses, and all the modern conveniences that come with houses in our time. Living in the cabin built character and reminded us to be thankful for what we have.

The cabin was built over one hundred years ago in 1895 by Marvin's grandfather, Bassford Cole. It was a wonderful experience to live in the cabin and just to look around the walls and think about all the family members who lived there. The hard work that was accomplished when it was a working farm; the ups and downs due to births and deaths and all the family memories is almost overwhelming. If those walls could talk … It reminded me how good we have it now with electric heat and lights that turn on with a flip of a switch. We don't have to worry about finding wood and chopping wood for the fire to cook and keep warm. There are some pictures in the cabin of our lost family members and back in the day they didn't smile for the camera. Some of those pictures are rather "creepy" and are a great beginning to a ghost story with the lights turned down low. In fact, I do believe there was a time that Andrew and his cousins were in the cabin telling ghost stores and Grandpa Marvin looked in the window and made a creepy dog bark that sent everyone into screams and hysterical laughter.

We lived in the cabin for just over a year while our house was being built. I remember being so cold and making comments that my "core" would never be the same. The funny part is that while our house was close to completion, we would sit in the cabin and look up the hill to see our house. The lights were on, and the heat was on so the wood floors could cure. I remember thinking, that house is warm, and I am not. It was close to Thanksgiving when I looked up at the new house, anxious to move in, and it started to snow. I called our builder and said, "Please, please, please can we sleep in the house tonight?"

He said, "Yes, go ahead and sleep in the house." We grabbed two inflatable mattresses and ran up to the house to spend the night. In my anxiousness, I made the bed with the mattress upside down so we slept on the plastic side and it was COLD! I was COLD! The first night in our new house and I was still cold. We moved in a few days later and just love our house.

While we were still in the cabin, Andrew wanted one of his friends from Batavia (Chicagoland) to visit. His name was Fat Tyler, apparently there were a lot of Tylers in the neighborhood, so each Tyler had a nickname. Fat Tyler stayed with us in the cabin for a couple of weeks. I know he wondered what in the heck we had done. We had a big beautiful four-bedroom house in Batavia and moved to this small, old cabin. During his stay we had a very bad storm in June with golf-size hail. There was so much hail it looked like it had snowed three inches. The hail was so heavy the roof collapsed over the kitchen, and there was a big hole. We had to put up big sheets of plastic to cover the hole until it could be fixed. We walked into the kitchen one morning, and a big, black snake had crawled across the plastic and was just lying there for all to see. Ugh! Talk about creepy!

We also had bats that lived under the carport at the cabin. They were easy to see because when the carport was painted white with a sprayer, the backs of the bats were painted as well. Black on one side, white on the other side. It was a sight to see. Every chance I got during the day, I went out on the carport and said hello to our painted bats while they were sleeping. The bats fascinated me. At night while they were in flight and thought they were invisible to the world, little did they know that white paint on their front side was like a neon sign. Fat Tyler liked speaking to the bats as well and watching them fly at night.

There is no telling what Fat Tyler told the neighborhood kids when he got back to Batavia. Andrew's family moved to the country and had all these wild animals living with them!

Throughout my career, I have also been very lucky with interesting and rewarding jobs. My first law firm job was working for David Sanders at Threadgill, Smith, Sanders & Jolly in Columbus, Mississippi. I soon found out that I had a lot to learn about the law, but I found it fascinating and wanted to learn as much as I could. After a little research, I found out the local university had a four-year Paralegal degree, which at the time was not offered at a lot of colleges. Usually a Certificate is awarded after a short thirty-, sixty- or ninety-day course and if the student has some college credits. I finally figured out what I wanted to do when I grew up. Up to this point, I had about a year and a half of "general" classes but just didn't know where to go from there. I applied, was accepted and started taking night classes while working full-time. I was close to graduating with nineteen hours left to go when it was time to start looking for our next adventure. I decided to finish it all in one semester but couldn't do it and work full-time. So, I let my boss know that I would be leaving the firm to finish my degree. Somehow, I walked out of his office with a part-time job. I was so mad at myself and thought, Man, you can't even quit your job! I went to classes every day but Sunday. I was in class Friday night for Biology and Saturday morning for Algebra, classes all the other days during the day and night and somehow worked and studied in between.

It was tough but I did it! After graduation, the firm promoted me from Legal Assistant to Paralegal and I continued to work there for another six months until we moved to Arkansas.

I worked for several law firms over the years, usually part-time because Andrew was little, so I worked when he was in school. When we moved to Woodridge (Chicagoland) the second time, I was working for a law firm when I was offered a job at McDonald's Corporation in the Investor Relations Department. Working at McDonald's was a wonderful experience, and I learned a lot about the corporate world. I was responsible for organizing the Annual Meeting for 1,200 to 1,500 shareholders. This included food, parking, giveaways, organizing buses, crowd control and most importantly, booking Ronald McDonald. There are several regional Ronald McDonald's but only one corporate Ronald, and his name was Archie. I will never forget the first time I called to book Archie as Ronald for the shareholder's meeting. My co-worker was thrilled I had taken over that role because she said "Archie is crazy." But, keep in mind, she was scared of clowns. Archie lived in Wisconsin. I called and got his voicemail, and when the message started it was Archie using the voice of Julia Childs. The message was . . . "This is Julia Childs, and I'm in the kitchen cooooking." It was hard for me to leave a message as I was overcome with giggles. Archie was definitely a character as I guess is not surprising since he made money being a clown.

Several months later when Archie arrived at the meeting, I met him at the entrance to escort him to his dressing room. He greeted me and said that I could call him Archie for now but must call him Ronald once he was in costume. He handed me his wallet, which must have been about five inches thick and said, "Hold on to this for me." He said, "You can take some cash out and buy yourself a pair of stilettos. So not only did I have a walkie-talkie in my hand, a cell phone and now this huge wallet to stuff in my pocket. He was quite the character. He told me he came from a family of Circus trapeze artists. He was very talented, because he sang, performed magic tricks and was very funny. I really enjoyed meeting Archie/Ronald over the years.

I worked for McDonald's for five and a half years and got the opportunity to travel to many places for investor shows. We were invited to several Ronald McDonald House Charity Dinners and saw Garth Brooks and Dennis DeYoung from Styx perform and attended many Black Hawks hockey games in the McDonald's box. It was a wonderful time of experiences but a lot of hard work and McDonald's was very good about rewarding hard work. Hard work pays off. I was promoted to Senior Representative after a couple of years and received many "cool" gifts from the department for successful annual meetings and projects, including a crystal miniature restaurant with 14k golden arches and a Limoges French Fry box. About two weeks before we moved to Wisconsin, I received a call from the McDonald's legal department. I was told that they had "heard about me" and my legal background. The attorney asked if I'd be interested in transferring to the Legal Department. My dream job was to work for the legal department in a large company. Unfortunately, the timing wasn't right as we were in the process of moving to Milwaukee. But, the opportunity for my dream job did come true several years later.

My next interesting job was working for the Mayor of the City of Aurora after our third move to the Chicagoland area from Milwaukee. Mayor Tom Weisner was a very busy mayor. He wanted to get out and meet the people. The bulk of my time was scheduling appearances, ribbon cuttings, speaking engagements and just walking through downtown Aurora on Friday nights, meeting and greeting people during the Friday Night Festival called Downtown Alive. Aurora was and is the second largest City in Illinois. When a new mayor is elected, it is common for the Mayor to "clean-out" the office and bring his new people in. I was working for the Streets Department for the City of Aurora and my boss, Rosario, recommended me to be the Mayor's secretary. It was a big promotion and would be a big challenge. Working for the City of Aurora was very interesting and a whole different world from working for a corporation or law firm. The Mayor and I hit it off and became friends as well as working together. He was very disappointed and sad when I told him we were moving after working for him 3½ years. But, we kept in touch and he came to visit us years later in Asheville. Mayor Weisner died a couple of years ago, and I know the City of Aurora misses him as he instituted a lot of changes that brought businesses, reduced crime and made Aurora a better place to live. The Mayor served three terms and prior to being Mayor worked for the City of Aurora for eighteen years. He also served in the Peace Corps. An interesting side note—the parking garage where I parked is the same parking garage that was filmed in the movie *Wayne's World*. One night I was asked to work late because the then Governor, Rod Blagojevich was coming to visit. I will say that Governor Blagojevich had more hair than body. He was not that tall but had a massive amount of hair on his head. He walked in and immediately shook my hand. He was very personable. If you will remember, Governor Blagojevich ended up being convicted of conspiracy to commit mail and wire fraud after he attempted to solicit bribes to occupy the Senate seat that was vacated by Barack Obama.

Besides working for several law firms, my other interesting job is working in the legal department for Volvo Construction Equipment (VCE) which is where I work to this day. This is the dream job I spoke about earlier. My background working for law firms, McDonald's Corporation and the City of Aurora have really helped me in my present position. I have worked for VCE for fifteen years and have been promoted three times. I get to do things in my position that most Paralegals dream about. I draft contracts, work on acquisitions of companies from start to finish, and I also work on the legal paperwork when we sell a business; I travel often and meet with executives and Dealership owners. I recently went to a legal conference in Sweden and was able to visit all the Volvo entities' corporate offices (Volvo Construction Equipment, Penta, Volvo Bus, Mack Truck) and drove many different sizes of Volvo and Mack Trucks—even a garbage truck (all clean of course). VCE was very good to me, and I am proud to work for them.

At one point, VCE decided to move the corporate offices from Asheville to Shippensburg, which is located in South Central Pennsylvania. Everyone was offered a job at the new location but I would have to move. It was a hard decision to make as to whether to move with the company or find another job. When we moved previously, it was always for Greg's

From this

To that

Good reasons to smile

job. This was the first time it was for my job. Greg was happy working for the State of North Carolina, and it was a very good job; we had built our beautiful home on the family property in Candler/Asheville. We didn't want to sell our house and we didn't want Greg to lose his job, so we made the decision for me to move to Shippensburg for a year in order to help the Legal Department get on their feet—then I would find a new job back in Asheville.

VCE made it very difficult to say no, and I was offered a number of incentives to move. It was a very stressful time trying to make a decision, and my boss and I had several conversations about the move and if I would go. She asked me at one point how I could be so calm about this huge change, I replied with, "Well, it is a huge change, but it was a business decision that VCE made—it was not personal. Does it affect me? Yes, but we can work through it." This was the lesson I learned from Greg about jobs and change, and it was a defining moment for me.

During all these conversations about whether to move or not to move, whether to sell the house or rent the house; what to do, Andrew said, "Mom, I will move with you and finish my degree at the Shippensburg University." Andrew had taken some courses at Western Carolina and at AB Tech, a local community college. The University waived the out-of-residency fee since this was a corporate move. So the decision was made, and Andrew and I moved to Shippensburg and our adventure began.

As we were gathering information about whether to move or not, we made several trips to Shippensburg and the surroundings and were very impressed by the University. Andrew applied and was accepted to the Business School. We got a two-bedroom apartment in Shippensburg and moved without Greg. My one year turned into three years—I would come home to Asheville every 5-6 weeks for a week. It was tough and I was terribly homesick. After three years, I decided it was time to move home. It's not good for a marriage to be apart. I had a conversation with my Boss, Chris Clements, and let him know that I was pursuing looking for a job. Chris suggested that I work for one of the law firms that VCE employs for specific work and I would be the ambassador so to speak to the VCE account. We had two law firms that were very interested and even wrote proposals. But then Chris decided he couldn't live without me, and we started the negotiating process of Lisa continuing to work for VCE but working from home. He finally offered a plan that I would work from home three weeks of the month and come up to Ship (nickname for Shippensburg) one week a month. I decided to play hard to get and said I would think about it. I waited two full days before telling him it sounded like a plan. That was five years ago and I still work from home to this day. Unfortunately, with COVID, I have only been back to Ship one time in 2020 and one time in 2021. Hopefully things will get back to normal soon because I miss seeing my colleagues in Shippensburg.

As I mentioned earlier, Andrew was born in Fayetteville, Arkansas, the home of the Razorbacks. Andrew was a very happy-go-lucky baby, easily rolling through each of the stages of babyhood. He loved having friends and made friends very easily. Through all of our moves, it wasn't long before our house was filled with his new friends.

Andrew loved sports and still does to this day. While we were living in Woodridge (the second time), he played baseball. He loved watching the Braves and playing baseball. In fact, when he was a baby, I taught him how to do the tomahawk chop. One of the years he played baseball, his team was the Texas Rangers and were very good and there was a chance they would make it to the Championship game. And they did. The night of the game, the other team showed up with all the baseball players in the bed of a pickup truck. They were yelling and screaming, "We're Number One," – trying to intimidate Andrew's team. The Rangers just stood there watching. Well, let me tell you, the Rangers had some spirit too, and their stunt did not intimidate them—it made them mad and the Rangers ended up winning that game and the Championship. Andrew got some great hits and RBIs. He also caught a fly ball that was over his head at second base, if he hadn't caught that ball, we would have lost. The Rangers were the Champions. It was a wonderful win! Our Basset Hound, Maggie Mae, was the mascot of the team and was in all the team pictures. Sometimes when you boast too loud or are too confident, things just don't turn out the way you thought they would. I think the boys learned a good lesson that day.

Andrew also was a wrestler and wrestled for many years. He was part of a traveling wrestling group while we lived in Chicagoland and wrestled all day on Saturdays and sometimes Sundays. He and his dad would travel to the meets, which could be as far as two hours away for weigh-in at 7:00 am. After weighing in, it was time for a huge breakfast and then they would wait for the matches to start around 9:00. That is when I would show up. There were wrestlers there as young as 3 all the way up to seniors in high school. I never understood wrestling and the mental and physical strength that it takes until Andrew started wrestling. At one of the wrestling meets, all the boys were chattering that one of the teams had a girl on the team. I told Andrew, if you end up wrestling the "girl" don't underestimate her. It takes a lot of guts, and it was extremely hard for her to become a wrestler in a typical boys' sport. She will be a tough opponent. Well, guess what? Andrew did wrestle that girl and her name was Ariel. It was a tough match, and she almost beat Andrew. But he was able to pin her and win the match. This was a tough lesson to learn. The bottom line is . . . "You can't judge a book by its color" and you can't underestimate someone. These defining moments build character. Andrew continued to wrestle in Chicagoland and joined the wrestling team when we moved to Candler but only wrestled for about a year. By the way, isn't it interesting that we still remember Ariel's name—I'm sure she went on to do great things.

Another one of my favorite wrestling stories is when Andrew went on a diet. When Andrew started talking about becoming a wrestler, I was very concerned. Over the years I had heard stories of wrestlers who had issues with bulimia and anorexia. Starving themselves and becoming dehydrated to make weight and to change to a different weight class. I had a long talk with Greg about my concerns, but he wasn't worried. Greg was a wrestler in high school and stated that doesn't happen that often, and when it does, it's rare. He said, "It won't be an issue."

I gave in but stated, "If I see just the beginning or a hint of starving to make weight, Andrew is done with wrestling." So, Andrew came home one night after wrestling practice and announced he was on a diet. He said the Coach talked to him about going down a weight class and Andrew was thrilled. I said, "Okay, you can go on a diet, but I will monitor your food so you don't overdo it." Now, keep in mind, Andrew loved food and still does. He is all about "what's for dinner?"

We were having spaghetti that night, and the aromas were throughout the kitchen. I made him a salad with balsamic dressing and placed it in front of him to eat. He ate the salad and then continued to sit at the table with a worried look on his face. I finished preparing the spaghetti and called Greg to dinner. As Greg sat down at the table, Andrew proudly announced, "I am no longer on a diet! I like the weight class I'm in, and I will now have some spaghetti please!" Andrew's diet lasted a total of maybe . . . fifteen minutes? I never had a worry again about Andrew and erratic eating behaviors.

Andrew currently works for UPS and has been there for over five years. When Andrew and I moved to Shippensburg, he worked on campus at the UPS store, which is a franchise of the Corporate UPS. It was an awesome place to work, and they made sure to work with his class schedule, he would go to class and then walk over to his job at the UPS store. They really liked Andrew because he was consistent and always showed up to work. He decided when he started working there that he would go by the name, "Cole." I had to drop something off at the store one afternoon and walked in and asked for Andrew. The person I talked to said, "There is no one here by that name."

I rolled my eyes and said, "Andrew or Cole, whatever his name is, please tell him his mother is here."

The guy looked at me strangely, and I know he was thinking, *You are his mother; shouldn't you know his name?*

Andrew graduated from Shippensburg University with a Bachelor of Science in Business with an emphasis in International Studies. Andrew had the awesome experience of studying abroad in Poland for six months and then had an internship in Shanghai, China. He had a tremendous experience at Shippensburg University. He graduated in December 2015 and returned back to Asheville. Greg's birthday is December 10, and I told Andrew that was his dad's birthday present. Andrew applied for a job at UPS in Asheville as a Driver Helper during the busy Holiday season. He had a wonderful driver that bought him lunch every day and encouraged him to apply for a permanent position at UPS. Andrew applied and got a position on the Preload crew. He was responsible for helping load the trucks for the deliveries the next day. They named the trucks by the locations they were going to—Chicago, Knoxville, Texas . . . Andrew got the job and wasn't in that position very long when they encouraged him to apply for a position in the office as a Supervisor. He has been an employee now with UPS for over five years and has excellent benefits.

Last year, when the COVID outbreak first started, Andrew started looking for a house. He found a house in South Asheville and closed in April 2020. He saved money for several years at UPS and was able to make a substantial down payment on his house. It is in a great location, and he is now a homeowner—a beautiful thing. And, his parents are happy because he is just thirty minutes away.

As a parent one always reflects back on whether one made the right decisions for the kids. Were they too tough at times and too soft at times? I sometimes wonder how our lives would have been different if we hadn't quit our jobs in Chicagoland and moved to Asheville. It was a tough move on Andrew as he was still in high school. But, my worries soon go away when I think about the relationship he has built with his grandparents and uncles. Andrew and Grandma Mimi love to talk about baseball, specifically The Braves. Andrew loves to talk about football with Uncle Tom, specifically Da Bears and the Falcons. And with his Uncle Mike, the conversation is about music and silly jokes. But the most interesting relationship is with his Grandpa Marvin. Grandpa would sometimes give Andrew a ride to AB Tech for classes. During those rides they would take turns choosing the music to listen to on the ride. Grandpa introduced Andrew to Mozart and the Symphony and Andrew introduced Metallica and Queen to Grandpa. Grandpa Marvin loves to listen to Queen and Metallica to this day (well, not so much Metallica) so Andrew bought him a Metallica t-shirt for Christmas. Grandpa Marvin and Andrew enjoy going to see the Asheville Symphony or concert pianists at the Asheville Amadeus Festival.

Moving to Asheville has been good for all of us in our own unique ways. Being close to our parents is a wonderful thing. Greg and I enjoy walking down the trail up to "the big house" as we call it for a glass of wine and talk of politics, current events or what the heck are they building down the street, to name a few. Mom and Dad's house became the big house when we were living in the cabin, and the name just stuck. We have also built a very strong relationship with Jim and Karen Moore, our cousins. Over the years we would have dinner together once or twice a week and go on fantastic adventures, from visiting friends in Daytona Beach to Savannah to long weekend trips to Oak Island Beach and concerts. Jim and Karen have since moved to Newton, NC, which is a mere hour and fifty minutes away, to live close to Karen's sister Kat and husband Trace. Greg and I often jump in the car to go visit them and do some porch sitting, talking and planning our next adventures. We still go on long weekend trips to the beach or to a mountain cabin with Jim, Karen, Kat and Trace at least twice a year. The adventures continue as we hope to someday make it to California and ride a train along the coast.

All these stories and memories are a snapshot of where we've been for the last sixty plus years. Reflecting back on our lives, it is evident that we have been truly blessed. To have the experiences of living in a foreign country and learning at a young age that no matter where you live, who you meet, where they're from, where we're from—we are all the same. We are mothers and fathers, brothers and sisters, aunts and uncles, cousins and friends. We bleed when we are hurt, cry, smile, mourn and celebrate our life events. At the beginning of My Chapter, I asked the question, "What did our parents teach us and continue to teach us?" They taught us many things—love, morals, ethics, humor, kindness, decency—but the most significant in my book is diversity and open-mindedness. My parents continue to teach me something new every day, and we are blessed to have them. Our collected experiences and our learnings from our parents have made us better people. Remember the story of the little girl who had an accident on the velvet pillow? Did I get in trouble? No, I guarantee that my parents, once they got out of the restaurant and that embarrassing moment passed, had to giggle just a little bit.

Keep smiling and seeing the bright side when you can. Life is short and we need to make the best of it. Laughter heals a lot of situations. Thank you, Mom and Dad, for the life lessons and helping me become the person I am today.

Father and Son

Another good reason to smile

Andrew and his own house

Lisa and Uncle Roi

And some people thought Jimmy Dean was handsome.

The Guither Connection

Life is good.

# 5

# Michael's Point of View
# Michael Patrick Cole

# The Cole Story

To obtain the essence of boy-world, a tooth-missing grin is one of the essential ingredients.

With friend Bubba at home in Kabul.

At the carpet bazaar in Kabul, Afghanistan.

# Michael's Point of View
# Michael Patrick Cole

My name is Michael, at least that's what those who consider themselves authorities, call me. People who know and tolerate me call me Mike. I've also been called Char (Cole), Dan, Red (from those without any creativity, P-Cole and Eloc Ekim, which is Mike Cole backwards. That is pronounced EE-lock EE-kim, for the record.

I was born in February in Morehead, Kentucky, in a Catholic hospital. I have been told that I was to be named something else, but when I was born with red hair in a Catholic hospital, a stern Nurse (Nun?) took one look at me and said "That's a Michael Patrick." We are not Catholic, but we generally follow orders. I'm the youngest of the three Cole kids. While each sibling is different, we are all very alike at the same time. We all love reading, music and food ...Just like our parents! I'm the quiet one, for the record.

We soon moved to Atlanta where my Father took a job at Atlanta Baptist College. Looking back on my childhood, I have realized how lucky I am to have the family I'm blessed with and to have had the childhood and adolescent experiences that I had growing up. Our parents instilled in us proper values and led by example.

We lived in a safe neighborhood—the only dangers we encountered were the dangers we created. Nothing too bad—our dangers were more like misadventures with BMX bikes or a brother who failed to mention he was going to pop a wheelie with me on the back of his motorcycle.

When I was 2 years old, the family moved to Afghanistan, or so I'm told. We were there when I was 2- to 5-years old. I wish I had more memories of our time there, but most of my memories are just of the front yard, our dogs, a VW wagon, and giant sunflowers. During this period, there were no TVs or modern appliances in Afghanistan, so I didn't know they existed. When we moved back to the States, it was, of course, a multi-flight

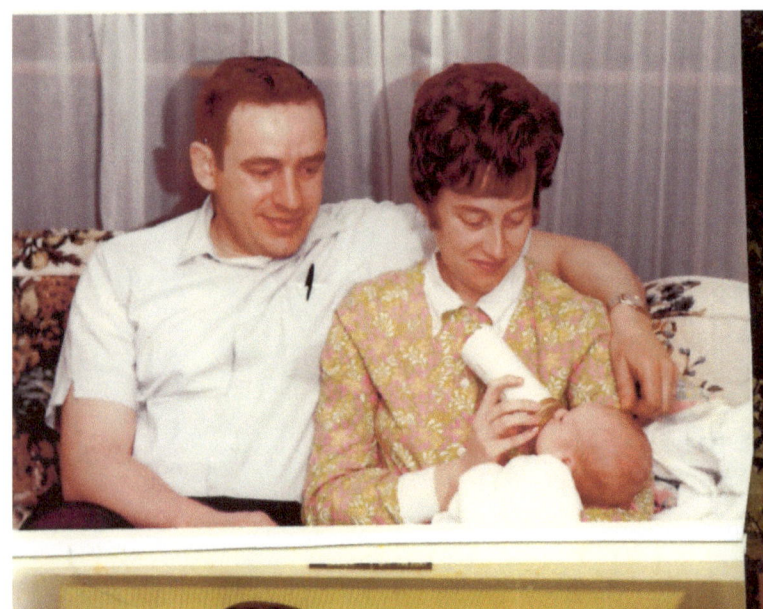

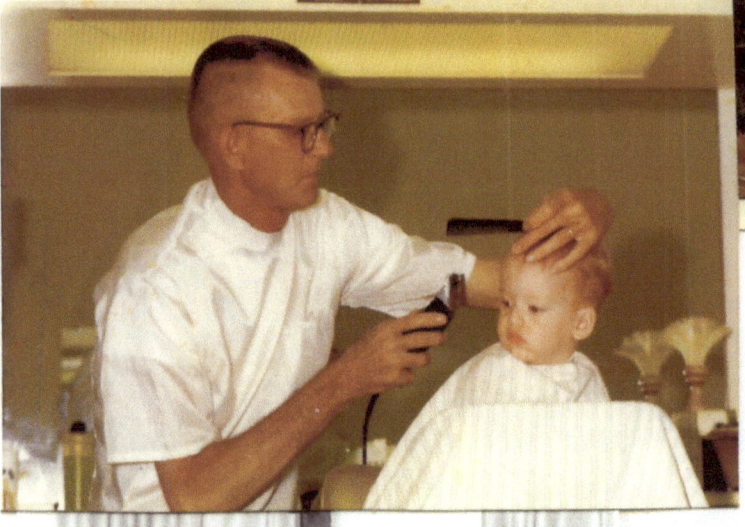

Morehead, KY 1968, Michael within two weeks of birth—with Granny Haynes in Clyde, NC—with Marvin on Hawaii beach on the way to Afghanistan in 1970—with Tom in Kabul—first haircut at Embry Hills (Atlanta) Barber Shop 1968.

process. During the journey back we checked into a hotel in Hong Kong and got in an elevator to go to our floor. I had never seen or heard of an elevator, so I guess I thought we were leaving this large lobby and cramming into a small closet for some reason. When the doors opened at our floor, I exclaimed, "Who changed that?"

In second or third grade, I met a girl named Lisa Reynolds while trying to go to meet another Lisa that I had met at school. I had been told explicit directions on how to get to Lisa Monroe's house, but I ended up at a completely wrong house, wrong street, wrong block (by several). I should have realized then that I have directional dyslexia. I walked up to the door, knocked and asked for Lisa. I received confused looks, but they produced a Lisa. Turns out a girl who didn't live there was visiting her grandparents, and her name was Lisa! So many Lisas. The girl eventually moved in with her grandparents and we became great friends—even though it wasn't cool to have a friend that was a girl in third grade, and I occasionally did get grief for it. Funny how things change. The original Lisa from school had a beagle—that's one of the reasons I liked her. Well, being the youngest kid of three whose siblings were much older than me, I was versed in 70's rock when most kids my age were not. I asked her what her dog's name was, and she replied, "Jeremiah."

I belted out, "Jeremiah was a bull frog!" from an old Credence Clearwater Revival song. She ran away crying before she ever knew he was a good friend of mine.

I remember we'd love it when Dad had to go to the grocery store for one thing, like milk. He'd be gone for an hour and come back with an assortment of cookies and snacks . . . and milk. The sweet tooth is apparently genetic.

My main pal, best friend, partner in crime was a lad by the name of Bill Foster. We met in kindergarten, and, while we currently live in different states, we are still great friends and keep in touch. Every once in a while, we still meet for dinner, a game, a concert, a bike race in Athens, no telling. Bill never had an issue with energy. In kindergarten, he was adamantly against naptime and didn't want to put his head down. He eventually got in trouble, and I suppose his parents had a chat with him because suddenly at naptime he started putting his head down on his arms folded on the table like the others. The only difference is Bill proceeded to move his arms and head back and forth on the table during the entire naptime! We were pretty much inseparable and rarely got into disagreements. However, there was one recurring disagreement in the early years of our friendship: "What is the proper time for dinner?" My family ate dinner around 6:00 p.m. and his family ate around 7:00. So, I would have to leave before his playtime was over, and it irritated him and he wanted me to address it with my parents. I, however, took offense and would always have the stance that his family was wrong (mainly because I was usually hungry by 6:00). Of course, those arguments disappeared as we aged, but we do still have an ongoing disagreement that will never change and that is related to our college choices and a football game in the fall.

Bill was my BMX buddy, my "Meet you at the corner?" friend. While we were growing up the authorities started to build a hospital right near his house. They dug a HUGE hole/crater, I guess for the foundation. Something happened. My guess is the neighborhood

complained about ambulance noise, and they abandoned the hole before any concrete was poured. Well, BMX bikes were just coming around, and this became our neighborhood Six Flags. There were jumps made from the red dirt and trails going all around. It was a blast! My friends had our BMX fun there and my older brother and his friends would ride their dirt bikes there. Of course, we got out of the way when we heard engines . . . but that was part of the fun. Avoiding the older kids (not including my brother's group) was part of fun and excitement. All of this was on top of miles and miles of trails that we had in the woods next to that crater. I knew those trails so well that occasionally I have a dream about them. Eventually that crater was filled with condos and those woods were leveled to make neighborhoods. We were angry, but we were also older then, and Bill and I (and company) were starting to be interested in things with four wheels. We went everywhere on those bikes without a worry in the world.

Tom was the older brother with all the cool toys that I was too young for (such as motorcycles), but he still shared, and I loved to ride on the back. I remember one summer he worked at JC Penny; there was a refrigerator problem, and they were going to throw away a bunch of candy. He came home with HUGE bags of slightly melted chocolate-covered peanuts. It filled most of the basement refrigerator and amazed my friends. You'd have to just break off a chunk—sweet teeth gotta eat!

I remember electric racetracks that summer as well. One day, Tom grabbed Mom's keys and offered to go up to the convenience store for sweet tarts and Coke. I mentioned that Mom was about to leave for her voice lesson, and he assured me that all was well. Well, we dallied and all was not well. Mom's car was not there when she needed to leave for her voice lesson. Needless to say, she was not happy upon our return. All for candy—guilty by association!

Lisa was the older sister with all the cool records. Bill and I would sneak in her room and play them when she wasn't there. I don't think she cared. There was one Hall and Oats song that we had to play at least four or five times in a row, simply because it had the cuss word that the radio had to bleep out. I remember when she got her first apartment in Clarkston and we were riding in her bright red Datsun B210 with the windows down with "White Room" by Cream playing, I thought, *It must be so cool to be older!* You could drink at 18 back then, so Lisa had a keg party for her 18th birthday. Feeling the pressure to be a proper host and provide the utmost in service and convenience, I started walking around asking people if they'd like a refill. Only, I'd ask the people with half a beer left and drink it before I filled it up. It was quite the plan. These days I'm a near germaphobe and can't believe I did that!

I remember there was a community dog named Old Red. He was at least partially Irish Setter. I say community dog because I never found out where he actually lived, but he was EVERYWHERE, and everybody knew him. He was obviously well fed because I've never seen an Irish Setter that wide. I'm pretty sure he spent his day making rounds for treats. You could be anywhere in a five-mile radius and Old Red might just pop up out of nowhere wagging his tail and asking for scratches.

One of the nation's most renowned Ferrari dealerships was located in Tucker, Georgia. When Bill and I started falling in love with cars, we would sometimes ride our bikes up there and just dream. Nobody ever bothered us. I'm sure they saw us sit in them, but they saw that we were just innocent kids … and fans … and let us be. I do not think that would happen today.

Bill is a month older than I am, so he started driving first. Both of us were adamant that manual transmission was the way to go. Some things don't change—my current car has a six-speed manual transmission. We were in love with the Porsche 911, and that hasn't changed to this day. He bought a 1972 VW Beetle at 16 and immediately put speakers in the back that were probably designed for a large vehicle, not a bug. I'll never forget how loud The Scorpions could be in that VW. I think V-DOSC speakers currently used in concert setups for sound reinforcement are based on the acoustics of an early 70s VW curved roof.

Bill later bought an early 70s Datsun 240z with three carburetors and an exhaust header, and we soon found out that coupe would do over 100 mph before switching to the final gear. We discovered this on Evans Road (35mph limit! Sorry, Mom). It was absolutely gorgeous inside and out and midnight black with diamond stitching on the seats and doors. I went on a two-week trip with my parents, and when I returned, I learned that Bill's father sold the Z because it was leaking oil. Much later I found out that Bill's father drove the car just before he made that decision to sell it. I think he came to the realization of just how fast that car was. As disappointed as I was then, he might have saved our lives with that decision. Nevertheless, Bill bought a Golf GTI and drove that thing on three wheels whenever he could.

Besides the friendship between me (Mike) and Bill (my pal), the other member of the **Three Stooges** was Sean. Sean was a transplanted New Jersey kid who was into three things:
- Early 70s Mach I cars
- 007 Movies
- ZZ Top

That sums up Sean's favorite things. So while Bill had the 240Z, which was so quick that doing a donut looked more like a cursive L and left us with no idea where we were at the end. Sean preferred a 351 Cleveland Mach 1. He had three while we were in high school. Anyway, the high school weekend experience involved a lot of unnecessary driving and circles. The thing to do on Friday and Saturday nights was to drive around the Northlake Festival shopping center parking lot. Occasionally a movie, but a lot of driving at night. Then, during a pretty Saturday afternoon, we'd switch it up and drive in circles around Stone Mountain. I can tell you that it made sense at the time, and we were not alone.

We were pretty much good kids doing what kids do. Probably the most deceitful thing we were guilty of was saying, "I'm sleeping over at Bill's house," when he told his parents that he was at my house. Those nights involved more intense driving in circles. Or the occasional sneak out. One night Sean was sleeping over, and we decided to sneak out. We meticulously stuffed the blankets with pillows and shoes to make it look like we were asleep on the couches and we quietly slid out the sliding glass door and tiptoed to a 351 Cleveland

Mach 1 that happened to be about as stealthy as a freight train. When we returned at 4 a.m., we found a note on our stuffed caricatures from my mother:

"I'm not as dumb as you think I am"

Short, simple, to the point . . . powerful. Let's just say Sean was nowhere to be found by the crack of dawn that morning! He did not want to face my mother and left me to fend for myself.

Overall, I had a great high school experience. DeKalb County at the time started high school in the 8th grade; so as a "subbie" or sub freshman, it's a pretty intimidating thing to walk into the same school as Juniors and Seniors. False rumors about drugs being forced on us and rampant bullying didn't help matters. Luckily I had older siblings to set me straight. They told me, "Don't buy a pool pass (because there is no pool) and other tricks." Henderson High was a long school up on a granite hill. It was called "Hell on the Hill." It was originally supposed to be shorter, and two stories, but when they discovered they'd have to blast through granite, they decided that, instead, it would be a long, one story structure on top of that rock. One morning during the bus ride to 8th grade, my stomach started rumbling. I could tell pretty quickly this was going to be a problem that wasn't going to just go away. For some reason at that age, the thought of a bowel movement in a school bathroom was horrifying. There were many unsafe daredevil stunts I would do instead, if giving a choice. Well, I wasn't given a choice, so my plan at that point was to go to the 500 hall—the hall farthest away from the bus lanes and morning activity. Did I mention it's a long school? Yes, I believe I did. Thanks, Stone Mountain, for your granite reach and everlasting impact. Probably mad about the circles. Well, let's just say I did not make it. I cleaned up as best I could, and in the process, flushed my underwear. I had to go commando the rest of the day. All of this was fine to me because the #1 goal above all was accomplished . . . nobody knew my secret but me. So, I went to first period, and then to homeroom where they began the announcements, which started off with:

ATTENTION: THE 500 HALL IS CLOSED DUE TO FLOODING!

At first nothing registered with me—then realization, then a brief snicker, and then total shock and fear. You see, to help keep the laundry straight, my mom would sew in names or designs on our underwear strap to identify them. The clues were out there! I went the rest of the day in total fear that someone was going to come to the door and call me in the hall and then everyone would know. Luckily, the FBI never showed up, and, thankfully, the statute of limitations is up! Henderson is a middle school now so I'm not even sure if I graduated high school at this point.

There was an older girl in the neighborhood on whom I had a HUGE crush. One day during the summer before 8th grade, Bill and I were chatting with her and asking her questions about high school . . . just stumbling around trying to think of things to keep the conversation going. Everything was going great until she asked about elective courses, and

I mentioned that I was taking Latin. She said, "Latin? Why would you do that? Coach Hogan teaches that, and HE IS CRAZY."

Great.

I do not know where to start with Coach Hogan, but I guess I'll start with the Buick he drove. It had dozens of dents all over it from temper tantrums and golf club strikes. He was a brilliant man. He had a slight Boston accent with very strange inflections and cadence (and a slight tick that sounded like a snort). The class was a mix of all high school ages—there were Seniors who played football in there, and here I am an 8th grader who has heard nothing but bad news about this teacher.

One of the first days. he was comparing active versus passive with the sentence, "I kick <snort> the can." During the lesson, he proceeded to kick a previously well-dented trash can across the classroom, sending trash everywhere. Obviously, the poor trash can was a common prop.

We did Coach Hogan's homework before any other homework. We did Coach Hogan's homework in other classes and on the bus before getting home. We did Coach Hogan's homework before we did fun things—that's how intimidating he was. I remember spending hours and hours at my grandmother's house over Christmas break doing future homework translations to get ahead. Future homework! Apparently Bill's parents had the same vision about the importance of taking Latin as mine, and he begrudgingly started Latin classes in 9th grade . . . after hearing a year of my horror stories. Bill's father is a lawyer, so he understood the importance of Latin as well. (As it turns out, both our parents were right about taking Latin . . . and pretty much everything else).

Another day while in Latin class, there was a man mowing the grass and every time he passed, at least one or two students were distracted and looked out the window. This was annoying Coach Hogan because he wanted all the attention. So after a few times, he exploded and screamed, "Is it SO interesting <snort> that the MAN is MOWING the GRASS?" So a few minutes passed, and the mowing man went by again, and someone made the mistake of looking toward the window. Coach Hogan proceeded to throw his podium down, and then got in a chair and started scooting in circles. He banged his head on the wall. Then he got up, grabbed his podium off the floor, and left the classroom. The class was shocked and bewildered to say the least. I don't think anyone was laughing. A short time later, here came Coach Hogan up to the window. He knocked on it and motioned for a student to open the window. A girl did—it was one of those old fashioned windows that will tilt out for a breeze. Coach Hogan then set up his podium and said, "If it's SO INTERESTING, <snort> I'll teach from HERE!" And he taught the rest of the hour from outside. The next day when we walked into class, he had turned all the desks to face the back wall just for our 5th period class. And he taught to our backs that day. So I got my hard labor Latin class time in during my first two years. High school was a breeze after Coach Hogan! It had been like basic training for high school.

***

Bill ran cross-country in 8th grade with a bunch of guys from my elementary school and some new kids that I liked. My brother was a runner—one of the first around our area—and sometimes people would ask him if he needed a ride because they didn't realize why he would otherwise be running. Anyway, I always looked up to my brother, and Bill kept asking me to run, so, despite the fact that I had never been a fast runner and was always sort of a chubby kid, I joined the cross-country team. I never excelled at it, but I had fun with it, hanging with my friends—or sweathogs as my mom called us—and ran for three years until my Senior year when I chose to work instead. There was a runner named Phil who was right around my skill level. We made it our season to battle each other, in a friendly way, and it made each of us better competitors. I usually started the season faster than Phil, and then he'd eventually creep up on me and best me a few times. The last two or three races of the season were a toss-up, but we were both competitive in our own ways, even though we weren't winning the races. We pushed each other further than we would have gone if the other wasn't there.

***

I worked at The Athlete's Foot at Northlake Mall, selling athletic shoes and apparel and eventually worked my way up to Assistant Manager. I was opening/closing the store and submitting cash and revenue reports while I was still in high school. I can tell you to this day that the foam in your shoes is EVA, or ethylene vinyl acetate! On slow days we would re-arrange the clothing racks to a baseball diamond and play baseball with posters and baby shoes (Nike Tyro had the best bounce). While we had our fun, I was serious about the job when I needed to be. The company didn't offer the safe combination and banking information to high school kids often, and I appreciated the trust. Counting the beans came easy to me, so it seemed. I think that's when I started to think about numbers instead of being a lawyer. So much for all the lawyer-training Hell with Coach Hogan.

One spring in high school, I met a young lady named Sage, and we started dating. I know it was spring because of her birthday, and that's when it always happens, right? I took her out to dinner and a movie on her 16th birthday. I had arranged for two dozen roses to be delivered to school before we even had a first date. I don't know what I was thinking in doing that, but as it turns out, days turned to weeks, months and years, and we were pretty much inseparable. We even had matching Honda Preludes, although different colors. People said we started looking alike, mostly because I was no longer a chubby kid, thanks to cross-country.

Sage's family was an Auburn family through and through. Her parents told her she could go to college anywhere she wanted to, but if she went to Auburn, they would pay for it! So, as you might have guessed, I found myself as a Freshman at Auburn University. The transition from metro-Atlanta driving to small-town driving was fast and drastic. Fifteen mph speed limits and manual transmissions are not a great combo,

Thank goodness Mike favored his Mother.

With Sage on prom-night.

My dad made me hold his smelly Pipe while taking this picture in Hannibal, Missouri.

and I got more than my share of speeding tickets to the point the State of Georgia sent me a letter.

Another Bill, this one Bill Allen (or Nella Llib backwards), was my college roommate for the first two years. He went to my high school, and lived really close to me during high school, but as it turns out, we were just in different circles and didn't really know each other very well. The summer before our first Fall semester, he called me saying some fraternity contacted him about a Chattahoochee River trip and asked if I wanted to go. I said sure, but I had zero intentions of joining a fraternity. We showed up, and there were about eight large rafts tied together in a circle, beautiful women everywhere, and a raft in the middle filled with beer and ice. We were only 18. Nobody cared. To say it was fun would be the understatement of the year.

We moved into Connor apartments in a brand new complex that had only twelve units. You could have probably made a movie about this apartment complex. With the exception of one weird guy, everybody knew each other. We hung out all the time. We played pranks on each other. One character named Scott got angry if we locked our door because he liked to just walk in. He constantly drank . . . he never studied. He drank tiny beers because, "They're easier to throw." He didn't know what a trash can was. He kept getting kicked out of school for academic reasons and would somehow find his way back in. Did I mention that his parents were wealthy? I think that had a lot to do with it. The third time was a charm though, and he eventually didn't return.

Ashley Snow lived across the hall. She let me drive her Mitsubishi Starion sports car whenever I wanted to. What a time to be alive!

Back to Nella Llib, one night he was going to fraternity rush at Chi Phi, the river-rafting bunch, and I tagged along with no intentions to join. Needless to say, we both joined. Those first two years there were no rules—colleges and universities had not cracked down on fraternities yet, and it was no holds barred. Alcohol was without limits or rules. Back then fraternity parties were open to anyone, and people would bounce from one to another. We weren't the coolest fraternity, but we had fun, and we won the Spirit contest every year I was there. The fraternity that wins Spirit gets the best football section closest to the 50-yard line. As crazy as some of those times were, they were also very strict on the pledges about grades. There were mandatory study nights, and if we didn't make grades, we couldn't attend parties. There was also a mandatory meal plan that ensured that I at least saw some vegetables . . . even though they were cooked in lard. That was also my first experience with true Southern sweet tea. Holy Cow! I still can't handle the sugar. Through all the chaos, it also brought structure and was an opportunity to learn about leadership. Sage also joined in the Greek system, but we soon grew apart and eventually broke up the summer after our Freshman year. I briefly considered transferring to UGA where Bill and many of my high school friends were going, but I quickly realized that Auburn had already brainwashed me.

There was one strange fraternity tradition: if a brother became engaged, a metal canister would be filled with rotten food, urine, dog poop, spit—anything nasty and vile that could be found. People would hold him down and spray him with the foul liquid. Then the chase was on. It was a scramble to get out of the basement and out of the house because the victim would chase everyone in the house and around the yard trying to tackle them and get the vile substance on them. It was strange and fun. Did I mention I've never been engaged? Every May we would hold our biggest party: King Party. We would dig a big hole in the parking lot, line it and fill it up to make a giant pool and would get dump trucks of sand to make a beach. Dozens of kegs, two sixty-gallon trash cans of hunch punch.

For the final two years of college, I moved farther off campus into a condo with three other guys (and a roommate's girlfriend as it turns out!). Basically, I moved in with two people from high school and one of the kids from Connor Apartments. The new place was much bigger with more amenities including multiple pools, but none of the neighbors talked to each other like those at Connor apartments. Sadly, it was more like the real world. While that couple whom I shared a bedroom with would later marry and divorce, all five of us still stay in touch to varying degrees.

During these years is when I really fell in love with live music and would attend a concert any chance I got. In 1988 I stumbled across a band named Widespread Panic in a little bar, and so far I've seen them close to two hundred times since. That first night my roommate Geoff and I were going to see a band named Nothing Personal at The Supper Club in Auburn. For some reason, we showed up early and Widespread Panic was the opening band. Our jaws soon dropped. I've met so many friends from the fans of that band. They're never on the radio, but are often in the top ten grossing for concert revenue nationally and produce a fun evening. One year I saw four concerts in a row at the Fox Theatre on New Year's weekend, and they repeated only one song: and that was a song of which they do two versions.

Oh, by the way, there was also a little education going on in Auburn, Alabama—here and there when I could fit it in my schedule. Often when I'd call home from school my father would say at some point near the end of the conversation, "Remember what you're there for!" But really, I'm proud to say that I never intentionally skipped a class in over four years. The only time I missed a class was a 7:30 a.m. Speech Class. I was terrified of public speaking then, and don't exactly look forward to it to this day. I was so nervous about my speech that I stayed up very late practicing and overslept. The teacher had a rule that if a student missed the class on one of his or her speech days, a doctor's note must be brought in. So I was stuck. I couldn't get a zero for a grade, so I went to the infirmary saying I had a sore throat, just to get that note. I was quite surprised to learn soon after that I had not one, but two types of strep throat! I was so confused! I didn't know whether to use my spending money on this prescription or beer, because I felt fine! For the record, I filled the prescription and eventually received an A on my speech.

I remember one semester I was struggling with a major choice and expressing that frustration to my parents when my father responded, "I still don't know what I want to be when I grow up." I know part of him was kidding and part of him wasn't, but it deflated my anxiety balloon. In the end, I switched from Accounting to Finance because I didn't want to be an accountant, which is pretty much what my whole career has been.

A proud day graduating from Auburn.

Wearing shorts visiting a Hindu Temple was not forbidden. So a cloth dhoti was provided.

Auburn graduates are educated to handle many conditions in life.

I graduated in December of 1990 in the middle of a horrible economy. The summers while I was in college, I returned to Atlanta and worked landscaping at DeKalb College, later Georgia Perimeter, where my father worked. So, after months of fruitless job searches I went back to landscaping to at least earn some spending money. The economy worsened, and Governor Zell Miller ordered a state hiring freeze. That situation means a manager can steal an employee from another department, but nobody can hire any new employees. Months later on one very hot day, I was working in the sun and the head of IT approached me on the lawn. I knew who he was, but hadn't really spoken to him previously—I was afraid he spoke in 1s and 0s. Anyway, he said, "Ain't you got a four-year degree?" I said yes and he replied, "Wouldn't you rather work in the air conditioning?" So, the IT department stole me from Landscaping, and that marked the beginning of "Mike, the Computer Nerd." I knew nothing about computers on my first day, but after six months, I could build one. That job changed my life—I have always been comfortable around computers since, and I usually end up being the interdepartmental IT guy at every employment opportunity. I enjoyed the problem-solving aspect of desktop support a lot. Thank you, Zell!

*** 

Eventually the economy improved, and I learned of an opportunity at the Board of Regents of the University System of Georgia as an internal auditor. We traveled all over the state of Georgia and visited state-operated colleges and universities. As an internal auditor, my job was to find problems in the current year before the state auditor would find it at year end. "We're from the Central Office, and we're here to help." As you might imagine, we weren't received as helping friends. However, it was a wonderful way to learn a little bit about everything at a college and provided many lessons on dealing with difficult people as well as the art of delivering unwanted news in a tactful manner. Most of the audits were routine and based on a time schedule, but occasionally we'd get a call on the fraud hotline and would have to do an unannounced audit. One such audit involved allegations of an employee loan fund being run through a fundraising department for the University's Gospel Choir. This University had suffered through a horrible flood two years before, and they were still rebuilding. Well I asked for checks to be pulled—all related to this Gospel Choir. For each one I was told that "the flood got it." This wasn't my first day on the job, so I asked for the checks numbered just before and after one of them and they produced both. I said, "So the flood came in and snatched that first check, but left the other two? Yep. Hmmm. There was plenty of evidence elsewhere and the Comptroller was relieved of his duties.

I moved up the audit ladder a little bit and eventually moved to the Financial Reporting side of the house and was Project Manager for the largest PeopleSoft Financials software implementation ever in higher education—thirty-four colleges and universities. A few years later I transitioned from the Board of Regents to working on a college campus using that same software. At first I was at Southern Poly (gobbled up by Kennesaw State), then

Georgia Perimeter (gobbled up by Georgia State), and currently Dalton State College (thankfully un-gobbled and hopefully unpalatable), where I'm the Director of Budget and Payroll. Still counting those beans!

The Cole family has always been a family of Atlanta Falcons and Atlanta Braves fans. We do not agree on college football, or whether or not mushrooms should be included with a meal. After my parents retired and moved to their home in North Carolina, I was surprised at how big a fan of the Atlanta Braves my mother had become—she was on top of the scoop well before the family most of the time. I've since heard rumors that my mother has moved to the dark side of football: the Carolina Panthers. I don't like to think about it. We considered football rehabilitation for her.

One of my favorite family traditions through the years was the family trip to Mexico Beach, Florida. We would usually go every other year, and it was a great time to relax, get away from work and catch up with family members. Tom and Lisa were much more adventurous with the places they lived, so these were rare opportunities to catch up with not only my parents and siblings, but my nieces and nephews when they could make it. My father made sure we always had educational programs while on vacation. I will admit that initially the thought of having a schedule on vacation was not a good idea—it sounded like what I was trying to take a break from. But it wasn't a bad idea. I remember one day at work somebody asked if I wanted to go to lunch, and I told him that I couldn't because I was going to the beach next week and had to finish a book for the book night. "What?"

I explained that we all read the same book and then discussed it one night; somebody takes the job of leading it, often the person who suggested the book. Then we have music night when everyone plays his or her favorite song for the year and we discuss them. There's Trivial Pursuit night and a night for the kids to go to the amusement park. I remember watching the Braves with my mom as they lost a twelve-run lead one year at the beach while Tom and the kids went to the park. What happened? The nightly events changed slightly over the years, but they were mostly the same. My coworkers first found this to be hilarious, but over the years, they kept asking about it, and I could tell that they thought it was neat. I think they were jealous.

As I said before, I'm very blessed to have this family, and so thankful that we all get along. Maybe it's because we all like the same things: reading, music and food. Oh, and the Atlanta Braves!

Tom's caption was "Which one is the clown"?

Andrew is a little skeptical about his uncle Mike.

A visit from Freya and Melia Kia.

Two peas, same pod.

Marvin, Tom and Mike after completing the Atlanta Peachtree Road Race.

**STEAMBOATING**

# 6

Riverboating Intermission

Mimi and Marvin on the Mississippi River.
Performing Mark Twain on one of the riverboats.
By the fence known around The world.

-Mimi loved to sit in the paddlewheel bar with this view while sipping something and reading a risqué novel.
-A happy LeRoi,
-Norine and Roi,
-Leah The Beautiful.

Leah, Roi, Norine and Janie.
Bob Swayngim, Sue Flynn by Kitty, Patricia, Roi and Norine.
Becky and Tony Candler.

LeRoi and Norine ready for a riverboat dinner, Marvin, Patricia and Janie, John and Debbie Brown with Granny.

# 7

## Cole Review by Bob Greenberg

# Cole Review
## by Bob Greenberg

It was August 1970, and I sat on a flight from Beirut, now landing at Kabul International Airport. Even from thousands of feet above ground, one could see that this was no ordinary place. It was surrounded by mountains, and most of the city's buildings were the color of the earth around them, a pale brown. The scene included colorful mosque roofs, a few trees here and there, a handful of structures more than three stories tall and an overall impression of aridness.

What was I, Bob Greenberg, doing arriving in Kabul that summer? It's a somewhat complicated story about how Afghanistan and I were brought together, and as a result, I fell into the circle of the Cole family. Much of the rest of my life was given direction by chance events that brought me there.

In 1966 I graduated as a history major from Carleton College, a small school in Northfield, Minnesota. My decision to go to Indiana University (IU) to enter a PhD program in Russian History was made difficult by my alternate choice of entering the U.S. Peace Corps in Kenya. I chose IU, hated the doctoral program, loved my job working with students in a residence hall and switched majors to College Student Personnel Administration (CSPA) while simultaneously reapplying to the Peace Corps. The Peace Corps accepted me to teach middle school English in Iran and I accepted them.

My two years in eastern Iran proved to be an incredible learning opportunity. At a time when I was ripe for life experiences, the Peace Corps offered a multitude of them. I learned passable Farsi (Persian), developed a deep sense of independence and experienced some much needed maturation. I taught English one year, then moved to an area that had been devastated by the Dashte-Bayaz Earthquake of 1968. While there I lived in a tent, designed and supervised the construction of a three-room school in a remote village, served as the "doctor" in a village, treated ringworm in children and lived among people whose lives had been turned upside down by a devastating natural disaster.

After the two years of Peace Corps, I returned to Indiana to finish my Master's Degree in CSPA. My realistic plan was to eventually become something like a dean of students, but my actual dream was to work again overseas. During a session of a course in International Education, our guest speaker, Dr. Tom Schreck, IU's dean of students, spoke about his experience with a team of IU advisors at Kabul University in Kabul, Afghanistan. The team was funded by the U.S. Agency for International Development (A.I.D.) and was helping Kabul University's central administration.

This was a bombshell! I made an appointment with Dean Schreck and asked if there was any way I could become a part of that team. It turned out there had been a position for a research associate on the team for a number of years, but it had never been filled. They needed someone who spoke Dari (an offshoot of Farsi), was in the Higher Education Administration Doctoral Program and who wanted to go there. That person had never shown up until I walked in and told Schreck, "I'll clean floors and cook rice if that's what it will take to get me on that team." My plea worked.

I was admitted to the doctoral program, hired onto the team, and not long after finishing a Master's Degree and newly named a doctoral student, was on that plane from Beirut to Kabul not knowing what to expect.

***

I wish I could remember more of my arrival and first days in Kabul, but after fifty-one years, I've forgotten many details. I didn't know what to expect from our advisory team or from Afghanistan itself. However, these two elements were vital to my experience, and I need to describe each.

Afghanistan was an Islamic nation of fourteen million people with a constitutional monarchy; it was making efforts to enter the modern age. It was described as the least developed nation in the world outside of Africa and was commonly said to be dashing out of the 16th Century into the 18th. Afghanistan was a "nation" that came together when faced with external threats from outside but was incredibly divided by its multitude of ethnic groups, languages, clans and urban-rural differences. The average family income in 1970 was the equivalent of $50. Women were abominably limited by religious, governmental and familial restrictions.

Kabul, the capital, had about 425,000 inhabitants and was growing rapidly, much of it the result of migration from Afghan towns and villages. It reflected attempts to modernize, and one could find a handful of modern restaurants, women dressed in Western clothing, hotels, movie theaters, schools, paved streets and bookstores. This was in contrast with the rest of the country where such modern "advances" were viewed with distrust and objection.

Kabul University (KU) was the only university in the country. It was experiencing rapid growth and, from its initial chartering in 1946, had grown to about 4,500 enrollees. Young high school graduates from remote provinces represented an increasing percentage of incoming students, many of them extremely unsophisticated. Some were unfamiliar with indoor plumbing, shower facilities, reliable electricity and mass-produced meals. They had never experienced the intermingling of Afghans from different parts of the country in one place.

As Afghanistan attempted to advance, it found a number of countries interested in helping it. This was sometimes done with good intentions but often derived from political rivalry to gain influence in this strategically located nation. Among these countries were The Soviet Union, France, Germany, Egypt and, of course, The United States. Though there are no figures for how many foreign employees were from each of these countries, it seemed as though the U.S. had by far the largest number. They covered a broad range of concerns and included the groups below:

**U.S. Agency for International Development:** developing roads, constructing a major airport in Kandahar, building a major dam in Helmand Province, supporting many other infrastructure and agricultural projects as well as assigning teams supporting Kabul University's Colleges of Agriculture, Education, Engineering and the Central Administration. Our IU team was charged to advise the Central Administration.

**U.S. Embassy:** There was a substantial State Department presence mostly housed at the Embassy Compound lying between the airport and downtown Kabul.

**Military:** There was a small Marine group stationed as Embassy guards. Other U.S. military served as advisors around the country, but we did not interact with them.

**Peace Corps:** The Peace Corps had a presence in Kabul and at some provincial locations. Many volunteers were teaching high school English.

**American International School-Kabul (AISK):** This was a school attended by the children of U.S. citizens stationed in Kabul. They also accepted students from other countries like India and Pakistan, and some Afghan children. Most teachers were American, and they covered a full range of elementary and high school subjects. Similar schools operated in many countries and at large U.S. military bases.

In general, representatives from one country did not socialize extensively with those from other countries (excepting Embassy personnel). Even among the various U.S. groups mentioned above, most socializing was done within groups. There was limited socializing with Host Country Nationals (HCNs) because their dealings with foreigners were watched by the Afghan police and they feared reprisals if they got too close to non-Afghans. Soviets returned that favor as their nationals lived on a closed compound where they were closely watched by their own security personnel.

***

I was met at the airport by members of the Indiana University team including Marvin and Mimi Cole with their offspring Tommy, age 11, Lisa, age 9, and Michael, age 2. It was very apparent that our team was warm and collegial and that the Coles were going to be good friends. I grew up in southern New Jersey and Chicago with one sibling, a brother more than eight years older than I. Marsh and I were close, but he went to college while I was quite young and I was similar to an only child from the age of 8. I was 27 years old, an unmarried stranger in a very strange place, and in no time, Marvin and Mimi and the kids seemed to accept me as one of theirs. Large family life was not normal to me, and as I observed the Coles and the bonds they shared, I was on unfamiliar territory. I loved it!

Our offices at KU were in the Central Administration Building where Marvin, as USAID Advisor in Student Affairs, supported the IU team and the KU Vice President for Student Affairs. I was his Research Associate, hoping to conduct meaningful student-affairs research that could also be converted into content for a doctoral dissertation after my return to IU. My contract was to last for one year.

Marvin treated me like a younger brother. He told me tales about life for Americans in Kabul. At the same time, he let me know how important my research work would be to him, to the University and to all of Afghanistan. A bit of hyperbole, maybe, because at the time I didn't even know what I'd be researching, but Marvin would be my director, and it was exciting that he was enthusiastic about what I was to do. I already had one older brother, but he was in the U.S. so it was great having Marvin assume that role.

We shared an office with a glass partition looking into the KU Records Office, rows and rows of file cabinets with thousands of files reflecting current and past students. Marvin pointed out that there was no meaningful demographic information on the University's students, and this might be a good place to start my work. There were no statistics reporting students' home provinces, first languages, father's occupations (very few women worked) or high schools attended. There were no computers on which to call up data. So how was I supposed to do something about a lack of data?

I acquired a large spreadsheet tablet and began by setting up columns for the demographics we hoped to collect. Marvin got permission for the records office to bring me these handwritten student files, in piles of ten or twenty at a time. They brought me over 4,500 files. I fought to read the Dari handwriting and to record data in hand-tallied groupings of five; four vertical lines and a crosshatch for the fifth. Over and over I went—file after file, stack after stack. I did this for weeks. No, make that months. Occasionally, Marvin would walk over to my chair to give me a robust series of pats on the back.

I was fortunate to have Marvin sitting across the room, constantly reminding me that these marks and crosshatches represented people who had never been counted. We'd cheer when I'd find a female student from a distant province. He'd roll his desk chair to my part of the office and tell me about how the top educators at Atlanta Baptist College, where he had previously been Dean of Students, were worse than the ultra-religious mullahs of Afghanistan. He'd regale me with tales of family events, their experiences working for A.I.D. in Lahore, Pakistan, or engage me in a discussion about ethics, news events or whatever else was on his mind.

A part of the USAID program involved selecting Afghan educators to attend American universities for graduate training. Our team sent a number of Afghans to Indiana for

Master's degrees in Student Personnel. One of those was Anisa Azamy, a bright, young woman who served as Assistant Director of Student Records. Anisa would often bring my stack of files and stay to chat with Marvin and me about life in Afghanistan and her memories of America.

Anisa would arrive for work wearing a Persian-style chador, much less confining than the burqa that most Afghan women wore. She was about five feet tall, beautiful, and a barrel of unrestrained energy. We looked at her as an example of the type of person who gave us hope that Afghanistan could advance into modern times.

In all, the dull monotony of recording data from file after file was relieved by the fact that about ten percent of the way into the work, we could see that the results would be worthwhile. I learned a big lesson from all of this regarding work done in relation to end product. The work is worth doing when the end product is of value. With Marvin as my cheerleader, the demographic report of students was completed, and the results were valued by the Afghans and by our team.

The other major part of my work involved developing, administering, tallying and reporting on a written survey of students seeking their opinions about KU's student services. These included: Admissions, New Student Orientation, Records, Health Services, Counseling, Student Activities and the Student Activities Center, Student Housing and Vocational Placement. This sounds like quite an array of services, suspiciously close to what one might have found at Indiana University. My role was to learn about each of these programs, get student input and make recommendations on how they might be improved. The survey would be in Dari, the verbal instructions in Dari, and the audience would be groups of students who had never been asked their opinions about much of anything, particularly not from a foreigner.

We'd enter a room of students selected for the survey, and I'd read a page in Dari, on what we were seeking and why we wanted the information. Afghans are not always trusting of one another and rarely trust foreigners, but they willingly gave us the information we sought.

We learned a great deal from the Afghan students, administrators and faculty members. Concerning some issues, our findings highlighted the obvious and, in other areas, brought problems to light. Above all, the report put on paper the status of student services at KU. For example, the large men's dormitory on campus, a modern western-style building, had overreached its capacity almost immediately. Its rooms, designed for four students, often housed as many as twelve. Students would awaken early to wash and say their morning prayers, so hot water would quickly disappear. Cultural differences among students representing Uzbeks, Tadjiks, Pashtuns, Baluchis, and even Hazaras from nomadic backgrounds could lead to discipline issues. Equipment would break down, and being a modern building, replacement of parts would be expensive and time-consuming. And, of course, the food was the least popular aspect of dorm life.

A program of student activities had been planned and the position of Director General of Student Activities could be found on KU's organization chart. Unfortunately, the position had never been filled. There were some facilities and resources that could have been used for activities, such as an auditorium and a printing press. But there was fear that they could be used for political purposes, so they received little use. A student government was prohibited for the same reason.

In the summer of 1970, a Counseling Center was established within The Faculty of Education. It was housed in the University Library, and the three trained counselors provided this service on a part-time basis. Within a short time, one of them died of pneumonia, a second died of hepatitis, and the third left to continue his studies in the U.S. Thus, the Counseling Center had no counselors.

The KU organization chart for student services might resemble that of an American university, but the substance behind the chart was not there. There was a willingness to dream of such programs, but lack of funds, lack of understanding and fear of giving students too much influence kept much from happening.

The report I produced, with Marvin's constant encouragement and guidance, was a picture of what existed at that time. I submitted it and left the country, so I don't really know to what use it was put. However, the experience of achieving something that had not been attempted before in that entire country was extraordinary.

*** 

My life outside of work was totally unexpected. As the initial flight into Kabul landed, I expected my life to be similar to that of a Peace Corps volunteer. Was I ever mistaken!

I was a penniless graduate student earning $500 a month and living in a very nice house with Abu Bakr—a full-time servant to cook, clean and shop for me. I also had Baba, an elderly man who was a full-time guard to watch over me. He had a small room in my courtyard and spent much of the nighttime hitting a stick against the ground to let any potential thieves know he was on the job. The house was surrounded by a wall, like all homes occupied by Americans and most Afghans, and the enclosed courtyard was like a front yard. There was no grass. Abu Bakr and Baba both were required to report regularly to the police about my comings and goings and guests.

Like many of the lead Afghan servants in Western homes, Abu Bakr spoke fairly good English and at times we'd parry back and forth from English to Dari and back to English. He decided I needed company and found me a parrot to keep me company. On the Coles first visit to the house, Michael saw the parrot and was fascinated. He proceeded to call me Kabob Greenbird, a name I was never quite able to shake for my entire Afghan stay.

Mohammad Razi was an Afghan administrator who had studied at IU, courtesy of our AID contract. He'd loved America and his experience, and we soon became friends. Razi was building a house in Kabul and at one point needed a place to stay. I had more room than I needed and invited him to move in with me. He accepted and, for a few months, was a part of the household. Razi was a great source of information about life in Afghanistan as well as a huge help while I was constructing my Dari questionnaire.

There was an American compound not far from where I lived. The compound contained medical offices, a commissary, tennis courts and other recreational facilities. This was commonplace for Americans working overseas, particularly in developing nations. During my Peace Corps years out in the hinterland, I never got close to the U.S. commissary. I resented the Americans who had access to peanut butter, U.S. cuts of meat, inexpensive and healthful dairy foods and eggs, packaged goods and especially alcoholic beverages. Now the "shoe was on the other foot," and I loved having this resource.

The compound had clay tennis courts with a Pakistani pro to give lessons. Our team chief, Dr. Chris Jung, was an avid tennis player, and I wound up playing more tennis than I had at any time in my life. Marvin took up tennis joyfully, and we took lessons from the pro. The lessons usually consisted of him hitting balls to us while we tried to return them with him commenting, "Very good, Doctor Cole," or "Excellent shot, Mr. Bob."

The American community in Kabul had one activity that brought the whole broad group together once a week during each fall. It was time for flag football. The Embassy compound had a football field behind it, and we gathered for three hour-long games every Friday. Refreshments were sold. Wives, daughters and girlfriends cheered from wooden grandstands. You'd have thought you were in Everytown, U.S.A.

Flag football is like touch football in that there is no tackling. The offensive teams wear belts that have flags attached to them. When a ball carrier has a flag stripped from him he is "tackled." Teams held practices, developed set plays and generally took the activity seriously. Teams included USAID, Embassy, Marines, Peace Corps, University (Afghan students, most of whom had studied in the U.S.), and AISK High School.

The 1970 United States Agency for International Development Flag Football Champions in Kabul, Afghanistan. Of course, if you have the broader educated vision, you would immediately conclude this team was the champions for the whole nation of Afghanistan, perhaps even Southeast Asia if you have really good vision. Greenberg, the "Blocking Quarterback," and Marvin, the "center who never needed a helmet," are on the extreme right.

I wound up playing quarterback for the AID team. Marvin was center. I spent the year complaining about my view. In flag football the quarterback could not run the ball. I wasn't much of a passer. If I did complete a pass, Marvin would pat me on the back and say, "Good pass, Kabob." We had Joe Lambert, quick and elusive. Other teams had trouble snatching his flag. I became known as "Kabob, the blocking quarterback" and our team rode Joe's speed to the 1970 championship.

This was a big deal! The Peace Corps had some really good athletes, the Marines were tough and didn't like losing, the Embassy guys played dirty, the AISK kids had unlimited energy, and we were viewed as a bunch of gristly over-the-hill old-timers. In sports, one can never be sure of what is going to happen.

After I'd been in Kabul for about six months, AID informed me that my house was to be changed. I was moved to a larger house with a backyard enclosed by a wall, which, coincidentally, bordered on the Coles' wall. In other words, we were neighbors. I spent a lot more time with the Cole family, it taking only a short walk around the block to be at their front door. Marvin and I played a lot of chess games. We shared a lot of happy hour drinks followed by dinners, and Mimi and I enjoyed sharing gossip about the community.

We lived in a purely residential part of Kabul that housed wealthy Afghans and much of the foreign community, particularly the Americans. The rest of the city was fascinating. Most of it was relatively primitive, streets shared by diesel buses and trucks, automobiles, donkeys, goats, sheep, camels and people. Almost all Afghan women from the age of puberty wore the very confining burqa to cover themselves. Their faces were covered by a mesh that must have interfered with their vision. Rough-looking villagers walked about with rifles slung over their backs.

The rug bazaar was located downtown on a busy street where there were newly knotted rugs spread on the street for intentional aging. All the traffic of the street softened the rugs and, after cleaning, made them more attractive.

The giant Used Clothes Bazaar was a commonly visited shopping area for Westerners. It was a bazaar hidden among downtown streets and was comprised of booth after booth selling used clothing from around the world. Much of it was worn-out, old and unattractive, and would sell for a few pennies. However, there were sometimes very surprising fashionable items to be found. It was a badge of honor to find good clothing there.

Another curiosity was The Money Bazaar. International exchange rates were complex, and sometimes official rates varied quite a bit from market rates. The Money Bazaar had dozens of moneychangers with piles of cash in different currencies, attempting to make money by these variances in exchange rates. Before travel to India or Pakistan, it was common for us to have dollars changed in the bazaar.

If one went to the city's main downtown gathering place, one would find small boys running about offering free samples of hashish to bystanders. Kabul was on the trail followed by thousands of European and American tourists beginning in Istanbul, Turkey, and ending in Katmandu, Nepal. Drugs had become commonplace and the Beatles"

*Magical Mystery Tour* was being lived by hippies seeking freedom, solace, truth and drugs. For some it was a journey of revelation and for others it ended early with the opiates of the area.

Kabul had a handful of modern amenities, but compared to the cities of Iran or Pakistan, it was far behind. The primitive nature of Kabul made it interesting, but the obvious levels of poverty, violence, poor health care and pollution made clear that it would take a great deal for it to modernize. A poor educational system and overall government ineffectiveness added to the difficulty in bringing forth improvements. Blatant discrimination against women and all sorts of minority groups made progress difficult.

***

Afghanistan is located in a frequently contested part of the world. Three times the British invaded Afghanistan from their Indian Empire, and three times they were violently expelled. The Afghan people can be fierce, and they unite when attacked from the outside. Recent wars fought by The Soviet Union and then The United States have not brought the Afghans to their knees.

Travel for someone like myself in 1970 was a remarkable experience because I knew I was on ancient routes that formed a significant part of Asian history. The ancient route heading east out of Kabul was used by armies from the time of Alexander the Great. It takes the traveler through the Kabul River Gorge, across the plains of Nangarhar Province and then through the Khyber Pass and into Pakistan.

This leaves a short distance to Peshawar, the remote northwestern outpost of the British Empire. In 1970 the population of Peshawar was about 250,000. In 2021 it is 2,000,000 and a good bit of this growth was a result of wars in Afghanistan that forced refugee Afghans into Pakistan. I was lucky enough to drive this route in my little VW Beetle in 1971 and I could still feel the clash of the former British Empire with the local traditions, religion and culture.

Travel inside Afghanistan was equally thrilling. It seemed that the longer one stayed in the country, the more things there were to see. Afghanistan is the size of Texas, and there was only a handful of paved highways in the entire country. Travel wasn't always easy, but it was almost always thrilling.

I flew Afghan Ariana Air from Kabul to Bamyan, a spectacular ancient Buddhist religious site. Bamyan sat on a crystal clear lake and was the site of giant Buddha statues carved into the mountain walls nearby. They were constructed during the 6th Century B.C. by Buddhists from India. They were spectacular. Unfortunately, the Taliban declared them to be religious idols and blew them up in 2001.

The city of Mazar-i-Sharif lies in Northern Afghanistan, on the plains near the Oxus River, which at that time, bordered on the Soviet Union. Now it is near the Afghan borders with both Uzbekistan and Tajikistan. I had become friendly with a Peace Corps couple who taught in Mazar and drove up to visit for a few days. During that stay I was fortunate to see a group of Afghans playing a fierce game of "buzkashi."

Buzkashi, literally translated as "Goat Drag," is a Central Asian sport played on horseback with the object of carrying the carcass of a dead goat across a goal or tossing it into a designated circle. There would be dozens playing at one time and they would whip and strike one another to try to get hold of the goat. A 1971 movie starring Omar Sharif, *The Horsemen*, depicted Afghanistan and the competition to be the best Buzkashi players.

The highway distance from Kabul to Herat in Western Afghanistan is approximately 650 miles. I took this trip, alone, in my little Beetle. Herat is close to the Iranian border and located at an ancient trade crossroads. It had a citadel built in the time of Alexander the Great. Herat was also a very interesting commercial city with beautiful hand-knotted rugs and numerous other crafts. The population of Herat has grown from about 100,000 in 1970 to over 649,000 in 2021.

In the summer of 1971, I was fortunate enough to be invited to join a team from the U.S. Agriculture project as they drove across the middle of the country. This was a small convoy of two or three Toyota Land Cruisers headed westward through the roughest and most beautifully desolate areas I've ever seen. The roads were narrow, rutted rocky paths, up and down mountainsides. The occasional villages or tea houses would be hours apart. There were precious few inhabitants, but the route still held ancient treasures. For example, in Ghor Province in a nearly inaccessible area, we passed the Minaret of Jam, a 203-foot, tall tower built around 1190. It was spectacularly beautiful with Arabic calligraphy and stucco and baked colored tiles. The Minaret is thought to have been built to celebrate a military victory at a time when the road was more heavily traveled.

*** 

That trip through the center of the country, then back on the main highway through Kandahar, was the trip of a lifetime. I got home in time to wash up and head to the Coles where a party was commencing. I was very tired and started feeling more than a little feverish, so I returned home. The next day I went to the clinic on the U.S. Compound where I was diagnosed to have contracted a nasty case of viral hepatitis.

Viral hepatitis was usually the result of consuming infected water or food. I thought back on that trip, and some of the water I had drunk directly out of cool streams, not knowing if there might be a herd of sheep a short way above. Anyway, my fever peaked at about 104 degrees and I was confined to my house with weekly blood tests to monitor my liver functions.

Weeks turned into a couple of months while I recuperated from the hepatitis. By the end of the "incarceration," I was able to enjoy the company of others and even hosted a Peace Corps party at my house. I loved everyone singing along to "My Girl" and even joined the crew of guys mangling dance moves of The Temptations. I was exhausted by 9:30 p.m. and went to bed while the party went on.

By some time in November, I was declared healthy enough to engage in normal (non-alcoholic) activities. Marvin made sure my contract was extended until April, which would give me time to finish tallying questionnaire data, by hand, and preparing a detailed report with recommendations.

However, The Cole Family was not yet finished with me. They had been secretly planning a party built around my being unmarried. The hepatitis had caused a delay in holding the party, but it gave Marvin and Mimi more time for planning, and that was a dangerous thing. Shortly after I was declared "recovered" from hepatitis, Marvin had me back on the football field, but that was nothing compared to his and Mimi's other plans for me.

In November, invitations to a party at the Coles' house were sent to many of Kabul's AID representatives and to our Peace Corps friends. Some of the teachers at AISK were invited, as well as a handful of other Americans living in Kabul. The invitations were to the wedding ceremony of Robert Greenberg to Ellie Mae Wampler of Polecat Creek, Kentucky. I knew there was to be a party but did not receive the invitation so I didn't know the theme.

Darryl Neat was AID Agriculture and the husband of Ethel, our team's secretary. Darryl wore white and played the role of the pregnant Ms. Wampler. There was a member of our football team dressed as Ellie Mae's father, and he carried an antique shotgun. Another football team member performed the ceremony.

The wedding ceremony was begun well after the guests had plenty of time to enjoy drinks and normal conversation. Of course, as a recent hepatitis patient, I was not permitted any alcoholic beverages. I experienced my mock wedding ceremony totally sober and seeking any means of escape. I didn't find one, and the words "You may now kiss the bride" left my knees wobbly. At the end, Marvin patted me on the back and said, "Congratulations, Kabob." The event went down in infamy.

*** 

My final months in Kabul were spent finishing our report on student services at KU. Winters were bitterly cold and outdoor activities were limited. In spring we played softball on the Embassy field for the AID team. I continued to enjoy the feeling of being a member of the Cole family, and as my April 1972 departure approached, I realized how difficult it would be to leave. Being so close to their family was a new experience for me and I never forgot it.

On an April day in 1972, I boarded an Air India plane for the first leg of my four-week trip home. The Coles had brought me to the Kabul International Airport, and we had said our goodbyes. As I waited for takeoff, James Taylor's "You've Got A Friend" was playing in the cabin. The flight attendant asked if I was all right because I was crying like a baby.

The plane left the ground, rose quickly to avoid the spectacular mountains to the north, and I was on the way home. My route included India, Thailand, Malaysia, Singapore, Hong Kong, Taiwan, Japan, Berkeley, California, and then on to Chicago. My mother insisted on meeting me at the O'Hare Field Airport because she said it wasn't safe for me to come home from the airport alone. In fact, I had only twenty-five cents in my pocket and am not sure how I'd have covered those last fifteen miles of the trip home without her.

***

In 1973 King Zahir Shah was dethroned while he was in Italy. There was hope that Afghanistan could develop a more progressive government, but struggles between left and right were matched by competition between Western nations and The Soviet Union for a controlling interest. In 1979 the Soviets invaded Afghanistan, took over the government, and thus began a war that lasted nine years and cost hundreds of thousands of Afghan lives. The Afghans fought fiercely and, with weapons from the U.S. and European allies were able to exhaust the Soviet forces. The Soviets finally left the country, and the monetary cost and humiliation from losing the war contributed significantly to the break-up of the Soviet Union.

The departure of the Soviet forces did not resolve Afghan political issues as competing groups sought power. These included the Taliban—ultra-conservative religious Afghans, who had benefitted from U.S. support during the war against the Soviets. Taliban groups gained control of many rural and isolated parts of the country.

Al Qaida, an extremist Sunni Arab group, with support from the Taliban, set up training camps for rebel fighters in central Afghanistan. This organization was responsible for the attacks on the U.S. on September 11, 2001, and led to a U.S. war against the Taliban that, at this writing in early 2021, has lasted twenty years and seen the U.S. spend hundreds of billions of dollars and cost over 2,300 American lives and more than 20,000 U.S. injuries. Over 110,000 Afghan civilians, soldiers and militants have been killed during the war. The future of Afghanistan is uncertain, but many experts feared that the Taliban would gain control and reverse many of the country's modest advances in women's rights, health care, education and political freedom.

***

I returned to Bloomington, Indiana, to complete the requirements for a doctoral degree in Higher Education Administration at IU. I was to be sent back to Kabul as a part of a new contract, but, as I completed my degree, the coup against the King took place, AID postponed awarding the contract, and when it was finally approved, The University of Nebraska-Omaha was the recipient. I was no longer part of the future KU group and never worked overseas again.

My life took on a more traditional career-oriented arc. I entered the field of university career services at IU's Business School as an associate director. After three years I moved to The University of Cincinnati as Director of Career Services, and four years hence, in 1984, I became director of Career Services at The University of Tennessee. I expected to be there three to five years. I loved the Knoxville area, loved the school and loved my job. Pretty soon I also discovered love with Cathy Kinzer, now Cathy Greenberg, and her two teenage daughters Julie and Meg. Cathy and I married in 1990 and, though retired for about fifteen years, we still live in Knoxville.

My life didn't intersect with the Coles during most of this work. I spoke on rare occasions with Marvin and visited them in Atlanta once or twice while he was at DeKalb County Community College. DeKalb County CC grew into Georgia Perimeter College, and when I learned that Marvin had become its president, I felt that occasionally occupational justice is served. They couldn't have had a better, more honest, and more inspiring leader.

Somewhere in our early years of retirement, I talked to Marvin about Cathy and me visiting him and Mimi. They were retired and living in Asheville, North Carolina, only a couple of hours from Knoxville. A trip was planned.

We began our visit with Marvin laughing, patting me hard on the back, and saying "Good to see you, Kabob!" He and Mimi adopted Cathy as though she were a long-lost sister, and we fell into conversation with ease, telling stories about our lives in Kabul and some about our lives since then.

Before leaving Knoxville, I had cautioned Cathy about admiring anything in the Coles' house. I tried to explain that such admiration could have consequences but she didn't take me seriously. Cathy commented on a beautiful pottery plate and vase set that had been locally made. When it came time to leave, Marvin and Mimi had them all packed up and ready for us to take home with us. Cathy, fearful of Marvin's generosity, is much more cautious about expressing her admiration for things in their house.

Cathy and I have visited Marvin and Mimi in Asheville numerous times, usually at a Mediterranean restaurant that we all love. In many cases, whether at the Cole home or at a restaurant, Tom, Lisa and Mike will join if available. It feels like a family gathering and Cathy has been enthusiastically greeted as a part of it.

***

I was surprised and honored that Marvin and Mimi asked me to write this chapter of their book. They were a daily part of my life for twenty months and have regularly been in my thoughts ever since. When that Air India flight left Kabul and I was sobbing like a baby, it was because I didn't know when or if I'd ever see my adoptive family again.

# The Greenberg Afghan Wedding
# Marvin's Version

Our good friend Robert, who was called "Bob," Greenberg was a frequent visitor during our stay in Afghanistan. After work one evening during "Observation of Libation," Bob was discussing the activities at his twenty-first Birthday Party and asked Mimi about her twenty-first party. Mimi replied, "I did not have a party for my 21st birthday. Bob took this as a cue for an activity.

Being isolated in some sense, people from the United States were always open for a chance to get together, exchange news from home, exchange books and dine. This community togetherness was beneficial, especially since we had no radio or television and our back fences usually selected for gossip were nine-foot walls with glass covering the top to stop persons with ill intent from entering. During our three-year stay, we had in our home, chess parties, a country music show—with live performers from various performers including a CIA Agent assigned to the Ambassador and a Veterinarian from the Wyoming team—and frequent dinner parties.

So Bob and friend Bill Heim, Coach at the American School, had a 21st birthday party for Mimi at the age of 35.

Mimi promised Bob he would be experiencing revenge and she started scheming and planning. She would do things like sneaking into their home while they were working and writing on Bob's mirror "Just Wait."

So since Bob had not married at the time, a wedding for him was arranged—which was the common practice in Afghanistan. A picture for an advertisement of a pregnant-looking woman was found and placed on the invitation. The husband of the Indiana team's secretary, a hefty man with very hairy legs, was enticed to dress as the bride. The Indiana team's university business advisor, Joe Trosper, dressed and played the role of the Mullah

# BROWN-GREENBERG VOWS TO BE SPOKEN IN AFGHANISTAN

The Reverend and Mrs. Lester M. Brown of Salt Lick, Kentucky announce the engagement of their daughter, Bertha Mae, to Mr. Robert Greenberg of Kabul, Afghanistan.

Mr. Greenberg is serving in Kabul with the Indiana University team as a Research Associate. He has an honorary degree from Carlton College and is presently a graduate student at Indiana University. Miss Brown is a graduate of Miss Perriwinkle's Charm School in Salt Lick, Kentucky.

The Rev. and Mrs. Brown are accompanying Miss Brown and her six months' old daughter, Roberta, to Kabul. The marriage will take place in Kabul with the Rev. Brown, who is Pastor of Stony Fork Baptist Church in Salt Lick, officiating.

Wedding activities will take place at the home of the Marvin M. Cole's at 349 Karte Seh on *October 28, 1971* at 8:00 P.M. A reception will follow. You are cordially invited to meet Miss Brown at this time.

Mostly informal
Regrets only
41529

The future Mrs. Greenberg knitting booties for her surprise bundle prior to her departure to Afghanistan.

Mr. Greenberg, known in Kabul as the blocking quarterback, anxiously awaits fiancee.

# Y'ALL COME ! ! !

performing the ceremonies. Another USAID employee, Art Fabricious, an agribusiness advisor from the Wyoming Team, played the role of the father of the bride and carried a rifle to insure his daughter's reputation would not be tarnished. Lisa is pictured in overalls and freckled-faced as the flower girl.

Invitations (depicted on the previous page) were sent out to the usual party friends, but the word got out and more came than were invited. Desperate for entertainment, the event became more than that envisioned by the Cole family.

We had more than thirty people in our rather large living room.

Bob's wedding was described later as the event of the year and therefore got Marvin in a bit of trouble with his boss. That boss was Taulman Miller, an economics professor at Indiana University who was a wonderful person but very calm and tranquil—the antithesis of boisterous. Mimi and I thought Dr. and Mrs. Miller might not be comfortable in our outrageous wedding activity. However, we did invite his boss, Tony Lanza, the AID Director for Education who loved the burlesque wedding show, but who subsequently asked Dr. Miller why he did not attend the Cole Wedding Extravaganza. So I had some "explaining" to do. (Dr. Lanza's son was Tom's best friend and is shown in the extreme left in striped pants in the picture.)

Our United States newspaper in Kabul, The Kabul American, posted an announcement about the wedding. We assume someone at the event reported it to the paper, knowing all the time it was "tongue in cheek" reporting.

Bob's reaction to the event was to keep smiling with a frown and he asked the question to Mimi, "Are you going to crucify me"?

Bob's wedding was remembered by many as a happy event in Kabul, Afghanistan, that helped build community and relieve our sometimes frustrating work efforts.

## The Kabul American
Published Weekly for the American Community by the American Embassy in Kabul

VOLUME 9, No. 44　　　　　　　　　　　　　　　　　　　November 4, 1971

```
        DEADLINE FOR ALL ITEMS IS TUESDAY NOON
        ADDRESS THEM TO:  ADMINISTRATIVE OFFICE
                          AMERICAN EMBASSY
                          FOR: KABUL AMERICAN
```

DUTY SCHEDULE

```
November 1 - 8   EMBASSY: Mr. Schifferdecker, 30089; Miss Patterson, Miss Lavery
                 USAID  : Mr. Hooker, 42921, Miss Bryant
                 USIS   : Mr. Bernier, 25963
                 MEDICAL: Dr. Reyes, 32709; Miss Murphy

November 8 -15   EMBASSY: Mr. Hawley, 30085; Miss Archer; Mr. Potter
                 USAID  : Mr. Meadows, 41318; Miss Bieler
                 USIS   : Mr. Peppers, 20215
                 MEDICAL: Dr. Moede, 41180; Miss Nielsen
```

Announcement: Mr. Robert M. Greenberg of the Indiana Team and Miss Bertha Mae Brown of Salt Lick, Kentucky were married in a quiet ceremony at the home of Mr. and Mrs. Marvin M. Cole on Thursday, October 28. The American Community in Kabul extends its heartiest congratulations and best wishes to the newlyweds.

(L-R) Vice Presidents with Marvin:
Bill Crews, Martha Nesbit, Flora Devine, Rob Watts

# 8

# As College President

# As College President
# by Marvin Cole

REMINISCING AND RECOLLECATING FACTS, OPINONS, THOUGHTS, FEELINGS, JOY, ANGUISH, AGONY AND A FEW DIGRESSIONS WHILE PRESDENT OF DEKALB COLLEGE

The unknown factors that go into making decisions may be more dramatic than the actual decision. I have often wondered about the decision process made by Congress, the Supreme Court, and our nation's Presidents and wished I knew the steps, the anguish, fear, arm-twisting, threats and theatrics that were involved in the process. To me, one current question is, "Why is Congress is so concerned about whether the person placed on the Supreme Court is liberal or conservative?" I thought the Supreme Court's main concern was justice, but it seems that Congresspersons, perhaps more than anyone else, feel that justice is either Democrat or Republican. I guess I want Justice to be above politics.

The behind-the-scene antics of our former "DeKalb College" are not as dramatic, and I did not have the power or desire to make threats or have people express fear of my office, but I want to tell you about some of the factors, tomfooleries and monkeyshines that were going on at the time of a few events that were stressful to me.

## FACULTY FORUM

As I have told before, I thought of dropping out of college after my freshman year because of the requirement to take a speech class. I was so shy and backward that to stand up and speak before a room of people ranked, for me, just below a firing squad. But my girlfriend, Mimi, shamed me into taking the course. And I survived a New Jersey Speech Professor who was brought in to help get the twang out of mountain talk. Although the "abject fear" was gone, I never got over being nervous when I had to speak to a group, but at some point in my junior year a group of students persuaded me to make a five-minute speech at a student assembly as a prerequisite to running for President of the Student Body. I was elected and it was that experience in my senior year working with Dean of Men Howard Almond that gave me direction for the rest of my life. I wanted to work in higher education. I wanted to be a Dean of Men.

One more big personal guide to my life was my mother's philosophy as a real person. When I received the doctor's degree, she said, "I don't think I have to say this, but just in case, never get the big head and always remember that your britches were once made out of the backs of your father's overalls—after he had worn out the front of them." She had no opportunity to go beyond the eighth grade. But her actions communicated that the only qualification I needed for success as a real person and success in a decent life's work was to always respect all people.

That gives you a little of my background for how I felt at the first Faculty Forum Speech when I became President in 1981. It was a great comfort to have a speaker stand to steady my shaking legs. The term "speaker stand" is used because of Agnes Donaldson—an English teacher who caused English teachers to watch their language. Many people call a speaker stand a podium, and when I first referred to a speaker stand as a podium in the presence of Agnes, she informed me that a podium is a platform upon which there is a speaker stand and upon which people sit. Obviously the lesson took, and to this day, it is why I think of Agnes Donaldson every time I hear someone use podium incorrectly.

The Faculty at DeKalb College contributed greatly to my education. They introduced me to a Huck Finn whom I thought I already knew. As a boy I had read the adventure story but missed the message. That experience made me wonder about a lot of books read and all that is derived is the story, or chemistry and math courses taken and solved the problems but missed the message. Can one go through college and miss the message—the purpose? Although I was relieved and grateful for all my educational experiences, I have had a psychological fetish for being educated. I firmly believe that one is never educated, but it is a mark of an intelligent person to always endeavor to become educated. My guideline also says that a Christian must always struggle to become Christian. It helps one to become educated if he or she happens to encounter a good teacher. Many people can pass on knowledge, or one can get it from a book, but a teacher can take something equivalent to a mud pie and turn it into a learning experience.

With that in mind, consider Van Gogh and one of his most famous paintings. When I first glanced at *The Starry Night*, I saw only a nice blue picture that I thought the artist had angrily brushed it in frustration to try again another day. Then a teacher came along and refined my art education. Van Gogh was a religious person, served briefly in England as an assistant to a Methodist preacher and tried to enter the seminary, but he failed the entrance exam. So he became a volunteer missionary, but annoyed people (he did struggle with mental health problems), and therefore was told he could not serve anymore. He kept his faith, but held antipathy for the church. So, we come to *The Starry Night*. You are familiar with it. Don McLean wrote a hit song about it called "Vincent." The painting shows a town and a church at night, and above is an amazing sky—the moon and stars whirl like pinwheels overhead. Many see the lights in the sky representing Christ, the light of the world. The light of God's love. Some of the houses show light, representing the hearts and lives of people. But right in the middle of the painting is a church. There is no light coming from the church, just a cold building with no light. What is the message? I missed that in Art Appreciation in college.

In writing a book *Essays After Eighty,* Don Hall, Poet Laureate of US 2006–7, talks about things that he experienced throughout his life. So looking back as I read this book, I remember being disconcerted at one time by what I missed in being educated. Now I know a person can never be fully educated, but it sure is fun discovering things I missed, and one of my bucket list items is to keep on trying.

When I was first employed at DeKalb in 1973, the Faculty Forums to me were a mundane, tedious affair, something to be dreaded. I did not feel that the President at the time, in his address, tried to get the faculty to explore horizons. Contrarily, I saw the remarks as speaking down to a group of college faculty and felt that was unacceptable. There were no prepared remarks but some sermonizing. At the first faculty meeting I attended at South Campus, the Executive Dean Seaborn Thompson called the meeting to order and then asked me to pray. I laughed out loud because I thought he was joking. The look on his face told me otherwise, but he recovered and went on to pray. I could not believe that there could be a prayer at a faculty meeting at a state institution. I confess I had become a religious pessimist from a previous job working for the Atlanta Baptist Convention in recruiting students and faculty and opening Atlanta Baptist College—opening in 1968, now Mercer University of Atlanta. There were 168 Baptist preachers involved in that organization. Believe me, neither ISIS or Islam can steer one away from Christianity more effectively than working for 168 Baptist preachers. The Baptist College closed after two years because of preacher-backward policies and the lack of money. Fortunately, at that time, Indiana University employed me to work in Afghanistan for three years and that was a religious recuperating period for me. Baptist preachers are not popular in Afghanistan. Obviously I retain a redemption blemish in the forgiveness part of my brain.

I will admit that my observing the Islamic Mullah's made Baptist Preachers look a little better. At any rate, at the former Faculty Forums, I remember the speakers looking like they had purchased their ties and suits from Wayne Cooper, a Sociology teacher at DeKalb. He told me that he purchased his ties for a dollar a dozen from the flea market. Although Wayne's education did not reach the doctoral level, he was a very frugal person and I remember the day he came into my office, sat down, and said, "Marvin, as of today, because I watched my pennies, I am a millionaire." I was impressed but did not have the strength to utilize his source of neckties.

The remarks at those fall forums were on a level of one I remember vividly: "The chalkboards are clean, the chalk is in the chalk trays, the student desks are in line, so you go in and teach." So I wanted a very different Faculty Forum. I wanted to speak up to the faculty rather than speak down to them. I read and sought out what I thought were meaningful trends and thought in higher education. I worked on those talks for over a month each year at night because it was hard to find quiet time in the office during the day. I also bought a new tie and shirt each year but not from Wayne Cooper's barrel. (Therefore I failed to become a millionaire.) And yes, I know, new ties, new suits and nice words do not a good teacher make or an effective college president, but to me it was a way of showing respect for people who were forming tomorrow's citizens. The unspoken message was that faculty hopefully would feel they were looked up to and appreciated and would feel good about the place where they worked. In trying to speak up to the faculty, I overcooked the communication, probably more than a few times, but one particular time in trying to impress faculty and "getting above my raising," I quoted W.E.B. Du Bois, the noted author and civil rights leader. I wanted to use the correct French pronunciation so the faculty would think "I was with it." So I stated his name as in "Dubwa." Flora Divine, Vice President for Legal Affairs, came to me after the speech and told me that "Black people do not appreciate your mispronouncing the name of their champion. His name is DOO BOYZ."

I could not afford a new suit every year for the Faculty Forum. Just a tie. When I went in as President, I made $40,000 a year. I still have the contract. Several faculty members made more than I made, and that was appropriate. Good teachers are hard to find, and their impact far outreaches that of a mere administrator.

Fifteen years later when I retired, I had reached the $70,000 mark. It was a lot of money compared to the $2,800 salary in my first job in higher education. But I spent a lot of money with various activities as being president. After paying off our mortgage and other bills when we left Atlanta after retirement, Mimi and I had $20,000 to start a new home in North Carolina.

## GOING TO THE BOARD OF REGENTS

In 1981 when I went in as President, DeKalb College was a part of the DeKalb County School System. The buildings on Central Campus were drawn like a high school facility. I reported to the Superintendent of DeKalb County Schools and had to defend, cajole, beg and sweet-talk once a month at a meeting with the Dekalb County School Board. The DeKalb Technical School was then part of DeKalb College.

It was while working with the school board that I became very sensitive about Democrats and Republicans. I felt I had to please both to get their approval for the needs of the college. Senator Joe Burton used to put his signs of his name on an elephant cut-out on our lawn. We were concerned that the Democrats on the Board would see the signs. Some of our neighbors who knew our dilemma would sneak around at night and remove the signs, but Senator Burton would replace them each time.

Part of our budget was provided by the state government as stipulated in the agreement Superintendent Jim Cherry got the legislature to pass when DeKalb College was created. After the DeKalb College Act was enacted, the legislature passed a law that stipulated no other county school systems would be provided funds for a college. So, DeKalb College was a unique phenomenon in Georgia, thanks to Jim Cherry who was one of the most powerful men in Georgia, because DeKalb County was where the growth and money were at the time. He was powerful and farsighted. But things change and I have wondered if the powers-that-be in the state government resented this one county getting funds for a college. After all, other counties around Atlanta were beginning to be big and powerful. As the cost of operating the college increased, the legislature refused to increase the initial allotment and the School System was running short of their funding needs for the schools—much less the college. I would walk the halls of the Legislature, groveling to Democrats and Republicans to increase the funding for the college. So did Travis Weatherly Sr. Tom Murphy, Speaker of the House, was adamant that the state would not increase the funding unless DeKalb College became a part of the University System of Georgia.

Meanwhile, back in DeKalb County, the DeKalb School Board refused to allow the college to go to the state system. Board Member John Truelove was adamant in the position of not going to the Regents. It was frustrating that we could not get across to the Board that we could not continue under current funding arrangements. To keep the college operating, our only hope was to join the University System. I remember saying at one meeting: "But Mr. Truelove, if we go to the Regents, we will not be moving to Bartow County; we will still be right here in your county." Finally one morning, I ran across Mr. Jackson, Chairman of the Board, walking the halls of the Legislature, and he pulled me aside and said, "I have been talking to Speaker Murphy and all the DeKalb Legislators, to all the "powers-that-be" here this morning and found you are right—we can expect no further help from the state. He said he would inform the Board.

Meanwhile, Superintendent Freeman was working on his own solution for use of the college campuses. He said since the state would not increase the funding, he was thinking of alternative uses such as model high schools for selected academic honors programs at one or two of the campuses. Somehow, Georgia State University got into the act and made overtures to Dr. Freeman. Someone pointed out that Dr. Freeman's name was listed as a Visiting Professor in the Georgia State Catalog. Georgia State was ONLY interested in the North Campus—had no interest in the South Campus or Central Campus.

Over the Christmas holidays, a very large sign was installed on the North Campus depicting it to be a campus of Georgia State University. Being merely upset does not come close to describing my feelings about this hostile takeover. Neither the president nor any administrator at Georgia State or DeKalb County Schools had said one word to me about this sneak attack. I told Travis Weatherly Jr., the Plant Manager, to remove the signs as soon as he could get a crew together. Then I informed Dr. Freeman what I had done. This was a time when Mimi thought she would soon be the sole breadwinner of the Cole family—fully expecting I would be fired. She would wake me up at night to stop me from grinding my teeth.

Dr. Freeman and I did not have an adversarial relationship, but we never became real friends. This is the person who had recommended me to the Board to become President of DeKalb College. There was something about him that kept me from wanting him as a fishing buddy. For one, he applied pressure for friends to be employed at the college. A couple of Board members also pressured me to employ individuals whether they were needed by the college or not.

One day, Dr. Freeman phoned that a friend was visiting in his office and he wanted me to come to perform about ten minutes of Mark Twain. I was flabbergasted. This would mean traveling to my home to get dressed as Twain, go to his office for a ten-minute performance, back home to get in office attire, and back to campus. I said no. I just could not get away from the office. Saying no to one's boss makes you uncomfortable for a day or two, wondering if there will be consequences. Besides, NO is a word I have always had difficulty in delivering.

Informing Dr. Freeman of my plans, I made an appointment to see Chancellor Vernon Crawford to see if there was any possibility of DeKalb College becoming a unit of the University System of Georgia. He gave some hope and arranged for me to meet with the Vice Chancellor, Dr. Dean Propst, to begin feasibility studies. Dr. Propst, who became Chancellor, and I met at the Barbeque Restaurant on Memorial Drive for breakfast. The Barbeque restaurant and The Waffle House were Dr. Propst's favorite restaurants. He was a very practical administrator. Dr. Ray Cleere was assigned as the liaison overseer of the details of our joining the University System.

Ray and Dr. Propst became my good friends. During the feasibility process, Dr. Cleere came to our DeKalb School Board Meeting and, after hearing the shenanigans of the members, said to me "You are going to love working in the University System." The Board of Regents personnel never allowed us to refer to the joining process as a merger. It made the attorneys nervous. Merger meant that we would join "as is" and therefore all tenured faculty would retain their tenure. This was a big issue with them and with us. So we had to go through the painful process of losing tenure and then reapplying twenty faculty per year. Faculty were given the option of keeping their tenure and work in the school system, but many did not have the proper credentials, and no one wanted to work in secondary schools. So all faculty stayed with the college and all were eventually "retenured." The Board of Regent's personnel never questioned any of our recommendations for tenure. So we became a unit of the University System of Georgia. We benefited because the College remained intact but they also benefited. Our addition solved a big problem for them.

The Board of Regents reaped great benefits for who we were. At the time the Federal Government was paying close attention to segregation and gender numbers. The University System of Georgia had not reached the satisfactory diversity level for majority white institutions. But after DeKalb entered the system, there were no such concerns. DeKalb College had more African-American students than any other majority white institution in Georgia. It had more African-American administrators, more African-American faculty, and more female administrators than any other majority white college in Georgia. I am proud of that record. Newspaper references to the Federal Government looking into the University System's discrimination numbers ceased to exist.

## ONE COLLEGE CONCEPT

Our college was composed of three campuses, ingeniously named Central, North and South. In several respects other than geographically, they were three separate colleges. There were some tensions involved and belittling comments made about the other campuses. This bothered me very much as I like harmony and teamwork. One reason my favorite sport is basketball is because it requires more teamwork than any other sport. We had three baseball teams that seemed to end each game with a fight. We had two basketball teams, three soccer, three tennis. Our biggest competitors were within our own college. When I expressed dissatisfaction over college teams fighting each other, coaches and others tried to tell me that it was inherent in the game. I found that reason unreasonable.

But the most malaise/malady were attitudes about the academic programs of sister campuses. I was informed that the people at the admissions office at the University of Georgia were told by a DeKalb faculty member that the transfers from one campus would be good students but not from other campuses. The informant named the South Campus as the one to avoid. The South Campus had a seven-percent African-American student population when I started there in June of 1973. That was the beginning of the white flight in the area. Seven years later, 1980, we had about a seventy-percent African-American student population.

Several people, mostly DeKalb School System administrative types, repeatedly informed me that when we reached a forty-percent black to sixty percent white population, we would experience demonstrations, disturbances, riots at the South Campus. I called the black members of the faculty to sit with me one afternoon and asked them to help me make an atmosphere to assure that "we are all for one, and one for all." We went from seven percent to seventy percent and had no racial problems at the South Campus. Our white faculty were as much responsible for good racial relationships as the black faculty. They only wanted good students.

Bill Gray, our Economics Professor, enjoyed a persona of being a grumpy, nasty, appalling person. First contact with him might cause one to expect disaster. But those who knew him, observed that he was trying to hide a big heart as a bulldog with no bite. He burst into my office one day and his first words were, "You son of a bitch." He was upset because I had reassigned one of his department's adjunct classes to a full-time person, and I had neglected to discuss it with him. He had a right to be upset, but I could not find him the day the decision was made.

Anyway in all our years together, Bill was always up for Best Teacher and I never received one complaint about his work. My point is, what went on in the classroom and in the halls and playing fields with faculty, to my mind, prevented racial tensions at the South Campus. I am proud of that. The South Campus was majority black. I believed then and now in one people as well as one college and wanted to eliminate any semblance of prejudice and segregation. Sadly, as a nation, as a world, it is still a frontier where we have yet to make meaningful progress.

In another area, each campus had its own committees to select textbooks so there were inferences to inferior text books on "other" campuses. So with my begging, and what I'm sure was considered persistence (as a nice term), we established textbook committees composed of personnel from all three campuses, so we ended up teaching from the same English textbook, same economics book, and books of other subjects across the three-campus college. At least on the surface, we were equal with textbooks, although I am not naïve. I know throughout the faculty world, professors use whatever book they like to get the point across, and that is the way it should be. We went from three baseball teams to one, as well as one basketball, one soccer, and one tennis. Of course it did not eliminate all jibes, but it was an effort for us to see ourselves as one team.

We started the President's Workshop with forty to forty-five people from all campuses for a three-day venture at one of the state parks exploring academic subjects from different perspectives. A book, movie, philosophy, a topic was looked at from the point of view of an English teacher, a biologist, a math teacher, a history teacher, and subject-areas professors—all from different campuses.

I remember being proud of Fred Hill, a Physical Education major (only because his coach made him stop majoring in math), giving an excellent report on his take on Toni Morrison's *Beloved*. One year, Jane Herndon suggested we invite her husband, a professor at Clemson, down to speak at the President's Workshop. He came for the entire three days, and the next year asked if he could attend again just as a member, and then every year thereafter. He said it was better than any conference he could get at Clemson. We tried to invite different people every year from the faculty, administration and staff. One person invited the first year grumbled about going, but complained three years later for not being invited again. There were a lot of good vibes about the President's Workshop. Betty Siegle, President of Kennesaw, heard about our workshop and asked me to come do one for Kennesaw. I told her the President had to do it, not a visiting potentate. I miss getting the education from the faculty as a consequence of those President's Workshops.

So along with some side bars, those are three behind-the-scenes descriptions of my worries and fun times while president. Looking back, I will have to say that the majority of the fears I had (that all of us working at the college had) were unfounded. I think most of us can say the same thing about our lives. Although I shivered and shook while giving the Fall Forum speeches, at least after a few years, I had the feeling that the faculty felt I might bumble and stumble, but I had good intentions as president. I tried to hold to some basic values that always pull one through, and I felt the faculty knew that. We did try to inform everyone what was going on through the Gray Letters and campus talks.

I also used to visit each campus for "Doughnut Sessions" and let faculty and staff vent and ask questions. I remember one session on North Campus when Walt Rogers complained that he was busy all the time outside the classroom because he had been appointed to too many committees. Walt was a tall, lovable person from Alabama. He taught math. He went on and on about the time he spent as he named the committees. When he finished, I told him I was sorry he had been selected for so many and then I said, "When I get back to my office, I will have your name withdrawn from those committees."

"Oh, no, no, no," he said, I do not want to be removed from any of the committees."

Walt just wanted to express a complaint but did not want anything changed. So a lot of times, it is just creating an atmosphere wherein people are free to express whatever they want. That helps good morale.

What I have written today were some of things that should not have been told then because it was not the right thing to do. Today, it doesn't matter anymore—no one cares. This brings us to today. Today, DeKalb College has become the academic part of Georgia State University. Things change, conditions change, people are slow to change. We expect our automobiles, cell phones and televisions to change and improve but we have less expectation for people. Yes, it did sadden me at first when I heard that our college was merging with Georgia State. So I took a walk among the trees around my house and had a one-man President's Workshop. And the result was: to me, one of the distinguishing marks of an educated person is willingness to accept, embrace and enhance change. You need to think about why we as a nation appear to love tradition and loathe change.

A common expression when and where I was a boy, and one I heard frequently from my mother was, "Don't get above your raising." Some values are forever, but one should always question. Throughout Mark Twain's work was the message to get above your raising; don't stay in the same old calf path all your life when there are straighter, more solid highways. The expression (adage) "If it ain't broke don't fix it," should ALWAYS be questioned, especially by educated people.

Rob Watts was Acting president during the merger with Georgia State University, and he went through a lot of discomfort and uneasiness with the change to Georgia State. I would not be surprised to find that Tina had to tell him to stop grinding his teeth at night. I have a lot of trust and respect for Rob Watts. He is more intelligent nationwide than ninety percent of the college administrators. My authority for that statement comes from Yogi Berra's belief, "I do a lot of observing by watching."

I made a study. Rob can read, really read. He can grasp the message between the lines, he gets the message, Rob also knows figures, a rare combination. But mainly he has good values. His main weakness could be resolved with a few lessons and more practice on playing the guitar. He is the best person I know to have held things together during the past few years.

*** 

A word about Katherine Martin: Katherine Martin was employed as a secretary for the Executive Dean of the South Campus around 1975-76. She was never just a secretary. She was an author, a painting artist, a reader and a drama teacher. Katherine received her

Bachelor's Degree in English and Drama at Mississippi College. A very private person, Katherine abhorred any resemblance of being in the spotlight. She excelled in ethical values and speaking out in her way for injustice.

As I was learning to portray Mark Twain, drama coach Katherine would stand at the back of an empty basketball court and yell at me, "Say those words clearly and distinctly, do not make small hand gestures, look the audience in the eyes, raise your eyebrows with that statement . . . " and a host of other do this – do that's that were unknown and difficult for this backwoods carpenter's son.

When I became president of the college, Katherine earned the title of Assistant to the President. Her writing abilities were of extraordinary assistance as we went through the enormous paper details and negotiations of DeKalb College becoming a unit of the University System of Georgia. She formulated the Gray Letters (so named by the faculty because they were issued on gray paper), which communicated activities, issues, concerns and helped tremendously in informing and relieving stress apprehensions to all college personnel.

If those who were affiliated with DeKalb College in the 1980s through 1994 perceived any semblance of success, Katherine Martin deserves a lot of credit for that perception, considering the work from the president's office.

*** 

Looking back, it was a wonderful experience for me. The good times won over rocky times. I was surrounded by a lot of good people—faculty, staff, plant workers, custodians. After being named President, I walked through the front doors at South Campus and Lucy Farley, a Custodian, greeted me with, "What are you doing here, turkey?" That was better than any plaque I ever received. As was Barney Sims presenting me with a badge in front of the convention for Black-American Affairs (or a faculty meeting) some public gathering with the initials SAWB – SMART ASS WHITE BOY. I still have dreams about faculty, administrators, committee meetings at DeKalb College. Early on in my career. I was impressed by a cartoon depicting a Chancellor of California Higher Education following a crowd of faculty members. The caption read:

THERE THEY GO. I MUST FOLLOW THEM
BECAUSE I AM THEIR LEADER

DeKalb College people made a world of difference to me. And I thank them for that wonderful experience.
Looking back, it was a wonderful experience for me. The good times won over rocky times. I was surrounded by a lot of good people—faculty, staff, plant workers, custodians. After being named President, I walked through the front doors at South Campus and Lucy Farley, a Custodian, greeted me with, "What are you doing here, turkey?" That was better than any plaque I ever received. As was Barney Sims presenting me with a badge in front of

the convention for Black-American Affairs (or a faculty meeting) some public gathering with the initials SAWB – SMART ASS WHITE BOY. I still have dreams about faculty, administrators, committee meetings at DeKalb College. Early on in my career. I was impressed by a cartoon depicting a Chancellor of California Higher Education following a crowd of faculty members. The caption read:

There They Go. I Must Follow Them
Because I Am Their Leader

DeKalb College people made a world of difference to me. And I thank them for that wonderful experience.

*Katherine and Bob Martin*

Above: Katherine's current art interest is creating these jeweled ladies. It started by using her mother's costume jewelry, her dad's railroad pins, brother's Air Force flight pins and husband Bob's fraternity pins. Then she began collecting jewelry from thrift shops and friends creating quite a collection of pin ladies some of which are now on display in shops in Lewiston, Idaho. The wood table was made by Bob Martin who is an accomplished woodworking artist and has created some wonderful pieces. The bottom pictures are art pieces created by Katherine as off-duty leisure time interests while working at DeKalb College.

DeKalb College friends: Martha Nesbitt and Marvin, Hartwell and Donna Quinn with Bill Crews, Ellen Sweatt, Edna Wilson and JoAnn Adkins, Randy Carol Copenhaver, and Fred Hill.

Some of our DeKalb College friends: Clockwise – Jarvis Hill and Jim Godwin, Rob Watts, IM Nur (Martin), Bari Haskins-Jackson, Gretchen Neill, Gary Roseman, Harris Green and John Michael.

Pam and Gary Roseman

Peggy Davis and Maimoona Sediqi on my last day as president of DeKalb College.

# 9

# Marvin the Teacher
# by Rob Watts

# Marvin the Teacher
## by Rob Watts

Marvin used the office of president to be a teacher. His classroom was the institution. He taught me and others how to be a college president, how to be a senior leader in the University System and beyond. He was my model, our model. He was the single-most important influence on my professional career. He also made it clear that he cared about me and others as people. Marvin was a teacher.

NOTE ON INSTITUTIONAL CONTEXT AND ABBREVIATIONS

From its opening in 1964 until June 30, 1986, DeKalb College (also named DeKalb Junior College and DeKalb Community College during this period) was part of the DeKalb County School System under the governance of the locally elected DeKalb County School Board. I will use the abbreviations DCSS to refer to the DeKalb County School System and DCSB to refer to the DeKalb County School Board. On July 1, 1986, governance of DeKalb College was transferred from the DeKalb County School Board to the Board of Regents of the University of Georgia, an agency of the executive branch of the state government of Georgia, led by the Governor.

The Board of Regents of the University System of Georgia comprises

(1) the actual Board of Regents itself, whose members are appointed by the governor, one for each Congressional district and five at-large;

(2) the Regents Central Office, staff to the Board of Regents, led by the chancellor, vice chancellors, and the like; and

(3) the thirty-four colleges and universities in the System, including research universities, four-year colleges, and two-year colleges.

I will use the abbreviation BOR to refer to the actual Board itself, the abbreviation RCO to refer to the Regents Central Office, and the abbreviation USG to refer to the entire

System, including the board, the central office and the thirty-four institutions.

DeKalb College was the official name of the college under the BOR from 1986 to 1997, when the BOR voted to change it to Georgia Perimeter College, as a recognition of its regional footprint. I will use the abbreviation DC to refer to DeKalb College and the abbreviation DC/GPC to refer to the college's entire history.

## COMING TO THE COLLEGE

I met Marvin for the first time in the spring of 1986 at breakfast at Evans Fine Foods at the corner of North Decatur Road and Clairmont. (It is now a pizza place.) Marvin was looking for a chief financial officer. The college would be making the transition to the BOR in a couple of months, and he was looking for someone who had experience in the USG or state government. At the time, I was working in the Legislative Budget Office, a staff office to the Georgia General Assembly. I was interested in making a career change. To be honest, I don't remember our conversation. He did not hire me; instead, he hired Levy Youmans, chief financial officer at a two-year college in the USG. He made the right choice for the institution, as he always did. Institution first. Generally speaking, people come to chief financial officer positions in the public sector in Georgia from two paths: Accounting and budget/policy. I was from the latter. Levy's expertise was in accounting, and DC desperately needed someone who could clean up its books, make the financial transition to the USG and state government, and bring the college into compliance with all the new laws, policies, rules and regulations of the USG and state government. Levy did a masterful job. The college received clean audits and became a USG leader in fiscal affairs.

A month or so later, another position became available, Director of Institutional Research. Marvin hired me for that job. He hired a number of people with USG and state government experience during the transition period.

I came to the college on September 1, 1986, after the college had made the legal transition to the BOR, so I had no experience of the college under the DCSB. As Director of Institutional Research, I did not work for Marvin directly, but for Fred Hill, Dean of Administration, a wonderful man himself. I had frequent contact with Marvin, but I was not on the president's cabinet and not privy to the senior-level decision-making. I saw the effects and could intuit the reasons for some of the decisions, but I was not part of making them.

On September 1, 1991, after Levy left for another job, Marvin appointed me first as interim and then, after a search process, as permanent Vice President for Fiscal Affairs. I worked directly for Marvin from that date to May 31, 1994, the date of Marvin's retirement. (I continued on at the college in that role after Marvin's retirement, for a year under Interim President Martha Nesbitt and then for the first half of Jacquelyn Belcher's ten-year tenure as the next permanent president.)

Marvin's presidency under the BOR (1986 to 1994) was marked by three major themes: 1.) Completing the transition to the USG, 2.) The dramatic growth of the college, and

3). Increasing the diversity at the college. A number of Marvin's contributions do not fit neatly into these three themes: Talent development, the value of the liberal arts, ethics, personal responsibility and humor. I will make some comments on these toward the end.

## COMPLETING TRANSITION TO THE UNIVERSITY SYSTEM OF GEORGIA

The college was legally transferred from the DCSB to the BOR on July 1, 1986. However, the academic, financial and administrative transition was far from complete. Most pressing, though, was dealing with the fallout from the transition with the current faculty and staff.

Coming to DC two months after the legal transition, I did not know anything of its experience under the DCSB. It took me awhile to realize what a traumatic event the transition was to the existing faculty and staff. Today, we would say many were feeling something akin to PTSD.

The BOR did not recognize faculty tenure granted by the DCSB, so all the faculty lost their tenure. (To my memory, there were 167 faculty members who stayed with the college even when they lost tenure when it went under the BOR. I don't remember the number of staff who stayed, but it was probably more than that number.) Faculty members had to wait two years to re-apply for tenure—and the BOR's policies for tenure were much different than those of the DCSB. The faculty anxiety was palpable; they worried about their jobs. Eventually all the faculty members who stayed did receive tenure under the BOR, but some did not receive it at their first opportunity.

Under the DCSB, there were no faculty ranks; all faculty members were instructors. All were, in this sense, equal. Under the BOR, all faculty members had a rank: professor, associate professor, assistant professor and instructor. Therefore, in the year prior to the transition to the BOR, the college had to institute a process to assign each faculty member a rank. As one can imagine, this process produced a great deal of faculty stress. Some faculty members did not like the process itself; others did not like rank assigned by the process, feeling their rank should be higher. Faculty members were no longer equal in this respect.

The BOR had a different benefits structure for faculty and staff than the DCSB. Many faculty and staff members felt that the health insurance and other benefits they received under the DCSB were better than those provided by the BOR. A few staff members had their salaries cut because they were outside the range of similar positions in the USG.

Under the DCSB, the college was relatively decentralized, with each of the three campuses having some decision-making power, which led to campuses having slightly different personalities. The BOR did not have any other multi-campus, decentralized institutions and insisted that the college be organized like the other USG colleges and universities. As a result, all decision-making at the college was centralized in the offices of the president and vice presidents. Many felt that the loss of campus semi-autonomy left them worse off.

Overall, my sense was that a significant number of faculty and staff believed that the golden age of the college was over. The college was no longer governed by elected members of the local school board, the school board that created the college, and whose members lived in the neighborhoods where faculty and staff lived and who were accessible to them. The college was now governed by a distant BOR in downtown Atlanta, appointees of the governor, only one of which represented the Congressional district in which the college was situated. They felt the college would have a greatly reduced influence over its own future.

Marvin knew otherwise. The college was in very poor financial shape during its final years under the DCSB. He knew the BOR would save the college financially, and this financial stability would prepare the college to grow and make an even larger contribution to higher education in the region, which is what happened. The college now had a dependable budget allocation, a regular allotment for repairing and renovating buildings, which started to make a dent in the college's deferred maintenance, and an opportunity for new facilities, the most important of which was the new $10 million dollar Jim Cherry Library on the Clarkston Campus, completed in 1993. The college could fill positions long held vacant and hire for new positions. The best years of the college were not in the past, but in the future. However, he had to change the focus of the college from the past to the future.

He used a number of strategies to accomplish this. First, he was a master communicator. In his president's address at the beginning of each academic year for all faculty and staff, at which he always sported a new tie and which set the tone for the academic year ahead, he was brutally honest about the effects of the transition on many—he acknowledged the pain some felt—but he was also relentlessly positive about the future. He highlighted the signs of stability and growth. He kept the emphasis on students, who would be well served by the transition as they transferred to other USG institutions for their Bachelor's degree. In his regular gray letters, so-called because they were printed on gray stationery and over which he sometimes agonized, distributed to all faculty and staff manually in an age before electronic communication, he detailed what was going on within the college, what was going on in the BOR and state government that affected the college, and specifically all items related to the transition. College employees could argue about the transition, but they could not say they were not informed about what was going on.

Second, as vacant positions were filled and new positions created, he hired a number of faculty and staff with prior experience in the USG. For them, the BOR was not the enemy; in many cases, the BOR was all they knew, and their experience was positive. As the number of new employees grew, both those with USG experience and those without, the tone of the conversation around the college began to change. The experience under the county was no longer the only benchmark; the comparison to other USG institutions began to take its place.

Third, he created opportunities for faculty and staff across the campuses to gather and get to know one another—open houses at his home, cross-campus committees and meetings and holiday luncheons, to name a few. This was critically important under the centralized BOR model. I met my wife, Tina, at one of these cross-campus holiday luncheons. She was in her first year of teaching on the Dunwoody Campus, and my office was on the Decatur Campus. I was behind her in the food line and struck up a conversation. Therefore, Marvin is indirectly responsible for our marriage.

Looking back, I think the most important of these cross-campus gatherings was the annual president's retreat. Many colleges have a president's retreat. Most use them for planning purposes: What do we want to accomplish in the academic year ahead and three-to-five years from now? They often just included senior academic and non-academic officers and sometimes a few senior faculty leaders. Marvin's president's retreats were much different. They were academic in nature; planning played only a small role on the agenda. They generally included about fifty people: half academic and non-academic administrators and half faculty, including some junior faculty members. There was a reading and viewing list, and the discussions about the books, articles and films were led by people in the related disciplines. It was a kind of liberal arts seminar, an opportunity to exchange ideas. It was a chance to show the depth of talent and expertise at the college and for people to appreciate the contributions that others make to the life of the college and the success of students. The evenings were social in nature. Marvin absented himself. It was a chance to get to know people on other campuses and share an adult beverage and a laugh with them.

In the end, some few souls were never reconciled to the transition to the BOR, but Marvin's insight that this transition would ultimately pay off for the college was demonstrated, and most people started looking forward rather than backward. Marvin's actions, in large part, saved the college.

## DRAMATIC GROWTH

In the fall quarter 1986, the first term under the BOR, the college enrolled 8,786 students. In the fall quarter 1993, in Marvin's last academic year as president, the college enrolled 16,349 students, an increase of 86%. No other USG institution had that kind of growth during this period. Of special note was the rise in international students, from 152 in fall quarter 1986 to 1,378 in fall quarter 1993, an increase of more than 800%.

Under Marvin's leadership, in 1987, the BOR approved leased space for the Gwinnett University Center on Sugarloaf Parkway in Gwinnett County. DC would offer the freshman and sophomore courses, and Georgia State University and the University of Georgia were included to provide upper division and graduate courses. GSU subsequently pulled out. UGA offered a few graduate courses, but did not make a significant investment in Gwinnett County until years later. Shortly after Marvin's time, in 1995, the BOR approved a permanent campus for the Gwinnett University Center, on Highway 316. DC/GPC moved there, and UGA started offering whole upper division and graduate programs there. In 2005, the BOR decided to convert the Center to a free-standing institution, Georgia Gwinnett College. DC/GPC transitioned out of Gwinnett in 2008.

In 1993, leased space for the Rockdale Center for Higher Education, a consortium including DC and Clayton State University, was approved by the BOR. Clayton State subsequently pulled out. After Marvin's time, the BOR approved moving the Rockdale operation to a permanent campus in Covington in Newton County, which opened in 2007.

The college now had five campuses. Marvin had taken the college from a county-based institution to a regional institution. In 1997, Marvin's successor proposed that the college be renamed Georgia Perimeter College, in recognition of the new regional mission of the college, which was approved by the BOR.

The enrollment growth spurred a corresponding growth in the number of faculty and staff members. The faculty grew from 167 to 374, an increase of 124%. Total full-time employees more than doubled as well, to 796.

The trajectory of DC/GPC, from 1986 when it entered the USG until 2016 when it was merged with Georgia State University, was set in motion by actions taken by Marvin.

## DIVERSITY

Marvin was always closely in touch with the demographics of the college and the surrounding area. The minority proportion of the student body grew from 22.1% (17.3% Black students) in fall quarter 1986 to 34.7% (27.2% Black students) in fall quarter 1993. He could foresee a time when the student body of the college would be majority minority. However, diversity among the faculty and staff was not changing at nearly the same rate. It was moving at a glacial pace. (This was also true of the entire USG.) Search committees tended to recommend people like themselves, which was true throughout the employment world, both public and private. The slow pace of creating a more diverse faculty and staff was a constant frustration for Marvin throughout his presidency.

He took many personal actions. He hired Flora Devine as the college's lawyer and put her on the president's cabinet, creating diversity at the senior level of administration. He invited Black speakers to college events. He put texts by Black authors, Beloved by Toni Morrison, for example, on the reading list for the president's retreat. He insisted that academic and non-academic officers create more diverse search committees and consider a broader range of candidates. He paid close attention to the make-up of important college-wide committees. He instituted diversity-related exercises for the cabinet. He let his cabinet know that diversity had a high value for him when it came to filling positions.

His actions did have a real impact. There was just a handful of minority faculty members in 1986. (Note: I apologize that I don't know the exact percentage of minority faculty members in 1986. Evidently, when the college merged with Georgia State University in 2016, some old DC reports were not transferred to the new website. I'm sure the information exists somewhere, but I haven't been able to find it. I do clearly remember, though, as the Director of Institutional Research at the time, that the percentage was low.)

By 1993-94, Marvin's final year, the college's faculty was 20% minority (17.1% Black). Still, the college did not move as quickly as he wanted on this issue.

The reasons for this are numerous and complex, and likely included both conscious and unconscious racism to some degree, unconscious always being the harder to identify and confront. A college does not exist in a vacuum. It reflects and refracts, at least in some ways, large or small, the culture in which the college finds itself. In addition, many people are simply resistant to change, even when it is occurring right before their eyes in their classrooms and neighborhoods; some are even threatened by change, any change.

Marvin was angry with me three times while I was Vice President of Fiscal Affairs, three times that I know of; there could be more he did not share with me. One of these three times involved diversity. We had an assistant director position available in the human resources department, which was in my area of responsibility. Marvin clearly wanted the department to hire a Black person; he did not think that the human resources department was sufficiently committed to his diversity initiative. The recommendation from the departmental search committee came to me—a candidate who self-identified as American Indian. I sent the recommendation on to Marvin for approval. Marvin came to see me and was livid. I felt terrible; I had disappointed him. I had failed in this part of my role, in spite of knowing how important this subject was to him. I should have given more personal attention to the search process for this position. Diversity in DeKalb County at that time meant Black. American Indians were a miniscule part of the student body (.3%) and the surrounding community. In the end, though, Marvin did not overrule the recommendation. He respected institutional processes. The college hired the candidate recommended. She only stayed a couple of years; her replacement was a Black person. I learned a lesson about my role and about leadership.

The more visible change in diversity came a few years after Marvin, with his successor, Jacquelyn Belcher, who is Black. However, the groundwork for the importance of diversity to the future of the college was laid by Marvin.

Since I said there were three times he was angry with me, I think I need to say something about the other two, even though they are not related to diversity.

First, just before I became vice president, the college had put its banking business out to bid, as required every five years under BOR policy. After reviewing the bids, my staff recommended that we stay with our current banker. Marvin was very upset. He said that the current banker had reneged on a promise to contribute to the college's foundation, and he had expected a recommendation that the college change bankers. I apologized, of course. I was not aware of the bank's failure to keep its prior promise. My staff may have known, or not known, but I didn't. I should have. Perhaps it fell through the cracks in the transition between Levy and me. I felt terrible again. However, Marvin respected the staff analysis of the bids and did not overrule the recommendation. Institution first, always. Another lesson for me.

Second, toward the end of Marvin's presidency in 1994, the other vice presidents and I wanted to find a lasting way to honor him. Marvin was always very supportive of the arts at the college. We thought it would be a fitting recognition to name the fine arts building auditorium after him. At that time, all naming requests had to be approved by the BOR. I drafted a letter to the chancellor, also signed by the other vice presidents, asking if he would be comfortable taking this naming request to the BOR. He responded right away that he thought it was an excellent idea. The chancellor respected Marvin very highly. (In fact, the chancellor asked Marvin to withdraw his request to retire in two earlier years.) Now here comes the complication. We thought that the chancellor would make this recommendation to the BOR personally. However, for formal reasons, all BOR agenda items related to an institution are characterized as a recommendation coming from the institutional president: President X recommends that the BOR approve . . . So when the agenda item was written up by the chancellor's staff, it read, "President Marvin Cole recommends that the BOR approve the naming of the fine arts auditorium The Marvin Cole Fine Arts Auditorium." You can just see how Marvin would react to this when he read it. He was not happy. He wanted to know where this came from; I had to explain. The agenda, of course, is public and distributed widely. Marvin thought it made him look vain, something he certainly is not . . . if anything, the opposite. If I remember right, which I may not, I think I called the chancellor and asked him to call Marvin and talk with him about it, how the vice presidents were just trying to honor him, which the chancellor supported, but his staff interpreted this as a regular agenda item and treated it as such. The auditorium was indeed named for him, which was fitting, and as time passed, I think it secretly pleased him.

## OTHER TOPICS

I want to make brief comments about five other topics that do not neatly fit into the three larger themes above.

**Talent development.** Marvin saw part of his role as developing talent in others, as creating future higher-education leaders. It is no accident that people who worked for him went on to senior roles at others places. Martha Nesbitt, Vice President of Academic Affairs, became President of Gainesville College, now part of the University of North Georgia. Randy Pierce, who opened the Gwinnett and Rockdale campuses, became President of Floyd College, now Georgia Highlands College. Levy Youmans, Vice President of Fiscal Affairs, became Assistant Vice Chancellor for Accounting at the RCO, essentially the chief accounting officer for the entire USG. Flora Devine, the college's attorney, moved on to two USG universities, first Kennesaw State University, then Savannah State University. Carol Copenhaver, Assistant Vice President for Academic Affairs, became chief academic officer at a community college in Florida. Bill Crews, Vice President for Student Affairs, became Executive Director of the Georgia Nonpublic Higher Education Commission, the state agency that regulates private colleges. Three other people who were hired as faculty members while Marvin was president subsequently became presidents of USG institutions: Virginia Carson at South Georgia State College, now retired; Ingrid Thompson-Sellers at South Georgia State College, still serving; and Margaret Venable at Dalton State College, still serving. A fourth faculty member hired while Marvin was president moved to a senior position at the RCO: Virginia Michelich became Assistant Vice Chancellor for Academic

Affairs, now retired. This list does not include the many DC people who moved to department chair, dean and director positions at other institutions. I moved on to the RCO, eventually becoming Chief Operating Officer, and also served as Interim President of USG institutions six times. Marvin was a great teacher for us all. The USG began looking to DC when it had senior leadership positions open. Marvin's successors wisely continued the talent development work that Marvin began:

**The value of the liberal arts.** Marvin preached the value of a liberal arts education. He often told students not to worry about their major, but just to explore the disciplines and get a good liberal arts education. You can use a liberal arts education to go in many directions in your professional life. He went several summers to seminars on great books put on by Indiana University; he continued his own liberal arts education. I agree with him and am an example. I got a broad liberal arts education and held a wide variety of jobs over my career, none of which was actually related to my degree. While creating the two-year college of the future, Marvin never wavered in his commitment to a traditional liberal arts education.

**Ethics.** Marvin was very ethical. He held himself to a high ethical standard and expected those who worked for him to do the same. He did not like dealing with politics, which sometimes required ethical compromises, though he did so when the institutional interest was involved. When important decisions were being made, he always asked, what is the right thing to do? When he knew what the right thing to do was, the task then was to get as close to it as possible, within all the constraints the institution faced. He was always disappointed when he couldn't do exactly the right thing because of some legal, financial or personnel restrictions. Marvin modeled ethical behavior for us all.

**Personal responsibility.** In the last few months of his administration in 1994, Marvin made a list of personnel matters he didn't want his successor to inherit. As I remember, there were six of them. He let a couple of people go and moved the others out of positions in which they had not performed well. He took personal responsibility for the personnel decisions made under his administration. He did his successor and the institution a great favor. While serving as interim president at a number of places, I have been involved in several presidential transitions. I can report that most presidents are happy to walk away and let their successor clean up the messes. Marvin's actions were and are rare.

**Humor.** For Marvin, humor could be found in almost any situation. He laughed easily and often. He had a great smile. He was famous, of course, for his Mark Twain impersonation, but much beyond that, humor was a daily part of the life of his administration. I have often thought that a sense of humor was an underrated quality when selecting people for leadership roles. I worked with several people without a sense of humor over the years, and they were always the most difficult people to deal with. Marvin's sense of humor certainly made him a better boss for those of us who worked directly for him and that sense of humor probably helped him manage the tremendous stresses of a college presidency.

## TO MARVIN'S GRANDCHILDREN

You should know that your grandfather is a great man. He saved a college, and once saved, made it a better college. His actions ultimately affected tens of thousands of students. He was revered by those of us who worked for him. He was our model; he had a way of bringing out our best selves. He made us better leaders and better people. He was the best teacher I ever had, the highest compliment I can hand out. He changed my life. You are so lucky to have him as your grandfather.

# 10

## My Neighbor
## by Marvin Cole

# My Neighbor
# by Marvin Cole

> I see the same stars
> through my window
> that you see through yours ...
> I see the same sky
> through brown eyes
> That you see through blue
> But we're worlds apart ...
> ... Together but worlds apart.
>
> "Big River" by Roger Miller

Why do humans have the intelligence to build a space ship housing a car-size, information-gathering vehicle plus a helicopter, programmed to take seven months to reach and operate on Mars for years, yet do not have the intelligence to learn to respect and appreciate fellow humans because they are a different race, sex or religion? I am not sure I have the words, or knowledge, or intelligence to express what I want to say to answer that question and know I do not have the insight to express what needs to be said; therefore I will begin.

We are going through another period during which I would think a person of color experiences disconcerting, discouraging and perplexing feelings. I suspect those feelings have always been there for Black people here in the United States, but current events must intensify those feelings, and I can only surmise what it feels like to have so many people thinking I am "less than." It would be grossly presumptuous of me to even assume any of my life experiences were similar to those of a Black person.

If I were a Black person today, I would feel like there are a lot of people out there who foster because of my skin an attitude ranging from "I don't like you," to "I hate you," or to "you are a lesser human." I would think it causes a lifelong skeptical cloud hovering over many of the non-white community members that hinders every aspect of their lives.

We also have many White people who think all the race differences have been settled. They dwell on how things "used to be" and think we can check "that White problem" off the "To Do" list. They see themselves as having Black friends with whom they eat, drink, and play tennis and never see the racial cancer working its way to another revolution. So many White people wonder why we periodically have these unrest demonstrations destroying people and property? But the Band-Aid applied never reached the problem.

There is a third group of people who have never accepted General Robert E. Lee's surrender at Appomattox to General Ulysses S. Grant. There were barefooted, threadbare, ill-supplied dogmatic soldiers and civilians then who could not fathom they were defeated. This low-level culture kept the Jim Crow laws—such as the requirement that all Blacks have to ride in the back of the bus—thriving for eighty years. Whether it is ignorance, family upbringing, religion, culture, or mental health reasons, the people in the third group are loud and obnoxious but still a minority when it comes to influencing the general population. They should be helped and educated as much as possible, but not be seen as the major cause of racism concern in our country.

My purpose in this missive is to describe some racial conditions, relate some personal experiences and give opinions of where we as a people need to concentrate our efforts to make us more tolerant, be less race conscious and become neighbors. Humans should always strive for understanding, healing and the common good.

I think of all the Black people I used to work with at DeKalb College in the seventies and wonder what was going through their minds when racial prejudice instances occurred. Those people became to me more than a colleague, and much more than an acquaintance. They were good friends. Some I would love to have as a brother or sister. They are my spiritual brothers and sisters. How could someone not like such good people? I had empathetic and sympathetic feelings when my Black friends had problems—when Harry Holly's wife died; when I learned Flora Divine's son, Malcolm, had died; and when Albertine divorced. I had arranged for her husband to become the first Black person to be a fellow member of the South DeKalb Kiwanis Club.

But I never experienced the feeling of being unwanted like so many Black people must have felt throughout their lives. I was an adult before I learned that there was a time that Black people had to step to the side when White people approached them on the sidewalk, or that black people were not supposed to look at White people in the eyes, especially White women, and were "Jim Crowed" to always be polite and deferential toward White people.

Be subservient. And we call this country educated? Whose standards declared the United States a Christian nation?

I became Executive Dean of the South Campus at DeKalb College in Atlanta in 1975. It was a time of great change in the area as White flight was in full process and Black people were moving in from Atlanta and elsewhere. The college was part of the DeKalb School System at the time and the administration kept sending me dire warnings to expect trouble when the campus population reached forty percent Black.

I had no rule about treatment of others except the one my mother gave me to treat people as people. I invited all the Black Faculty and Black Administrators into the conference room one afternoon and asked them to be my teachers. I told them what the School System administrators had predicted and asked them to guide me, and particularly to tell me if any of my decisions, words or actions were prejudicial against any group. Although appreciative, the group did not have a lot to say, and I have often wondered what they said or thought when they went back to their offices. Were they too embarrassed that the subject had to be brought up in the first place? Did they think that Dean was crazy and didn't have a clue as to what he was talking about? Or did they think, "If he doesn't know by now, there is no chance we can teach him now."

I recall addressing the faculty one time and giving a quote from W.E.B. Du Bois. Coming from an unassuming background (as Mark Twain says: "We were poor and didn't know it, happy and did know it), I was perhaps oversensitive to the perpetual disease of faculty finding fault with administrators. One of my school teachers made the statement, "Marvin is a nice boy but will never go to college." So with the faculty, I always wanted to have my tie straight and shoes shined on the lower end of the spectrum, and especially pronounce words properly on the upper end. So when I pronounced the name W.E.B. Du Bois to the faculty, I used the French version of "Boise" (as in Bwau) and felt good about it. Surely the faculty would be pleased I was "with it." When I returned to my office is when Flora Divine, the Vice President for Legal Affairs, came to me and gave me the come-uppance as to how to pronounce Du Bois. The good feeling was that our relationship was to the level that she knew she could correct me.

The School System administrators were wrong. We never had any trouble even when in a few years the campus grew from ten percent Black to seventy percent Black Students. And I am proud of the fact that when we joined the University System of Georgia five years later, we had more Black administrators, more White female administrators, more Black faculty and Black students than any other major White-populated college or university in Georgia. And since I am old enough to brag, one of my prize possessions is the President's Award presented at a Convention of the National Council on Black-American Affairs. My next-to-best award was a pin-on nameplate given by Barney Sims at a faculty meeting with the inscription S.A.W.B., i.e. Smart Ass White Boy. And my top award was when I entered the doors of the South Campus after being named President of DeKalb College and the maid Lucy Farley said to me "What are you doing here, turkey?" She was a jewel.

# My Neighbor

***

Martin Luther King Jr., in his classic "Letter From Birmingham Jail," chastised White ministers who had asked him to wait for a better time. He was not the first, but among rare people to make that appeal. William Dean Howells[1] tells of Mark Twain wanting action on putting former slaves on equal footing:

> *Clemens was entirely satisfied with the result of the Civil war, and he was eager to have its facts and meanings brought out at once in history. He ridiculed the notion, held by many, that 'it was not yet time' to philosophize the events of the great struggle; that we must 'wait till its passions had cooled,' and 'the clouds of strife had cleared away.*

Twain maintained:

> *. . . [T]he time would never come when we should see its motives and men and deeds more clearly, and that now, now, was the hour to ascertain them in lasting verity. Picturesquely and dramatically, Twain portrayed the imbecility of deferring the inquiry at any point to the distance of future years when inevitably the facts would begin to put on fable."*

Why are we still waiting?

In 1947, Jackie Robinson felt the waiting period had finally arrived. Jackie was the first Black person to play in Major League Baseball. His sacrifice made a big impact on the Civil Rights Movement. What made him different? What motivation made him willing to withstand all the crude and indecent calls made to him from the bleachers and the streets when he was displaying being a model for baseball craftsmanship as well as a model human being in public life? And on the other hand, what illness caused those people in the stands to display inhumane behavior to a fellow human being?

In 1952, Jackie wrote the following piece for the *This I Believe* series on National Public Radio:[2]

> *At the beginning of the World Series of 1947, I experienced a completely new emotion when the National Anthem was played. This time, I thought, it was being played for me, as much as for anyone else. This is organized Major League Baseball, and I am standing here with all the others; and everything that takes place includes me.*

Looking back from the year 2020, we say isn't it sad that we had to wait all those years to allow a fellow human being, Jackie Robinson, to have the same experience as White people.

Jackie Continues:

> *And what is it that I have always believed? First, that imperfections are human. But that wherever human beings were given room to breathe and time to think, those imperfections would disappear, no matter how slowly. I do not believe that we have found or even approached perfection. That is not necessarily in the scheme of human events. Handicaps,*

---

1 Howells, William Dean, *My Mark Twain*, New York, Harper and Brothers, 1910, page 36.

2. Usher, Shaun, *Speeches of Note*, Compiled by Shaun Usher, "I Believe In The Human Race," by Robinson, Jackie,. Berkely, CA, Ten Spreed Press, 1918, pp262-263.

*stumbling blocks, prejudices—all of these are imperfect. Yet, they have to be reckoned with because they are in the scheme of human events. . . . And this chance has come to be, because there is nothing static with free people. There is no Middle Ages logic so strong that it can stop the human tide from flowing forward. I do not believe that every person, in every walk of life, can succeed in spite of any handicap. That would be perfection. But I do believe—and with every fiber in me—that what I was able to attain came to be because we put behind us (no matter how slowly) the dogmas of the past; to discover the truth of today; and perhaps find the greatness of tomorrow.*

Jackie at that time rightfully felt that he had broken a chain of racial evil in the United States. He must have had thoughts that not only was he playing in America's top athletic sport, but helped to open the way for Black people to be on an equal playing field in all aspects of life. The other side of the story in later years is he did not realize his hope for equality. In his autobiography *I Never Had It Made*,[3] he observed "I cannot salute the flag; I know that I am a Black man in a White world. In 1972, in 1947, at my birth in 1919, I know that I never had it made."

But Jackie withstood a lot of verbal and physical abuse that many people would not have been able to handle. What made Jackie Robinson different? What in his background made him see the big picture? Contrariwise, why do we see the Confederate Battle Flag on beat-up pickup trucks in shantytown and trailer parks, and why do these same people refuse to recognize one of God's creations?

Prejudice, narrow-mindedness, bigotry, intolerance exist in all ethnic groups. As a current example, why has it taken one hundred years for men in this supposedly educated country of the United States to approve equal rights for women? Some so-called "Christian" churches are now obstructing gay LGBTQ people just as they did and do Black people. People are attacked as Muslims because their skin color tells the narrow-minded ones that this person is from the Middle-East. A 2020 newspaper article reports on hundreds of attacks on Asian Americans.[4] It stated one 41-year-old Korean-American was attacked by a Latino man "because your people are the reason coronavirus is happening." Why do some people use the brain God gave all of us and other people put it in cold storage?

***

Where can you go and not find prejudice? We are more inclined to punishment and retribution than to discerning why.

Why, in all the time since humans first inhabited the earth have we perfected many methods to kill people; become expert in increasing wealth for some; and excelled in machinery, media, mansions and making potato salad, but earned a failure grade in love and respecting our neighbor? There is a line in one of the songs from the musical "*Big River,*" which is about Twain's *Adventures of Huckleberry Finn*, that goes:

*People reach new understandings all the time*
*They take a second look, maybe change their minds . . .*

3 Robinson, Jackie. , *I Mever Had it Made*. New York City, NY. Harper Collins. 1972.
4 *Asheville Citizen Times*, Sunday, April 26, 2020, p 3B.

What makes us predisposed to find someone to blame and denigrate?

One of my after-college philosophy teachers, Tom T. Hall, has a wonderful line in his song "Old Dogs, Children and Watermelon Wine." The line goes:

*Old Dogs care about you*
*even when you make mistakes,*
*God bless little children,*
*while they're still too young to hate."*

As a young boy, I was not taught to affront and offend Black people at home or by the clergy. There was only one Black family in the entire community, and my mother used to take me on a couple of miles walk through the woods to visit that family. The father was Wheaton McMickins, a respected farm owner, but I suspect he was never invited to the local White churches.

We were influenced to beware of Catholics by the local uneducated preachers following the ignorant code that people had to have some group to look down on in order to feel worthy. My mother also had been friends and made lye soap with a Cherokee lady who lived about a mile from our home. My father, a carpenter, invited a Black man to have lunch with us one Saturday when I was a boy, but what is so sad to me today is that the poor man, after my father's repeated requests, could not sit down at a table with White people. That scene stuck with me. He had been so conditioned by our culture to be less than a normal human being that society would never be allowed to benefit from his skills and learning. But I did not understand that cause at the time.

Four years in the U.S. Air Force gave me a wonderful education on working, playing and partying with Black people and Catholics. It made me cautious about my previous training (as opposed to education) of listening to uneducated people—especially preachers, educated or uneducated. Our first son was named for two Catholic friends I was stationed with in London. I remember one occurrence a few months after I had arrived in England. A big, Black Air Policeman named Hunter woke me up in the barracks late one payday night, said he and the fellows were having a little game in the latrine, and asked to borrow ten dollars. The pay then was $33 per month. We were not even in the same barracks, but I gave Hunter the money and went back to sleep. Hunter paid me back a couple of days later. But I wondered later in life how this Black man from New York, knowing that I was from the South, somehow knew I would be amenable to loaning him the money. I have a strong feeling that in the Air Force, Black and White people were placed in an environment in which everyone was equal, so a new code, which no one wanted to break, was established, and thereby a new genuine human culture was in effect. Why do we not have that code in a non-military, civilian, freedom-of-choice setting?

I wonder if there exists a people of any country or religion who do not possess skin prejudice. While I was working at the University of the Punjab in Lahore, Pakistan, in 1963, our team was visited by a group of college presidents and administrators from the United States. One of the presidents had a very dark skin and was asked why Black people in the United States didn't adopt the Islamic Religion as it was devoid of racism. That

Muslim audience was quiet when that president responded that she had never felt the prejudice in the United States like she had experienced since coming to Asia. The shade of skin color is very important in Pakistan and India—the darker the skin, the lower level of jobs and treatment.

In the early 1970s, while working in Afghanistan, we observed great prejudice between provincial groups (tribes), with most groups having a particular disdain for a group in Mid-Afghanistan called the Hazaras. The Hazara ethnic group was descendants and has facial features of the Mongolians who had conquered much of Central Asia by the 13th century. Kasim Husseini, a Hazara who fled to Sweden, made the statement "We used to say that we had been born as something redundant, something unnecessary, into the world." In today's world, many Hazaras are leaving Afghanistan because the Taliban see them as heretics. Hazaras are Shi'ite Muslims and the Taliban are Sunni Muslims. Both are the same religion, same God, same Quran but each found a reason to split and hate each other.

Look at the Irish both at home and in the United States. Recall the "help wanted" signs in store windows and newspaper advertisements in the mid 1800s in New York, which stated:

## IRISH NEED NOT APPLY.

The persecution of Jews has existed probably as long as Jewish history. They have been blamed for whatever the current problem was of the time and place, such as the death of Jesus, the Bubonic Plague, World War I. Since skin color cannot be a reason, I suspect a predominant reason revolves around Jewish people having the reputation of being smarter than other ethnic groups. One study did show intelligence scores ranging from 7 to 15 points above the average for the total general population. Some intelligence discrepancy is noted in Adolf Hitler's policies, wanting to establish a superior race of his own people so he tried to eliminate Jews, the most intelligent citizens in Europe.

Reverend Rob Blackburn of Central United Methodist in Asheville relates an experience of when he was a boy picking oranges in Florida during the summertime. The groves were long and at the end of one day, he found he was at the end of the orchard. He started walking a long road back to the owner's station when it started raining very hard. The owner came along, stopped and told him to get in, so my friend opened the door and climbed into the cab of the owner's truck. The owner yelled at him "DON'T YOU KNOW WHO YOU ARE BOY? You are hired help. Get in the back of the truck! These were two White people.

When we hear the word "racism," we tend to think of African Americans and Caucasians. It is the most obnoxious form of racism in the United States. Other types include biological, sexist, cultural, disability, religion, physical, social class, sexual preference, xenophobia, age. Internalized racism is when a person of color, for example, internalizes the negative messages they receive and come to feel ashamed of themselves for being different.[5]

5 Eighteen Forms of Racism In The World, Life Persona, Internet.

***

So today we are looking for whom to blame for the protests, the riots, the harsh words, the ravaging and the stealing. So far we have not blamed the Jews, but we have been quick to blame a President, a Congress, a Governor, a Mayor, China and the virus. There is a cry from some people to do away with police as if that would eliminate all elements of racism and criminal activity. We are looking in the wrong direction. Political types can balm the wound and chastise the culprits, even promote a more amicable mood or tone for us to follow, but the cure resides elsewhere and either alludes us or we as a nation are not that interested.

One fabricated solution is to eradicate all monuments, which could have some connection to slavery and the Civil War. If we removed all the monuments and statues in the world, would that be sufficient to cause people to respect one another?

In Asheville, the City Council and Buncombe County Commissioners have made the decision to remove a sixty-five foot obelisk built in 1889 to honor Zebulon Baird Vance who was a Confederate soldier, Governor, and U.S. Senator. When I was growing up, I looked on the monument as a nice piece of rockwork. I was well into adulthood before I learned it was in honor of a person, but it still meant more to me as an artistic piece, which added aesthetic beauty to Asheville. However, I am a White person, and it was only after I dined with, played sports with, sang with, worked with, laughed and cried as good friends with Black people that I became aware that the Confederate Flag meant the same to them as the Nazi swastika meant to Jewish people.

So the Asheville City Council and County Commissioners have decided to build a platform and place a shroud over the Vance Monument. So the art piece is being covered up, and the city, which spends enormous efforts to attract tourists, will have people coming from everywhere to take pictures of art in a sack. But the standard operating procedure is whatever brings money to Asheville or helps the hotel business and their owners is sacrosanct.

Years ago, I remember reading newspaper articles and hearing on newscasts how the school textbooks in Germany, Japan and elsewhere were being rewritten to eliminate the atrocities in which they were involved during WWII. Are we doing the same thing in obliterating our history? Remember how our history books and media ignored our treatment of Native Americans in driving them out of their homeland to the desert and interning 120,000 Japanese Americans during World War II. When I visited the Gettysburg Battle Fields and saw old Civil War monuments throughout that park, I was reminded of how sad we once were to engage in such a war.

Do we need to be reminded of how ignorance can cause families to be miserable, how war devastates a beautiful country, and how religion and leadership failed to set a decent moral standard? It is important for us to see movies like *Saving Private Ryan, Battleground,*

*Apocalypse Now* and Ken Burns' documentary about our Viet Nam War, to remind us what war is like so we can keep watch on our Government and try to keep them from going to war to make money for Halliburton and other industries.

Governments throughout history have never had interest in improving our moral capability. White people have not universally shown that they possess the freewill to change racism without some kind of motivation. All major religions, if not all religions, have in common the belief of a Golden Rule to follow for instruction on how people should relate to others. If governments and religion had been diligent in raising the level of morality throughout history, we would have never heard of Martin Luther King Jr., or Rosa Parks, or Gandhi, or Vietnam.

It is too bad that it takes arthritis to give proper direction to our fingers to identify the proper source for many of our difficulties. The finger pointing is directed to us, the privileged.

Several recent advertisements for politicians depicted the candidate holding guns. Have we the citizens painted the picture to potential politicians that we want a leader who totes a gun? Do they think the way to get elected is to swagger in like John Wayne? If so, we can look for a John Dillinger gangster society on every street and road in the near future. What message did we citizens of the country send to politicians that we want fast-draw, tough guy or gal to lead us to the land of good neighbors and the intelligence of the common good? We elected them, and Pogo was correct in his observation, "We have met the enemy and he is us."[6]

It would be interesting for some genius statistician to depict a graph ranking the ethical position of humans throughout history. Does the line go up or down or remain unchanged when looking at our moral progress? Is our only hope to have some Asian or European scientist develop a Genetically Modified Organism (GMO) to cure the Moral-Virus-666 prevalent in the world? If we had the vaccine for that moral virus plague, Covid-19 may not have existed. And the reason I say it would be an Asian or European to discover moral virus vaccine is because we the people of the United States have decided to downgrade having an education, and that reading, writing, science and philosophy are of little value as a means to improving a nation. We know the diminishing interest in the quality of education by the kinds of people we are electing and then allow to stay in office with their continuing balderdashery.

***

In 2019, the Economic Policy Institute states "Among racial and ethnic groups, African Americans had the highest poverty rate, 27.4 percent, followed by Hispanics at 26.6 percent and Whites at 9.9 percent. Also, 45.8 percent of young Black children (under age 6) live in poverty, compared to 14.5 percent of White children.

Why do we have such disparity of income and wealth attainment in the African-American and Hispanic communities compared to the White community? Are we still

---

6 We have met the enemy and they are ours, part of a message from American naval officer Oliver Hazard Perry in 1813 after defeating and capturing Royal Navy ships in the Battle of Lake Erie We have met the enemy and he is us, Pogo creator Walt Kelly's 20th century parody of Perry's quote

trying to keep non-White people from reading and writing? If I were a Congressperson or Representative, it would haunt my soul that so many of the people in my county are struggling to have a decent living. Is it because 33,000 plus lobbyists in Washington who are paying Congresspersons to support various enterprises are the ones really running our country? It would concern a Congressperson with integrity that decisions that have been made to send jobs overseas to obtain cheap labor, cause our poverty levels to increase by cutting jobs in America and benefiting whom? You answer that.

The *Wall-Street Journal* on July 2020 quoted a Trade and Manufacturing Policy study that "since 2000, America's defense industry has shed more than 20,000 U.S.-based manufacturing companies. . . . much of it going to China." More than five million American manufacturing jobs have been lost since 2000. Someone please explain why our elected leaders could not realize that when they send our vocational jobs overseas, that means less jobs and more poverty for people in the United States.

One answer to an earlier question about what made Jackie Robinson different aside from his athletic prowess is the obvious reason: that he was educated. He left UCLA the last semester of his senior year and soon after joined the military. He was educated.

One of my all-time favorite books is *Man's Search For Meaning* by Viktor Frankl.[7] The book tells the story of Frankl's experiences as a prisoner at Auschwitz, Dachau, and other Nazi Death Camps and stresses that it is the ultimate test for all of us to find meaning in our lives. Frankl and his fellow prisoners had everything taken away from them—their families, jobs, health, friends, possessions, even their names and the hair on their bodies; but there was one thing that remained truly their own. He explains it this way: "We who lived in concentration camps can remember the men who walked through the huts, comforting others, giving away their last pieces of bread. They may have been few in number, but they offer sufficient proof that everything can be taken from a man but one thing: the last of the human freedoms—to choose one's attitude in any given set of circumstances, to choose one's own way." Frankl's decisions about attitude and meaning helped him survive the concentration camps. But Frankl was a person who was educated.

Yes, I know that is a sample of only two, but there are many more examples of how education has made a difference in peoples' lives. We have looked to education and to religion to make us a better kind of people and to have a better kind of life. The poverty areas in our cities of majority Black or majority White tend to be the site of less education. The White poverty neighborhoods are more likely the scene of the pickup trucks with the rebel flags. Do some people have to have others to look down on? Why do we see trash discarded near run-down trailer parks? Come to think of it, in this country of supposedly educated people, why do we have to hire people to pick up trash on our streets and highways and especially our National Parks?

This is not to say that racism does not exist in affluent neighborhoods. Being educated is not necessarily a cure for racism as can be seen by looking at Germany

---

7 Frankl, Victor, *Man's Search For Meaning*, Boston, MA. Beacon Press. 2006.

prior to World War II. Germans were considered highly educated but succumbed to the world's premiere racist in the personage of Adolf Hitler. But we like to think that education does enhance morals and better values for most people. Why were and why are people afraid of African-Americans being educated? In his autobiography, Fredrick Douglass made the observation that he "knew that there was something magical about reading, because it was forbidden."

In the 1896 Plessy v. Ferguson case, the Supreme Court ruled that the Fourteenth Amendment guaranteed political rights, such as voting, and not social rights. In the eyes of the nation's highest court, Blacks had attained political equality but not social equality.

We often forget that less than one hundred years ago, even in the 1960s, most African-American, Latino and Native American students attended completely segregated schools that were funded at rates many times lower than those serving Whites. The same students were excluded from many colleges and universities entirely. It takes decades to recover from malevolent neglect for both the partaker and the people who established the neglect. The "powers that be" did not listen to Frederick Douglass in 1875, and still do not have the ability to listen to his wisdom that "The world has never seen any people turned loose to such destitution as were the four million slaves of the South. . . . They were free without roofs to cover them or bread to eat or land to cultivate, and as a consequence, died in such numbers as to awaken the hope of their enemies that they would soon disappear." [8]

After many years of research and study, psychological scientists are still pondering whether genes or environment has the greater impact on a person's intelligence. They do agree that both are involved on a person's intellectual and behavioral make-up. On Intelligence Quotient (IQ) tests, statistics professionals use 100 as the average score for the population, with 68 percent of the total population having IQ's between 85 and 115. Ninety-six percent of the population have IQ's between 70 and 130. Approximately three percent of the population has an Intelligence Quotient below 70, and approximately three percent have an IQ above 130.

While six percent of the population in poverty are in the 90-110 intelligence category, thirty percent fall in the below-75 IQ measure.

How do we help that thirty percent below the 75 IQ level that are in poverty? They are the most vulnerable to be swayed by bad people or good people. We know that education is a process that develops skills, not one that indicates a level of intelligence. Working with homeless people over two years made me well aware that some people, for post-war reasons, are intellectually challenged for some reason and cannot get or maintain a normal job. But somehow an educated country should find a way to employ or make sure they have a decent life—not leave them to the wolves.

The Brookings Institution for Public Policy states that ". . . [E]ducational outcomes for minority children are much more a function of their unequal access to key educational resources, including skilled teachers and quality curriculum, than they are a function of race." [9]

---

8 Douglass, Frederick, Celebrating the Past, Anticipating the Future, 1875.~

9. Darling-Hammond, Linda. *Brookings,* "Unequal Opportunity: Race and Education." 1998.

In spite of apparent gaps in funding, teacher quality, curriculum, class size and community interest, we White people are still heard to say if students do not achieve, it is their own fault. Educational experiences for minority students continue to be substantially separate and unequal. *Why?*

I recall Governor Lester Maddox of Georgia objecting to the request to build more prisons to handle the wrongdoers. He stated, "We do not need more prisons, what we need is better prisoners." We can reduce the poverty areas by getting better parents. These are acquired by having better teachers and curriculum to make better parents so they can obtain better jobs while recognizing patience required for generations to break the cycle.

Educational outcomes excel when funds are used to employ qualified teachers, their having the freedom to discipline, and a high quality curriculum. The ultimate good setting is having parents that support the child's education. Our North Carolina poet Maya Angelou states:

> *If you don't plant the right things, we will reap the wrong things. It goes without saying. And you don't have to be, you know, a brilliant biochemist and you don't have to have an IQ of 150. Just common sense tells you to be kind, ninny, fool. Be kind.*[10]

Education can help people of all IQ levels to achieve. The big challenge is getting exceptional teachers to teach at all levels. Currently, it is difficult to obtain exceptional teachers because of the poor working conditions, safety concerns, lack of respect, the freedom to teach, atmosphere, pay not too far above the poverty level and society's not realizing that education and living require discipline.

Beginning teachers in North Carolina start at $35,000 and are responsible for teaching thirty-five plus individuals with multiple skills and attitudes. They are subject to harassment from parents and community, receive little to no respect, adopt a practice of constant study to improve, purchase teaching materials from her or his own finances, and require a lot of preparation after work hours. But a truck driver for $80,000 a year, can listen to lectures about Plato, Shakespeare, Mozart, Bach, Stravinsky or Willie Nelson all day long, and have no one to harass her or him. And to show the comparison to the extreme, the beginning teacher in San Francisco earns $55,000 a year while a family of two adults and two children in San Francisco would need to earn $148,440 to live comfortably. Imagine having to recruit teachers in San Francisco.

The needs of people in poverty are adequate education, jobs, security, adequate housing, respect and equal opportunity in all phases of life. Poverty and lack of education lead to bad decisions, being vulnerable to cult-like people, poor health and trucks with rebel flags. We have had several major Government Commissions and studies on poverty and racism since the Great Depression, all saying the same words, and all ending in inaction. The main people who benefit are the people hired to write the reports. Meanwhile, we live with the practice that by abandoning the weak, the strong survive.

The Democratic and Republican parties do not exhibit behavior to help us distinguish which if either is in support of education. But they do verbalize a lot about it while running

---

10 www.brainyquote.com/quotes/maya_angelou_634462

for election. As a boy, I knew everyone was a Democrat and all Southern states were solid Democratic and all one had to say to verify their conviction was "Hoover." President Herbert Hoover was blamed for The Great Depression and that situation dictated the Democratic Party vote until war hero General Dwight Eisenhower broke the chain as a Republican in 1953. Democrats at the time were known for "helping the common person" and Republicans were known for helping business.

The average income in 1942 when I was 10 years old was $1,885. My father was a carpenter, and I do not know about his income. We were not affluent, but we always had sufficient food on the table and a home. But we were taught to always keep a civil tongue and respect other people. Somehow from a good mom and pop, I acquired the belief that people who used bad language were of much lower class than we were. My mother cautioned me to stay away from those people who did not have a sufficient capacity for language to express themselves without "cussin." She would say, "People of that 'ilk' are bad people." Today our new movies cannot get through a scene it seems without using the "F" word and utter blaspheming. Why did that change? What caused us to degrade ourselves to the level of ignorance as a way of life? What educational principle or moral or political leadership led us to "F" mentality? Why did that happen to us? And remember, my mother and father had access only to an eighth grade education.

One other aspect of our poverty puzzle related to White racial blindness was written by 26-year-old Alyssa Ahlgren in an article entitled "Blind to the Prosperity."[11] She states her generation is blind to prosperity and that we are so well off that our poverty line begins thirty-one times above the global average. Alyssa claims, "Virtually no one in the United States is considered poor by global standards. Yet, in a time where we can order a product off Amazon with one click and have it at our doorstep the next day, we are unappreciative, unsatisfied and ungrateful." Her generation is "being indoctrinated by a mainstream narrative to actually believe we have never seen prosperity." So we have a generation of young people who believe they have never seen prosperity, and she says that her generation has seen only prosperity. But, she claims "We have no contrast! We didn't live in the great depression or live through two World Wars, the Korean War, The Vietnam War and we didn't see the rise and fall of Socialism and Communism." We don't have a prosperity problem. We have an entitlement problem, an ungratefulness problem, and it's spreading like a plague."

The ungratefulness problem of young people expecting everything to be given to them has at least helped our neighbors in other lands. We citizens now see that when work is being done, it is done mainly by Hispanics. Americans are too spoiled now to work.

Our formal, religious or informal education did not possess the component value to inform White people of the ability to recognize and humanely heal the cultural issues that Black and Brown people have dealt with for centuries. What really hurts at least since WWII is we who thought we were civilized and educated and called our country a Christian nation have taken no interest in discovering Black and Brown issues. We

---

11 Ahlgren, Alyssa. https://fee.org/articles/college-student-"my-generation-is-blind-to-the-prosperity."2020.

have had too many incidents in that time that cry out "take a look," but our moral pot sits dusty on the shelf.

We need an inoculation to cure our good neighbor-lacking virus. The drawback is presently we learn our values from each other. You might think that an attack on earth by the Martians is what it would take to instill in us an interest in respecting and caring for each other. However, the COVID-19 that attacked our world has not reduced animosity between countries or instilled the practice of some people in the United States to wear masks to prevent spreading the disease to others. The practice of proper moral values would eliminate the causes of poverty and should reduce a lot of social and political diseases.

If we could have a good number of people start a movement for moral aptitude to replace the prevailing greed and possessions aptitude, the education and equality problems would be solved. If we could elect people to Congress who would have the integrity to work for our country as opposed to working solely for their party, that measure would significantly demonstrate cooperation and reduce our divisiveness. But one must be educated to obtain a level of physical and mental comfort to reach sufficient knowledge to accept our neighbor. Then perhaps we will have the common sense to the extent that we will elect leaders who will stress proper values over goods and wealth.

## REAL PROBLEM NOT SOLVED

Supposedly by 2050, the United States will be composed of fifty percent Caucasian people and fifty percent of other races. At that time, it is anticipated that one will observe a tremendous increase in mixed marriages. This pattern has already started. Therefore there will logically be a big decrease in the prejudices observed in the past history of our country. So one could surmise that prejudice based on color will have ceased.

But that condition will not eliminate prejudice. Racism is only a symptom of the main problem. The preponderance of immorality in the majority of people dominates our behavior. Why do I say the majority? Because if unhealthy behavior was only in a small number of people, then our world would be vastly different. So say racism is eliminated, then because of the uneducated, depraved, immoral culture and mind of man, we will find other ways to practice evil through prejudice. We might choose redheads, or obese people, or Harvard graduates, Baptists, women, or men, or homeless people. I realized that by observing that in places I have lived where Black people are not available, the people find another group to hate. Something in us makes us want to have someone to look down on, to blame, and to make us ignoble people look good. We can work on that too, if we have a mind to.

The year 2021 has arrived, and still the Equal Rights Amendment for Women has not been approved by the North Carolina Legislature. Men in Congress waited until 1923 to introduce the Equal Rights Amendment, and it was finally voted on in 1972 and sent to the states for ratification. It was finally ratified by the States in 2020 but now held by the

National Archivist over a deadline technicality. Why are men so afraid of women? My only conclusion is men are afraid of the superior intelligence of women. Other than our history of prejudice against People of Color since 1619, nothing proves the condition of ignorance and lack of education in North Carolina as well as the country, better than men delaying the Equal Rights Amendment.

But the bottom line I know is we cannot blame Congress or the State Legislatures. After all, we put them there, and we let them stay. Can we hope for a time when we will have sufficient common sense, if not intelligence or education, to elect people with integrity and good character who will enact and pursue laws that benefit the growth and health of all humans everywhere?

Racism is not the main problem. It is a problem, but only a symptom of the real struggle. Perhaps it is from my study of *Adventures of Huckleberry Finn*, or my observation of people, or just living for 90 years, but I know that elimination of prejudice against Black People will not solve the basic problem.

The two things needed for happiness are breath and love. Why do we make life so complicated?

## Bari and Martin

RESPONSE FROM BARI HASKINS-JACKSON

Dear Marvin,

Let me begin by saying that I really appreciate that you put so much time and effort into your comments and that you have opened yourself up in this way for feedback from me and from others. Most importantly, I want to thank you for even wondering how I, and other Black folks, might be feeling, to care enough to ask, and for being the type of man that you are. If there were more Marvin Coles on this planet, the world would indeed be a better place.

I'm sure you will get a different response from everyone that you ask. So much is tied into our own individual life experiences, what we have encountered throughout the years and how we have chosen to deal, or not to deal with those events. My perspectives are a reflection of my life's journey and do not necessarily reflect the feelings of others, but I came by my philosophy honestly and often painfully. As you know from previous conversations, I am at the "slap everybody" stage of my life right now, so, sadly, with each day of stupidity that plays out before me, the disappointment deepens, and I have no real hope or expectation that America, or humankind, will ever do the right thing or if that capability even exists. (Oh boy, that sounds depressing! I'll need to climb into bed and pull the covers over my head for at least a week when I finish writing this response!)

I have been a loner from childhood and never fully embraced mankind as my friend. I have made a variety of exceptions along the way and have tried to be a loving and caring person most of the time.

I marched as a teenager, sat in at protests, carried signs demanding equal rights and sang "We Shall Overcome." I lived in New York and Atlanta and now North Carolina and have dealt with racism, both overt and covert, in every location and in everything that I have been involved in from kindergarten through graduate school, from employment to housing, from social activities to relationships and everything in between. I have been mistaken for the help numerous times, followed around while shopping, accused of cheating when I excelled on exams, told to stay in my place, and reminded repeatedly that in the eyes of many, not only was I invisible, but I was also perceived as a threat. Such an interesting dynamic . . . to be invisible and threatening at the same time. And yes, it is hard to explain the unexplainable, the ugliness, the divisiveness, the anger, the humiliation and the despair to someone like yourself, who has had a totally different life experience, simply by not being Black.

Rather than the red-pencil technique, I am responding to your "letter" with general comments and reflections. I hope you don't mind and that you are able to follow this approach even though I do ramble on periodically. You will notice that I capitalize the "B" in Black when I am referencing people as opposed to the color black.

The first letter is capitalized as it is for Latino, Asian, Indigenous People/Native Americans and previously Negro. It is consistent with that practice and is also a sign of respect. (Even capitalization of the word black became a debated issue although many Black folks have been capitalizing it all along.) There have been recent articles discussing this that you might want to Google and check out. The July 5, 2020, *New York Times* opinion article "Why We're Capitalizing Black" might be a good start.

As I am writing this, yet another Black man, this time in Wisconsin, has been shot by police, in the back multiple times, while his children watched. With the use of cameras capturing these incidents, the world now gets to see what so many people of color have witnessed over and over again on our streets and in our communities. As a Black mother of a Black child I have had to live every day fearful that my child will not return safely as he ventures into the world. My son's name could easily be on the never ending list of Black lives lost. These are my sons and daughters being murdered. The cry for change within our police departments is a legitimate one. There might be different opinions as to what this change should look like, but the assertion that only a few officers are bad and that there is not a systemic problem is bogus. There is a gang mentality that has developed within the force that is dangerous and disgusting. The police have never been my friends. The list of the times that I, my son and other family members and friends have been harassed and belittled by police is lengthy. In many Black communities calling the police for assistance has not been a pleasant option and has only led to more problems.

Meanwhile, around the neighborhood, people are excited and eager to greet their "awesome" president as he arrives at the airport for his farm visit here in Mills River. They are ready to line up, cheering and excited, along the streets that his motorcade will follow. RNC speakers include the couple who pointed guns at peaceful BLM demonstrators. They are being promoted as role models for law and order and symbols of the right to brandish, and ultimately use weapons for protection against the ugly mobs and terrible people that are coming to get them. (I wish you could have seen the expressions on the faces of the people in the Hendersonville gun shop/shooting range when Martin and I walked in last weekend to purchase ammunition. From the looks on many of their faces, I'm guessing that the philosophy of protecting your life and property wasn't suppose to apply to Black folks, or, that it never occurred to them that it could.) So many lies and so much hypocrisy surround us that finding the truth becomes a journey that many are unwilling to take. The leadership in this country is pitiful and the alternate choices aren't totally appealing either. We could be looking at four more years of this current leadership and what happens then?

Even with changes, promises have been made for generations and actions have been minimal at best. Just enough to try and appease, settle things down and pretend like everything is all better. To make matters worse, to ensure supremacy and continued control, Black people have been systematically taught to hate themselves and each other. Fortunately many of us have not fallen into this trap or have come to the recognition that "Black is Beautiful," but there are many who have taken a different path and are filled with loathing and self hate and a desire to be anything but Black. What a cruel and effective method to attempt to divide and destroy an entire race.

And so, when you ask "Where can you go and not find prejudice?" I do not have an answer. I wish I did because I would be on the first train/plane/bicycle headed in that direction! As you state, "prejudice, narrow-mindedness, bigotry, intolerance exist in all ethnic groups."

This is the world we find ourselves in and the reality is that the saga will continue and probably intensify. So where does that leave us? In chapter one of your "letter" you ask why? and address the situation nicely. And yes, the feelings that you mention that you think Black people experience are there, along with other feelings too varied, intense and numerous to discuss. As you've stated, those feelings have always been there for Black people here in the United States. Meanwhile, the denial and "head in the sand" approach has worked effectively for many people, including people of color, to soothe a ruffled conscious, to pretend that racism is a thing of the past, to bolster our expectations when moving forward. And yes, humans ideally should strive for understanding and healing but when, if ever, does enough become enough and ignorance, family upbringing, religion and political affiliations are no longer used as excuses for atrocious, amoral behavior; especially when those excuses are applied to one segment of the population and not to others? When does society recognize that the "third group" of people that you reference is greater than a small minority and that this same mentality is cleverly disguised in business suits, college degreed scholars, educators, politicians, and lawmakers and enforcers throughout this land? When do the blinders come off to the realities of what we are facing? I am amazed at how surprised many were by the increased, blatant display of racist actions in the past few years.

Our current leadership has done nothing but pour fuel on the ever smoldering embers of hatred and bitterness in this country. And, many people are loving it! It is truly pitiful. You have been blessed (or cursed, depending on how you look at it) with a soul and morals and the capability to empathize and sympathize. And, you have accomplished much in your efforts to do the right thing. These are things you should feel good about and continue to applaud and defend. These are the characteristics that have hopefully been passed on to your children and grandchildren as they were passed on to you by your parents through their deeds and actions.

As depressing as it sounds, as I have said previously, I fear that as a nation there is no genuine interest in finding a cure, as you put it. If there were an interest, perhaps I wouldn't feel like I've been singing the same old song and getting stuck on the same note repeatedly. There are so many lies that this country was built on that continue to be expressed as truths. For example, it's not really about the monuments or the Confederate flag but it is about the attitude. The deep undying love for what they represent, the "I wish I was back in Dixie" mentality, the "how dare you take this away from me" entitlement that permeates the air. It is often about the attitude and not the event or object itself. (Of course, if I wanted to place statues of Malcolm X, Minister Farrakhan and the Black Panthers throughout different neighborhoods there would be a totally different response and immediate action taken.) Many of those distasteful monuments that people are fighting to preserve were not even built to actually honor the Confederacy but were placed strategically throughout communities many years later as a visual Jim Crow reminder to Black folks to stay in their place. And from the looks of how things are going, including voter suppression rearing its ugly head, Jim Crow is still alive and well.

As you state, "It takes decades to recover from malevolent neglect for both the partaker and the people who established the neglect." This recovery cannot even begin as long as the neglect is ongoing and even denied. Yes, all of the statistics clearly show the patterns and this virus has further highlighted what was obvious all along.

People of color are getting hit hardest in all categories including educational access, health care and economic stability. We are also experiencing death rates at alarmingly high comparative rates. This in itself speaks volumes to the plight of people of color in this country. And yet there is still the constant denial chant that there is no such thing as systemic racism in this country.

Yes, there are things that can make a difference. I dedicated my life to working with students, many of them termed "under achievers" because I believed, and still do, that being educated can make a difference in the direction that a life will take. And yes, educators are not valued or properly rewarded for their efforts and some of them have become so disheartened and overwhelmed that they become part of the problem. Fortunately, I have many examples of students who were able to survive because of the education they acquired. It is only part of the answer but certainly has its benefits, as it did for me. Sadly, much of what happens educationally in this country is not about knowledge but rather a regurgitation of principles and premises that have been embraced from generation to generation. There is often an atmosphere of competitiveness and arbitrary evaluations of progress as opposed to a communal acquisition of information and the sharing of ideas. knowledge, true knowledge does not have to be gained through formalized education and, the act of gathering information does not always trigger a functioning moral compass. As you so aptly put it "our moral pot sits dusty on the shelf."

The simple rule that your mother gave you to "treat people as people" has been lost in a society that has lost focus on so many important things. Our religious affiliations, practices and beliefs are often more divisive than healing in nature. The basic tenant of "love thy neighbor," that trickles through most religious teachings in one form or another has faded away in the process. In the last week alone, thirty million households didn't have enough food to eat and thousands of homeless were sleeping in the streets. And yet, millions of dollars are being spent on campaigning efforts and speeches are being made that are full of hollow promises with testaments about how great America is. Examples of people, including Black people, who feel they are living the American Dream, have been paraded before us as if they were the rule and not the exception to the rule. We continue to be programmed and buy into the hype.

And so, what happens next and how do those of us who still have functioning moral compasses come to grips with where we are and how we got there? In my moments of deepest despair, I think about my 5 year old granddaughter and the world I would want her to live in. It is that thought that gets me out from under the covers to fight the fight even though my efforts might be futile. For her, I know that I must keep hope alive.

I hope that you have found this helpful in your efforts to "learn and get it right." I don't know that any of us will ever get it right but at least some of us are trying.

Wishing you all the best.
Bari

# RESPONSE OF I.M. NUR (MARTIN)
# GREETINGS OF PEACE, MARVIN:

It's interesting seeing and hearing exasperation coming from the voice of a modern day abolitionist. How strange the times! And, what has really changed?

Let me begin my response to your missive by reviving that old expression: "Give a carpenter a hammer, and every problem he sees becomes a nail." Based on this idea, I would suspect that as an "educator" you necessarily see the solution to perhaps the greatest evil to blanket the world is undereducated people expressing their ignorance by way of bigotry and intolerance. That if we could just educate the lot of them, all evils would end up as relics on the waste heap of history.

Extending on this idea, governmental agents who want to champion the cause of equality might think they can propose legislations to make such attitudes illegal. Religious leaders might think that their commitment to the faith causes them to preach that such vile attitudes are against God's commandments. That we should just "love ye one another." Or, that together we might just pray away the sins of racism, hatred and greed. But is any one of these realistic? Is it so easy to change what's in the depths of peoples' hearts and souls?

As we peruse over the landscape, we see that different levels of education actually stratify the population into classes, from rich to poor. We also see that laws tend to become draconian instruments that eventually are used as blunt instruments to ensure power, using statutes to constrict the freedoms of the masses and enhance the lives of those who reside in the upper tier of hollowed halls. As for religion, it's perhaps the most insidious of them all. I call it a once-necessary evil. We only need to listen closely to hear the moans of those still strapped to the racks in those dark, dank underground dungeons.

Today, however, it's just our minds that are on the rack, deluded into having absolute faith in false and misleading dogma.

We might even say that we are predisposed (or programmed) to look for answers "in all the wrong places"...

\*\*\*

In 1859, John Brown sought the aid of Fredrick Douglass as he planned his military assault on Harpers Ferry. Before that, he had successfully led troops in several anti-slavery campaigns in Kansas. He wanted Douglass to help recruit slaves from neighboring plantations to fight for their freedom. Isn't it interesting how a New

## I.M. Nur's Response

England boy from Connecticut, a skilled dairy farmer, wound up in Kansas, killing fellow White citizens in an effort to free Black people, people he probably didn't even have an intimate knowledge of? Yes, it's interesting how some people are just wired in their brain to want good, even if their methods might be wrong-minded. And, isn't it just as interesting how local farmers, militiamen, supported by US Marines, led by Robert E. Lee, in just thirty-six hours, rooted out, killed or captured Brown's entire assaulting force?

I digressed . . .

Marvin, do you remember the first time you and Mimi drove Bari and I to Morganton? Along the way our conversation meandered in more philosophical directions. During the discussion, I asked you one salient question, "What was the Will of God?" In response, I remember sensing that the question was received like that dreaded "pop quiz." I could see both of you searching for "that one right answer." Quickly both of you agreed that His (or Her) Will was "that we should live together in peace" or something along those lines.

I didn't pursue the logical follow up to that response because I didn't want things to get too heavy during our first exploration together. So I backed off.

The logical follow up to your response would have been, "Where in the Bible (or other book) does it expressly say that [living together in peace] is the singular Will of God?"

Marvin, as you are probably sensing by now, unlike most people you share profound concerns with, people who are acculturated to see every problem as a nail, or the need for a law, or more broad-based education, or for a sermon to soothe their soul, I approach understanding the nature of the problems we have before us today not from a political or educational or religious perspective, but rather from a direction I believe really addresses the nature of the problem—the real problem. Fact is, one can never get an answer to a problem if strategy for a solution is predicated on wrong premises. This is simple logic.

Like you, for many, many years, I too wrestled with understanding the problem of mankind's aggressiveness against other men. Why are wars waged? Why are murders perpetrated against innocent people? Why are taxes structured to retain people near poverty? And, why nails so often bend when you drive them into wood?

Understand that unlike most average Americans, I didn't have a straight sequential line of progress through school. I didn't go into the military, travel the world, or have a homestead to return to for solace and reflection. At the ripe old age of 4, I learned my father was killed one night in an automobile accident in Florida. He was one of those who was in pursuit of the American Dream.

He went to grade school. He decided to join the Navy rather than stay on the streets and suffer the fate met by most Black youth of his day. He committed himself to raising a family. And, he was just six months away from retirement, after serving 19.5 years in support of America's global interests. During his time, he fought in two wars (WWII and Korea). He suffered Jim Crow abuse on the streets of America, as well as in the military. But through it all, and until his death, he "kept the faith." So now I ask, to what end?

Following that tragic event, my two sisters and I lived in Louisiana for a time with my aunt and uncle and their three children. However, the bulk of the ensuing four years was spent living with our grandparents in Picayune, Mississippi. From the age of 5 through 7, I got to see the heart and soul of America, up close and personal. I saw that my grandmother couldn't hope to get a job doing anything more than serving as a domestic cook for a middle class White family. I saw how my grandfather, even though he was highly respected in our local section of town, and even though he as a 33rd-degree Mason (Prince Hall), and even though he was a Reverend in the Christian religion, could at best get a job as a laborer in a creosote plant. I also got to see the horror in my grandmother's face when one day some White boys on a school bus threw a wad of paper at us while we were walking on the white side of town, because that was where all of the stores were located. Not being schooled in the acumen of race relations of the mid-1950s, I was headed on the bus to kick some butt. My grandfather instilled in me the idea of respecting everybody and not taking any disrespect from anybody. Even now, some sixty-five years later, I still feel my grandmother pulling me back, as I was marching up the steps of the bus; and, I can still see the terror in her eyes, at what might have been. Needless to say, she knew it was time to send us back up to New York. It was clear that I just wouldn't fit in to the relationship Blacks had worked out with White folks in Picayune. And so, before the start of the next school term, my sisters and I were packed up and put on a train to live with our mother in New York.

Within a day or two after arriving, I was herded around the corner to the local public elementary school where I was to register for the 3rd grade. I remember there was a lot of hustle and bustle as the administrators sought to "properly place me." To them, coming from schools in po'ass Mississippi had to mean that I was "slower'" than Northern "Negro" kids. I didn't know at the time, but what they were doing was aligning me to within tolerance of an unwritten policy, to winnow Black youths—and especially Black boys—out of the system and on to the streets. Over the next seven years, although I had moments of brilliance, inexorably forces moved me in the direction of "the streets." And by 16, that magical age, they were successful. I was out. Funny thing, at around the same time, most of the young boys I knew coming up were in the same situation; but not so much for the girls. (That warrants a different analysis, for another time.)

However, unlike most of the other boys I grew up with, I had had those few formative years in the Deep South, an experience that laid a firm foundation of moral and ethical responsibility that so often was there to redirect me during times when life steered me in dark and haunted places—places so many of my peers were never able to recover from.

I lingered on the streets for nearly two years—going from pool room to pool room and from bar to bar, as I sought some semblance of purpose in my hyper-confusing life. And in spite of my wanderings, I never thought that my future would be fulfilled in either place because I witnessed the feat of others before me who had tried.

By a miracle, I began to read at the start of this period. At 16, the first book I read cover to cover was Claude Brown's *Manchild in the Promised Land*. It taught me about prison life that awaited those of us who fell into any of the alluring traps set for our real education.

The over-arching theme here is this. People who looked like me had a huge "target on their backs." I learned early on that the police were trained to kill or arrest me at any given moment. That any interaction with them constituted an existential threat to my life. And if not them, the military was there seeking my body as a sacrifice for their master's aims and ambitions in Vietnam. Preachers were there beckoning me to come on board to further their mission of bearing-witness to a relationship with an unbelieveable, unnamed god. And, industry was sometimes there seeking only my time and labor to enrich the rich, and those striving to become rich. I came to see America and all of the Eurocentric world as a system arrayed with a host of focused institutions aimed at exploiting any of us who, by our very existence, were deemed to be "ENEMIES OF THIE STATE!"

Some might think these are the machinations of a paranoid, deluded mind. However, for me, these are things that news programs on TV show every night, and they are real.

It was in spring 1970 that I first met Bari. She was working a work-study stint in the library at City College in uptown Manhattan. I was entranced before first sight. During those days, I saw myself as a political revolutionary. I, like so many others, believed there was NO reforming Amerika. No way, No how! I believed that only by way of an armed revolution would this deplorable adventure come to a definite end. This was the era of Farrakhan and the Nation of Islam, and Huey P. Newton and the Black Panther Party. And although I didn't see either as being the organization that would bring about the changes we needed, I supported them because they were the best revolutionary options we had at the time.

I thought it only appropriate to provide you with some highlights of my formative years as a benchmark for who I became—Albeit it Abbreviated . . . Cleaned up . . . and Sanitized, so as not to offend! In response to the history you shared, in my early analysis of things, I saw Jackie Robinson as a "token Negro." He was deferential to Whites and disagreeable with radical Black leaders. And I saw Frederick Douglass as a puppet of abolitionist forces. He obviously was a person who could, through eloquence and intellect, stir the indignation of White people with the hope of "changing the hearts of Amerika," a sentiment later championed by Martin Luther King Jr. During my intellectual development, I had no time for them or for their hopes in Amerika ever fundamentally changing. And although by that time I was becoming a voracious reader, I didn't read any of their writings and still don't to this day.

It was during this period that I began thinking about and asking those fundamental questions regarding our relationship with creation. But first and foremost I wanted to know how could there be a "Loving God," given the depth of evils in the world? This seemed incongruent with reality. Everyone could see that evil was at the very core of this entire society, and it was directed by way of political, economic, religious and military, as well as entertainment (sports and play) institutions.

From my indoctrination in the church in Mississippi, I was told that God was our benefactor, our protector, our judge. But what I continuously saw was White people, at every level, from presidents to bus drivers, giving Black people hell. This to me could only mean that either there was NO god, or that God was incompetent and weak against evil. And what these possibilities meant for Black, Brown and other oppressed peoples is that we were in for a rough ride in life, since White people, being more blood-thirsty than other people, would obviously continue to impose their brand of world domination, until they drove all of us including themselves toward oblivion.

Not a very bright future for Black people or anyone else, if this were the end of the matter. Still, my inquiring mind led me on in the pursuit of a more thorough understanding of "What it's all about."

My readings evolved to include psychological treatises like those written by Erich Fromm: *The Art of Loving, Man for Himself: An Inquiry into the Psychology of Ethics, The Revolution of Hope,* and others. But even with hope, he too painted a bleak picture for man's future. But despite the preliminary assessment, I plowed on in my search for answers.

I won't get into the genesis of my theosophical beliefs, but suffice it to say that as I began really studying the Bible, then later the Qur'an, and as I expanded my purview to include the *Tao Te Ching* (The Way) by Lao-Tzu, the *Lotus Sutra*, the *Bhagavad Gita* and many other texts, I began to sculpt a very vivid image of the Divine Creative Force, along with the overarching design we are all a part of. Each source gave me an appreciation for the good, the bad and the ugly of it all. And by 23, my eyes were becoming open to an expansive new comprehension of what was happening on this plane of existence. For the first time, things started to make perfect sense.

During my survey, I started to see how people, although having good intention, were guided not by what was in the books, but rather by what was pumped into their blood and brain by preachers and teachers who were themselves blind and tone deaf to higher wisdom—A classic case of the "blind leading the blind." Further, I understood from reading that there was indeed "a time and season for every purpose in creation," which included a time for evil to rule; at least for a time and a season. It's what the Qur'an calls, a respite. What it meant is that there was nothing you or I could do to change the power dynamic of the time we were in. At best, we could only strive to endure and perhaps share what little knowledge and wisdom we accrued. Fact is, this is what the entirety of the Bible, Qur'an and others admonish us to do. Again, neither you, I, nor our leaders, teachers or preachers can change the course of the river on which this Eurocentric world-age travels to its final destination.

Today, the spirit that ushers in persons like a Donald Trump into power makes clear that this world reached its apex sometime ago. In fact, since 1972, we've witnessed social structures increasingly implode on themselves. Still hopeful citizens, in desperation, eagerly voted for anyone who promised them the moon, to be great again and money in the bank. From then until now, supporter and critic alike have increasingly been able to see Amerika's demise looming, this side of the horizon. As the title of one of my recent essays states, people all over the nation and the world are desperately trying to "Reconcile the Irreconcilable."

In ignorance and arrogance, so many Amerikans are not satisfied with wisdom that says, "no one can turn what is evil to its core into something that is good for all." Still, in disbelief, Republicans, Democrats and Independents promise things that fundamentally support evil. Take this land, for example, which was literally stolen from peoples who were unprepared for the level of brutality that encroached on their world. They were driven off the land by gun-toting, Bible-intoxicated hordes, hunted like prey and murdered; the remnant of them was sequestered out of sight and out of mind. For generations their voices have been muted. Even now, their cries for justice go unheard. Today, no one raises a voice to acknowledge that the people who luxuriate themselves, from sea to shining sea, do so on the bones of some five hundred million people who were murdered to secure and defend stolen lands; not Republicans, not Democrats, not Independents.

This is why I tell my students, "I have absolutely NO HOPE in Amerika." But unlike Arjuna in the beginning of the Bhagavad Gita, I am not despondent. And unlike those who imagine a political solution or a revolutionary solution or an economic solution or a religious solution, I have intensely studied all of these and know that none of them offers us any hope of reconciliation.

But, unlike most of my people, I am not without hope. And I'm not talking about the vain hope that preachers spew from the pulpit about dying and going to an undefined heaven, if you're good. Or, an immature hope held by some of our most prodigious leaders who say that we will force Amerika "to live up to the true meaning of her creed." All of their hopes and dreams are in actuality, a form of insanity; delusions wrought by miseducation, as so eloquently stated by Dr. Carter G. Woodson in his 1933 book, *The Mis-Education of the Negro:*

Like Lebron James who is presently the undisputed master of basketball, a man who has spent thousands of hours studying and practicing every facet of the game, I have spent even more thousands of hours studying the greatest wisdom of all times. And, by so doing, I know with certainty that justice will prevail . . . and soon—that what was stolen by greed and avarice will be returned. That what was destroyed for vile and evil motives will soon be restored. I know this not just because the "Bible Tells Me So" (as the song goes), but rather because virtually all of the greatest works of sacred wisdom affirm this as fact.

Moreover, I know it from all the signs we are told to look for and are living through in these last days and times of this world's age. It's why daily we see the specter of wars, earthquakes, hurricanes, floods, fires, polar vortices, and the like. I may not know the day or the hour, but through wisdom I know the year; and it is coming soon.

Marvin, I don't say all this to negate the sentiments you expressed for a better life for people of all walks of life, of all colors and hues. But, in keeping it real, in my first book, The Meaning of Blackness: Uncovering the Secret of secrets, the Nature and Destiny of a People (currently out of print), I ask the question, "What is slavery?" and, the best answer I could come up with was, "It is when a person or people make choices that are against their long-term interests, especially if their mind is under the influence or control of another people. That relationship represents servitude, slavery, or the state scriptures call oppression." Yet, because virtually none of us has any other perceived alternative world to aspire toward, we, by default, find ourselves willing to defend this world's reality, as slaves, with our blood. Again, we see no other alternative. In this reality some of us survive and some thrive, as slaves. So, no matter if you're Black, White or somewhere in between, you function to further the only world you know—even a world that is hell to the majority of the planet's people. Enmeshed in it so thoroughly, the hell we know and are familiar with is preferable to any heaven of which we have no practical knowledge.

In ignorance, arrogance, avariceness and selfishness, too many are induced into surrendering to fear, lust, and hatred. It's why we have wars. It's why one person abuses another. And, if one reads the small print above, it's why we call on God, but seemingly get no answer.

Marvin, again, there's a "Time and Season" for all things under the sun and beyond. But be assured that this time and season has literally run its course. What we are witnessing, with Trump-ism, QANon and the like, with continued murders of Black people by police and common citizens, by "wars and rumors of wars" are the death rattles of a dying world. In my view, a new world based on Truth and Justice is dawning.

All good folks can do in the meantime is speak out against injustice; proclaim the passing away of this world age of evil; strengthen themselves in their commitment to go(o)dness; and know that there is a Masterful Creative Force that has a grand plan for this creation story, as it flowers into its perfection. Also know that what we see happening all around us isn't personal. It's business . . . divine business fulfilling a much grander purpose. Know that in this drama, God is not doing evil to us. It's just that True Justice demanded that evil had its time to manifest its design for creation. And over the past 5,125+ years, evil has absolutely manifested what it can produce, at its very best, which is pain, suffering, and meaningless death.

And as Forrest Gump said, "That's all I have to say about that!"

But, if you'd like some brief references for what this expository declaration presents, you might read Chapters 38 to 42 in the Book of Job in the Bible, Sura 15:36-39 and the short verses of Sura 103 of the Qur'an. And, if you'd like insights from an economics point of view, it would be instructive to read an under-appreciated work by Henry George entitled *Progress and Poverty* (1879, not the abridged version).

Anyway, these few words are my humble retort to your plaintive cries in the wilderness. I sincerely hope they suffice and bring you some measure of comfort.


With Best Regards for Sanity and Peace,
I.M. Nur
A.K.A. Martin

## RESPONSE OF DOUG WINGEIER

# Doug Wingeier

ii

Hello, Marvin,

I've re-read your paper and the comments from Martin and Bari. Rather than respond point-by-point (could lead to a forest-and-trees problem), I'll offer some thoughts in several general categories:

A. EDUCATION. You place a lot of faith in education as the means to enlightenment, responsibility and morality—understandable because of your long and successful career in education. Martin calls such faith in education into question for its contribution to stratification and tendency to indoctrination. My field of specialization was religious education, preparation for which required study of philosophies of education, among other things. A major influence has been Theodore Brameld's typology in terms of:

(1) Perennialism – discovering the eternal, archetypal principles/ideas ingrained in the universe, for example, Plato's Ideas of Truth, Beauty, and Goodness. Implanted by

nature, appreciation and practice of these will follow in one's thought and behavior (drawback—sets apart the leisurely intelligentsia from other "inferior" beings who must work for a living).

(2) Essentialism – imparting the basic facts, knowledge and skills needed for a successful, responsible life (drawback—possible indoctrination and production of a docile citizenry who absorb what they are told; discourages critical thinking).

(3) Progressivism – encouraging individual self-esteem and fulfillment (drawback—can produce self-centered individuals preoccupied with their own development without regard for the needs and well-being of others and society as a whole.

(4) Reconstructionism – developing skills of critical thinking, analysis, and organization equipping one to work to transform the system (drawback—could get you crucified). All this is to say that whether education is to be useful in addressing systemic racism depends on what TYPE of education is employed. I had a ride with a Lyft driver the other day who had been a teacher (middle school and high school) for over a decade, then gave it up out of frustration with "teaching to the tests" (Essentialism), lack of parental support, and low student motivation. Education as we practice it will not address racism because it leaves the system intact—even supports it.

B. RACE. Bari's comments are most poignant here. She has dealt with it all her life, and neither she nor Martin see much likelihood of change. Like you, I believe that exposure to and relationship with "the other" breaks down stereotypes and prejudice and helps one experience others as human beings like us, with the same needs, fears, hopes. However, this needs to happen in a setting where norms of respect and appreciation prevail. You established such a setting as an administrator by demonstrating your readiness to listen and learn from your coworkers. People responded to that with openness and cooperation, and a learning community was formed. I honor you for that. Your instincts for accepting and trusting others are indeed commendable. I had a similar experience in Singapore, where as a white minority in a predominantly Asian society, rather than standing on my "colonial" prerogatives, I learned the language, joined Asian rather than American groups for the most part, and sought out opportunities to learn their history and culture. This was in large part due to the kind of missionary training I received and the good sense my mother had earlier instilled in me to follow. We white Americans take for granted that we deserve the privileges we enjoy (whether through effort or inheritance) and refuse to acknowledge the systemic racism in our societal and individual DNA that perpetuates and disadvantages people of color. People like Bari and Martin have overcome this, which is greatly to be admired, but they still bear the scars.

C. MORALITY VS. FAITH. You put a lot of emphasis on morality, wondering why we Americans seem to lack a moral sense/compass when it comes to race (and other issues), and yearning for its restoration. Morality consists of a set of codes or guidelines providing direction for responsible living. But these are on the surface, learned, adopted, and (attempted to be) practiced—sort of like New Year's resolutions we make each year, then break shortly thereafter. They do not go to the heart of the matter, which is faith. Not faith as a set of beliefs, but as a deep-seated trust in a Spirit/Presence who loves, accepts, forgives and redeems us and provides us with the strength and will to "love God and neighbor." St. Paul says this best in Romans 7:21-8:2:

> So I find it to be a law that when I want to do what is good, evil lies close at hand. For I delight in the law of God in my inmost self, but I see in my members another law at war with the law of my mind, making me captive to the law of sin that dwells in my members. Wretched man that I am! Who will rescue me from this body of death? Thanks be to God through Jesus Christ our Lord! So then, with my mind I am slave to the law of God, but with my flesh I am a slave to the law of sin. There is therefore now no condemnation for those who are in Christ Jesus. FOR THE LAW OF THE SPIRIT OF LIFE IN CHRIST JESUS HAS SET YOU FREE FROM THE LAW OF SIN AND DEATH (NRSVA).

Because of our innate self-centeredness (sin) we do not/cannot live moral lives on our own. We need the transforming love of God to make this possible. This is faith.

D. RELIGION. Martin has little use for religion as a solution, and rightly so. Religion is not the same as faith. Organized religion is infected by the same original sin (DNA) of racism as the rest of society. Witness the churches' support for slavery, segregation, (the Central Jurisdiction; 11:00 on Sunday morning), consumerism, militarism and sexism. However, I still participate in church because it offers me challenge, guidance, support, encouragement, hope to continue the struggle. On some occasions, I have found more compatibility and courage among non-Christians than in the church and so align myself with them and their causes. But it is what the church teaches and stands for that points me in that direction and remains standing when other ventures lose heart or collapse. So, we don't put our faith in religion or church, but in the God of whom the church proclaims. Where did Huck Finn learn this?

E. INDIVIDUAL SUCCESSES. You point to Jackie Robinson as an example of one who rose above his racist surroundings to achieve stardom—due to his amazing God-given abilities, his pluck and determination, and (we might add though you don't mention it) to a white Methodist named Branch Rickey who took the risk and endured the ire of fellow owners to give him a chance. It takes the cooperation of both. I'd also cite the example of Satchel Paige, arguably the best pitcher in baseball history, who was confined to the Negro leagues until in his 40s and well past his prime, and then used only as a reliever for a year or two. Our society repeatedly loses incredible talent such as this due to the discriminatory attitudes, barriers, and policies in areas such as immigration, employment, education and law enforcement, which stultify people's ambition, development, and hope. Again the product of our racist DNA.

F. CAUSE/REMEDY. You repeatedly ask, why are people this way? Psychologically speaking—and you say this too—it's because of their lack of self-esteem. We are told in a variety of ways that we are not as good as the next guy, so the only way we know to compensate is to put the other down—like the old schoolyard game, king of the mountain. Here I'm informed by Maslow's needs hierarchy—physiological, safety, belongingness and love, esteem, self-actualization. I add to this a sixth—unity or community with others and a Higher Power. Our needs at each level must be met before we can move on to the next. When they are not, we become fixated at one level and inhibited from growing beyond it. This leads to lashing out, blaming, looking for scapegoats, competition for scarce goods and services, conflict—and even war. So, from a purely human point of view, our society must address itself to meeting these needs, one level at a time. Until we do, racial (and other) conflicts will continue.

HOPE. Neither Bari nor Martin seem to hold out much hope for change in their/our lifetime. Yet, curiously, and paradoxically, Martin ends by saying: "... there is a Masterful Creative Force who has a grand plan for this creation story, as it flowers into its perfection. ... Divine business fulfilling a much grander purpose ..." Seems like he is "hoping against hope." But his hope is mine as well. I try to avoid using the term God out of concern that it will evoke in others images/concepts far removed from what I intend. I prefer to speak of a Creating, Sustaining Energy/Mystery in what/whom I "live, move, and have my being," and out of which I come, in which I rest, and into which I shall continue to abide. I wish for you that kind of hope as well.

Your friend,
Doug

# FOR YOUR NEIGHBORLY CONTEMPLATION
## by Marvin

Humans were created with the option to choose between right and wrong. We can choose our behavior. The Good Book says we are to love our neighbor, but that choice must constantly do battle with human nature. Pundits have identified several different properties of human nature, and many are against being concerned about your neighbor.

When another person has a different point of view,. human nature makes some people want to confront and lash out at the offending party in various ways. Some vow to depart the company of the group or person and avoid future get-togethers. This attitude ignores the adage that differences of opinion make good horse races, or that one's education is enhanced by hearing and learning about different philosophies.

But to lash out, condemn, or walk away from another's view then terminates an opportunity for one to provide an alternative view, show the person another way, and it prevents your learning her or his assessment and position, and thereby abolishes the chance that you might grow to appreciate that person. Allow the other person to speak, and sometimes it is best to not reply at all, which also can give a message. Wait for another day and time to give alternative views. Sometime later one can calmly convey about another stance or interpretation that might trigger another attitude.

Mr. Twain said, "Loyalty to a petrified opinion never yet broke a chain or freed a human soul." One of the great hindrances to the United States attaining a thriving democracy is our incapability to discuss the differences between democrats and republicans, between conservatives and liberals. That inability is indicative of our lower status as being a cultured·and educated nation. Human nature makes us attach ourselves to one party for one reason or another and never consider either cause, just like a high school teenager. If God crated us, and gave us a brain, why do we fail to activate it?

Rational, reasonable, educated individuals should be capable of discussing anything without expressing the behavior of a backwoods simpleton. I have been fortunate in my life to not have a lot of money and to have many friends. They come in all colors, shapes and sizes and countries. Getting to know them forced out all previous learned assumptions and suppositions. One such family was the Nawaz's from Pakistan. His name was Muhamad Nawaz, but he was always referred to by his last name Nawaz.

IQBAL NAWAZ

DR. MUHAMMAD NAWAZ

I met and worked with Nawaz at the University of the Punjab in Lahore, Pakistan. We were the same age and both interested in counseling and psychological stuff. He was born and grew up in a town named Multan in a modest home and background. Nawaz is difficult to describe since, to most people, he would be unbelievable because he was so kind, humble, unpretentious and down to earth. He obtained his doctoral degree at Indiana University. Nawaz was an inspiration to me and provided one of the transformation experiences of my life.

Iqbal was also a different kind of person, particularly for Muslim culture. Her career position was as a Librarian and she was the first educated Librarian in Pakistan. She used her mind and spoke it when she needed to without cultural or religious restraint. That is one reason Nawaz and Iqbal got married. Nawaz loved her brain, enthusiasm and forthrightness.

After a period of work at the Institute of Education and Research in Pakistan, Nawaz and Iqbal moved to the United States. Nawaz was Chair of the Department of Educational Psychology and Iqbal, a Librarian at the University of West Alabama. They had two children, Sara and Salmon. Because of the color of their skin, they were subjected to uncomfortable racial prejudice in Alabama, but Nawaz stayed calm and just considered the level of the source.

Later, they moved to Cincinnati, Ohio, with work at the University of Cincinnati. Iqbal authored geography books for children. Nawaz authored books on comparative religions with the unwavering hope of advancing peace, compassion and understanding. Nawaz died in 2020 and Iqbal died in 2021. Dr. Sara Nawaz is a psychiatrist in Cincinnati, and Salmon is computer guru in Irvine, California.

One time when Sara was a teenager, she asked her father why neighbor country India was so much more advanced than Pakistan. Nawaz told her that it was because Pakistan had chosen to only educate half its population while India was educating females and males, and that is the reason we chose to come to the United States. That was/is Nawaz.

Twain as Marvin
painting by Katherine Martin

# 11

# My Literature Education after Meeting the Real Huck Finn
# by Marvin Cole

# MY LITERATURE EDUCATION AFTER MEETING THE REAL HUCK FINN

> Catalonian, the bookstore owner in
> *One Hundred Years of Solitude*,
> after being told by train officials
> his three boxes of books
> would have to travel in the freight car stated,
> "The world must be all (messed) up
> when men travel first class and literature goes as freight.
> Gabriel Garcia Marquez,
> *One Hundred Years of Solitude*, p 431.

For my 13th birthday, my sister gave me a copy of *Adventures of Huckleberry Finn*. I read it—thought it was a good story . . . but not as exciting as Zane Grey's *The Last Trail* or *The Mysterious Rider*.

Once every month or so, my mother walked a mile to catch the Pisgah and Leicester bus (P & L) into Asheville. One of her purchases would be a book for me and it was usually by Zane Gray. They cost one dollar.

Sometimes she did my chores to allow me to keep on reading. My parents went only to the eighth grade, but they were intelligent and believed in education. Sitting in a rocking chair with my feet propped up against the fireplace rock, I would be with that Zane Grey built-in-America hero, riding on a horse chasing bad guys. There was a clear distinction between good and evil. White hats for good guys, black for the bad; bad girls smoked. Life was so clear in the old days.

It helped me think about what I would do when I grew up—chase bad guys. Therefore, I became a college president and chased bad faculty. Of course the real world is not that simple. I think my growing-up involved the discovery that evil did not wear a costume or carry a flag. My first reading of *Huckleberry Finn* resulted in my judgment of it being a nice story but nothing special. It was put on the shelf behind Zane Grey's Old West stories. And for many people, it still holds that position.

I grew up feeling that I was not the sharpest guy in the county. And I am okay with that. It bothered me in the early years that I could not fathom all those algebra and geometry configurations, but that was eventually overcome by the knowledge that I had skills in other areas. I also found out that math people couldn't read and write.

Some of you must have watched Captain Kirk of *Star Trek* run the Enterprise. He was not the smartest guy on the ship. Mr. Spock was the always-logical intellect on board. Dr. McCoy had all the medical knowledge. And Scotty, the chief engineer, had all the technical know-how to keep the ship running even when it was under attack by aliens. Captain Kirk respected the skills of his colleagues, consulted them and never presumed to know more than they did about their particular area. He knew what he didn't know, was perfectly willing to admit it and kept asking questions until he understood. Kirk specialized in vision, tone and morale. He was a leader.

When I first read *Huckleberry Finn* I did not realize there were questions to be asked or lessons to be learned. I saw good people and bad people and the good guys won in the end. I missed the essence—the soul of Huckleberry Finn. I needed a Dr. Spock. That was before television. We did not have a telephone at the time. We had a radio we turned on in the evening. I listened to *The Lone Ranger*, my father listened to the news, and the Lux Radio Theater enchanted me. (Lux was a dishwashing soap). The stories on radio gave me pictures that television and film cannot depict.

One of the professors at Western Carolina refused to let his Shakespeare students read copies of the plays that had photos or illustrations. He said the photos "limited our vision." No photograph could equal the image that we had in our own minds of the doomed lovers. That was the charm of radio.

No actor could equal the Matt Dillon that I saw in my mind, crossing the street to the Long Branch Saloon, pushing through those swinging doors and flipping a silver dollar on the bar that clattered and whirled as he said, "Evening, Miss Kitty." Compare that setting with today's competition for reading and getting the essence of a good novel.

William Falk, in *The Week* magazine, told about today's world with the constant inputs of Facebook and texting and tweeting and messaging; no teen can be alone for more than a few minutes. He says, "Truth is, there were times in my teen years when I would have killed for the distraction of some online friends. But I don't envy the Facebook generation, living in the blab-o-sphere, with a half-dozen open channels at all times, seems more like a burden then a pleasure, and the endless back-and-forth—more an addiction than a choice."[1]

In the past, at least my past, there was always plenty of time with just myself to think. I know, I sound like old crotchety, bushy-brown-eyed Andy Rooney of *CBS-60 Minutes*, scowling at this newfangled world from beneath the disapproving hedge of my eyebrows.

---

1 William Falk, ed., *The Week*, March 28, 2021

But there is something to be said about looking for solace ... and clues ... inside one's own being. Alone, you have no choice but to make friends with yourself; if you never manage that, your virtual friends won't do you much good. There is not anything on television or the blab-o-sphere that can come close to the pictures you get in your mind as you read a good book. And intelligent people around the world know that nothing can alter your life and the lives of a nation in a positive, growing way as much as the observations and interpretations of a good writer. But it is not always easy to find meaningful ideas in our best books. It takes a good reader to find humor in Thoreau's *Walden* or Twain's criticism of Christians in the *Adventures of Tom Sawyer*.

After my Zane Grey period, my next great awakening in reading was as a junior in college. I was a business administration major and therefore not attuned to reading good books. Looking back, I should have been an English major, but I knew at the time that would mean teaching, and I was too shy to think about speaking before a crowd of more than two people.

But a friend told me to read Somerset Maugham's *Of Human Bondage* and then I fell in Love with the story and good writing. But here again, someone else told me about the book. For many of us, it takes someone else to inform us of the meaning below the surface of a good book. Sometimes it takes a gifted reader.

I was enthralled with Azar Nafisi's book *Reading Lolita in Tehran*. For two years before she left Iran in 1997, Nafisi secretly held a class at her home for seven young women to read and discuss forbidden works of Western literature. I admired the courage that took, but I envied the insight and wisdom she had for our literature. Here was someone from another culture giving the core and heart and spirit of American novels. I was impressed (and shamed) by the courage of those women who risked their lives to read American novels. These were novels that we no longer read because we have grown complacent and lazy in this art that is open to everyone. Perceiving the gifts inherent in those novels as "old hat," we watch television pseudo-actors with capabilities limited to using the "F" word every three or four sentences and dull ourselves to the point of missing value and message in books like *The Great Gatsby* or *The Grapes of Wrath*. Imagine those women in Nafisi's book huddled in a secret hiding place, in love with our literature. Reading is the most depressed art in our culture. And many times those who do read the words miss the message.

And aside from all that, in the United States, *Lolita* did not exactly make the top ten on the Methodist approved list of books. Here are Nafisi's wise words about people: "Every individual has different dimensions to his personality. Those who judge must take all aspects of an individual's personality into account. It is only through literature that one can put oneself in someone else's shoes and understand the other's different and contradictory sides and refrain from becoming too ruthless. Outside the sphere of literature, only one aspect of an individual is revealed. But if you understand the different dimensions, you cannot easily murder him or her."

That reminds us of Joseph Campbell's observation that we cannot kill our enemies in war unless we convert them to "other." Make them something alien. I guess it works in reverse, too. If we take our enemies and give them hearts and eyes and debts and grandchildren, they become like us and therefore, we cannot kill them.

My personal Dr. Spocks and Nafisis began with some English teachers at DeKalb College, which became Georgia Perimeter College and now merged with Georgia State University. I was Dean on South Campus at the time and was asked to sit in on a panel discussion of *Adventures of Huckleberry Finn.* The English faculty wanted to show the students that a Dean could read and write. So, I had to reread *Huck*, and that experience made me see a completely different book than I had read as a 13-year-old. Since then, I have become a "Child of Huckamania." Getting to know one author makes a person want to discover the meaning behind the words of other authors. For example, when I first read *Grapes of Wrath* by John Steinbeck, and even after seeing the movie, I knew it was about a place and time that I certainly did not want to visit. It was an interesting story—a "rags to riches" kind of story from the depression days. I was born in 1932 and remember stories from my parents about life on a dollar-a-day. But the real story from *Grapes of Wrath* passed me by. The title comes from "The Battle Hymn of the Republic."

> *Mine eyes have seen the glory of the coming of the Lord,*
> *he is trampling out the vintage where the grapes of wrath are stored;*
> *He hath loosed the fateful lightning of his terrible swift sword;*
> *His truth is marching on.*
> *– Julia Ward Howe*

The song was written by Julia Ward Howe and was a 1861 camp meeting tune. The main characters in *The Grapes Of Wrath* are mainly the Joad family (Tom, Ma, Pa, Grandpa, Grandma, Al—Tom's brother—), Roseasharon, Jim Casey, Uncle Noah). During the depression years, the Joad family are prisoners/slaves to a worn-out, drought-controlled farm in Oklahoma, with a lot of the Midwest referred to as the "dust bowl." The banks are taking over the farms and bulldozing the homes to clear the way for better business ventures. Tom Joad has just been released from prison for killing a man and leads his family to California. Tom Joad represents Moses, leading his family to a promised land. Moses also killed a man and was away for a while. California is the promised land because they have heard of plenty of jobs and there are green orchards, vineyards and wonderful farmland.

The Joad's story is a direct parallel to that of the Hebrews. So they pile on an old truck—two-by-two—as in Noah's ark. Twelve people—twelve tribes of Israel. Even the name of Joad reminds one of Job. One person is Jim Casey, a friend, called the Preacher, who represents Jesus Christ. Notice the initials J.C. One of Jim's lines: "A man ain't got a soul of his own, just a part of a great big soul." Jim is a good man. Like Christ, he is killed by the police later in the novel. Tom encounters a snake on the road. The snake gave Adam and Eve forbidden fruit. California is forbidden to outsiders and migrants. The snake betrayed Adam and Eve. California betrayed the Joads. There are many biblical allusions and imagery in this book. Some say it was in many ways America's *Les Miserables.*

Steinbeck provides in *The Grapes of Wrath*, a powerful message.[2] He presents religion as a double-edged blade; one can go to the path of being truly a devout, kind person, or one can choose the path of those who zealously condemn the views of others. Steinbeck speaks out against those who kept the oppressed in poverty ... And therefore, he was branded as a communist because of his "voice." It was also called a blasphemous book. It was banned and burned throughout the United States because it could not be read with understanding. There are always some who do not want such books to be read with understanding. At the end of the book, Tom Joad is again having to leave his family because his struggle for justice has made him an enemy of the government. As he leaves his family, he tells his mother where he will be in the future. Although he will not physically be with her, "Wherever they's a fight so hungry people can eat, I'll be there ... wherever they's a cop beatin' up a guy, I'll be there ... I'll be in the way kids laugh when they're hungry an' they know supper's ready ... "

The grapes have been a central symbol throughout the book: first of promise, representing the fertile California valleys, but finally of bitter rage as the Midwesterners realize that they have been lured west with false bait and that they will not be permitted to partake of this fertility. The wrath grows, a fearsome, terrible wrath; but it is clear that wrath is better than despair, because wrath moves to action. Steinbeck would have people act, in concert and in concern for one another—and finally prevail over all forms of injustice. Today it is listed in the list of the top 100 books in the World. The song "Brother, Can You Spare a Dime?" preceded *Grapes* ... A catchy tune—it really is a protest song as is *Grapes of Wrath*, both anthems of the great depression. It tells of a worker who helped build the country—with his labor—and finds himself out of work in tough times.

It was seventy-five years after *Huckleberry Finn* was published that special reader by the name of Ernest Hemingway said, "The first and best book written in America was *Huckleberry Finn*—all since have been copies of that." When the very respected Hemingway said those words, others had to take another reading of *Huck*.

Thoreau's *Walden* and Whitman's *Leaves of Grass* were not recognized as classics for one hundred years after they were published. So my mission here is to encourage you to find your Dr. Spock ... someone or something not connected to your occupation and find yourself by reading good literature.

English teachers are notably good readers. So listen to the Dr. Spocks and Scottys and Hemingways and English teachers when they tell you about books that made an impact on their lives. Remember that turtle did not get on top of the fence post by herself—but, oh the change in perspective when she got there. Find a rocking chair hideaway and read good books. Then I encourage you to pick an author or artist or woodworking—some area in which you become something of an expert. It opens up other worlds for you.

When I hear a reference about something occurring in 1885, I think about what Mark Twain was doing at the time, or what Huck would have thought about some frivolous happening in today's world. When I am in church on Sunday morning and I am not

---

2 Steinbeck, John. *The Grapes of Wrath*. New York City, NK. Viking Press, 1939.

particularly interested in the sermon, usually because the minister seems to be centering in on my sins, then I send my mind to *Huck* and silently recite a section of the book. It gives one all kinds of outlets. But mostly, I think it helps develop character and a way of life. Mark Twain, and particularly Huck Finn, have given me great pleasure although I really only discovered them after I was 50 years old. Good readers can begin much earlier. So here are a few gleanings from my harvest of *Huck Finn*.

## HUCK IN BRIEF

This is a brief review of *Adventures of Huckleberry Finn* in case you unfortunately did not have a teacher. The book was published in 1885 and banned immediately by the New York Public Library. In speaking for the library, Louisa May Alcott said, "If this is the best Mark Twain can write for young people, then he best stop writing." Actually, the book is not just for young people. It is a story that young people can enjoy, but its themes are rather more for adult readers.

*Huck Finn* has been banned every year since its publication, but for different reasons. The N.Y. Library and Louisa May Alcott condemned the book because of its coarse language. It was not New England. Prior to *Huck*, all books used proper English—they followed the European style and all authors were from New England. Later on, when Ernest Hemingway stated that *Huckleberry Finn* was the best and first American book written, and all since have been copies, the reason he said this was because Twain used the language of the people of the United States outside the New England area.

The book was written twenty years after the Civil War, but the setting was before that war. To touch on Huck's background and upbringing, he was staying with the Widow Douglas whose sister, Miss Watson, made Huck read the Bible and follow good table manners. Miss Watson also made the slaves gather every night so she could read the Bible to them. Huck's father was known as the "town drunk." His father steals Huck away from the Widow Douglas and takes him across the Mississippi River, keeps him locked up in a shack, abused, and living in fear of his father.

Huck escapes from Pap Finn and finds Jim, the slave of Miss Watson. These two escape from "civilization" and initially live in a cave on Jackson's Island.

Huck wants to know what is going on in the town, (named Petersburg in the book, Hannibal in the real world.) So he visits a lady across the river—Mrs. Loftus—and finds out a search party is coming to find Jim. So Huck rushes back to the cave on the island and tells Jim they have to leave. And here is a significant clue to what this book is about. Huck says to Jim: "THEY ARE AFTER US." He did not say they are after you, Jim, which was the case, but Huck ties himself to Jim by saying, "THEY ARE AFTER US." So they float down the Mississippi River on a raft. They were acquaintances before, but NOW have become friends.

The friendship causes Huck a dilemma. He must confront himself with obeying the law, obeying the Bible, obeying his culture, society, or obeying his gut feelings. Much of the conflict in the novel stems from Huck's attempt to reconcile Jim's desire to be free to be emancipated. Initially Huck is concerned only with his own freedom and doesn't question the morality of slavery. He wants to be free from his father and free from civilization.

As they raft down the river, catching and cooking fish, talking and laughing, having no one to look down on either one of them, attitudes change and friendship develops. Jim tells Huck that he feels "all a feverish and a trembling to be so close to freedom." He tells Huck that he plans to steal his own wife and children. This causes anxiety and consternation to Huck that Jim would steal another man's property—a white man's property. He says, "My conscience got to stirring me up hotter and hotter . . ." So Huck decides to turn Jim in to the authorities and as he leaves the raft in the canoe to go to a nearby town, he hears Jim say, "There you goes, the old true Huck, the only white gentleman that ever kept his promise to old Jim."

And Huck says, "I jus felt sick." He went back to Jim and the raft and did not disclose his Black friend as an escaped slave.

So after spending time with Jim on the raft, and observing the unsavory acts of people on shore that he calls "civilization," Huck's conscience tells him that he needs to help Jim because Jim is a human being. Jim does not act like those "civilized" people on shore that hurt people. Over time, Huck develops an inner conviction that he cannot return Jim to slavery. And despite feeling guilty for acting in a way his society considers immoral, Huck decides he must treat Jim not as a slave, but as a human being.

Huck says, "I knowed I'd done wrong . . . Then I says, 'hold on.' If I had done right and give Jim up, would I feel better than I do now? 'Why no,' I says, 'I'd feel bad. I'd feel the same way I do right now.' Well, then I says, 'What's the use of my learning to do right, when it's troublesome to do right, and it ain't no trouble to do wrong. And the wages is just the same.' I was stuck. I couldn't answer that."

Huck theorizes that if he had just gone to Sunday School that they would have "learnt you there that 'people that tries to make Black people free goes to everlasting fire.' It made me shiver." Then he decides to pray to see if he could get help in being a better person. But he finds he cannot pray a lie. So as his conscience gets hotter and hotter he says, "Alright then, I'll go to hell" rather than turn in his new friend.

The scene where Huck says he will "go to Hell" rather than turn in his friend Jim takes place at the end of Chapter 31. Hemingway said that is where the book should have ended. WHY? Because it was an honorable decision that Huck made in spite of all his upbringing to decide he had rather go to hell than to turn in his Black friend Jim.

But the book did not stop there. It went on for twelve more chapters, which has been debated many years as to why Mark Twain "ruined this magnificent story." And the reason was because Mark Twain was a prodigious observer of people. He knew human nature. He was a realist. He thought a windsock guided human behavior. What is a windsock? It is a cone-shaped sack with stripes used by plane pilots for landings and takeoffs. The wind blows through it and thereby determines DIRECTION and STRENGTH of the wind. Twain saw humans as changing directions according to which way the wind blows.

So he did not leave Huck with a noble Christian act. He was a realist. Tom Sawyer comes on the scene visiting his aunt and uncle on the farm in which Jim is being held captive. Tom knows that since Huck and Jim left Petersburg, Miss Watson had signed papers setting Jim free. BUT TOM DID NOT TELL THIS FACT. He wanted to play with an adventure. Tom is a romantic, representing society with rules and regulations and devoid of freedom. So he had Jim and Huck go through all kinds of escaping shenanigans that takes up several chapters, knowing all the time that Jim was free. Huck has always believed that Tom has knowledge about things and is intelligent. So he goes along with Tom's antics.

This book tells about Black people who had been freed from slavery but entered a bizarre inexplicable period in which they had LESS RESPECT than when they were slaves. They are still struggling to get respect. Jim, the Black slave, ran away from home because he heard that Miss Watson was going to sell him down the river for $850. He told Huck it made him feel good, because he was somebody for the first time. He was worth $850. So these last chapters depict what the Jim Crow laws established for the freed slaves what many are still exhibiting today as a nation, and as Christians, about people considered to be "other."

*Adventures of Huckleberry Finn* is an adventure story with a message. The word to describe the message is FREEDOM. NOT freedom of slave Jim, but freedom of Huckleberry Finn. How many of us could have made such a decision to "go to hell" as Huck did? To throw away all we have been taught, our culture, and going in a completely different direction. Can Huck, can we, cast aside all the culture and training we have received, ignore the windsock, and do the right thing?

That, to me, is the main message of *Adventures of Huckleberry Finn*.

## Special Literary Edition
(see pages 4, 5, 6)

# In The Spirit: A Review

*by J. Pair*

Mark Twain lives on in the spirit if not in the flesh. Dr. Marvin Cole, Vice President of South Campus, performed during Student Activity Hour on Wednesday, April 30th, assuming the role of America's first humorist and fiction writer, Samuel Clemens, better known as Mark Twain.

Cole's performance began as he stepped onto a dark stage illuminated only by the small flame from a match to light his Twain-like corn cob pipe. Brilliantly keeping in character as the picturesque, legendary Twain, Cole began to present himself as "an honest Man" in the presence of a lawyer who, surprisingly enough, kept his hands in his own pockets. Entrancing the audience which packed the theatre, Cole's personal appearance so resembled Twain's that the possibility existed for one brief moment that the old story teller had reappeared to put, once again, man in his proper foolish perspective.

With his performance of sketches of that all-American boy, Huck Finn, Cole drew the audience further into his magic land of make-believe. First Cole introduced the character of Huck Finn as Huck was first captured by his drunken Pap. Playing both characters, Cole brought to life first the boy who longed for freedom and then the drunken father who kept him prisoner. Cole portrayed Huck's tribulations as he escaped from Pap and joined up with the runaway Jim to head down river toward freedom.

Switching between the characters of Huck and Jim, Cole vividly brought to living reality the crux of the novel, **The Adventures of Huckleberry Finn**, and the dilemma of Huck. The adolescent boy, forced to choose between the call of his heart to help the runaway Jim whom he loves, and society's laws which imprison man, Huck opts for love, even if he does "go to Hell" for breaking man's laws.

Cole's evocation of Huck recalled the American dream of freedom which has existed since the Mayflower Compact was signed by the Pilgrims before they stepped upon the North American continent. Speaking in the character of Jim, Cole warmly revealed the honest values of the true American as Jim lectures Huck about his knavery.

Brilliantly conceived and professionally polished. Dr. Cole's performance was delivered apparently from the heart sincerely. Although he received a two-minute ovation, Cole, like Twain, slipped away.

*Dr. Marvin Cole as Mark Twain. (Staff photo by J. Pair)*

High School photo of Marvin. Wide shirt collars were "the in" in the late 1940s.

Bottom: Celebrating ninetieth birthday with an inexplicable crew.

PEACHTREE ROAD RACE
July 4, 1997
MARATHON**FOTO**

I never had to outrun anyone. To me, if I finished the race, then I won.

# About the Author

# About the Author

Marvin Mallonee Cole was born in Candler, North Carolina. The Mallonee part of his name came from a circuit-riding Methodist minister who was admired by his father. He graduated from Candler High School in 1950 and attended Mars Hill College for one year before entering the US Air Force for four years as a Military Policeman. He then attended Western Carolina College (University) for Bachelor's and Master's Degrees. At Western Carolina he was elected President of the Student Body for his senior year. He then attended Indiana University for the Doctor of Education degree (EdD).

Marvin has worked as Dean at Morehead State University and Atlanta Baptist College (Now Mercer) in Atlanta. Through the auspices of Indiana University and the United States Agency for International Development, Marvin worked as advisor for two years at The University of the Panjab in Lahore, Pakistan, and for three years as advisor to the President at Kabul University, Kabul, Afghanistan. The last twenty-one years of his professional career he spent eight years as Dean and thirteen years as President of DeKalb College in Atlanta, Georgia. As a hobby, therapy, avocation and advocate, he has been an impersonator in one-person shows and lecturer of the works of Mark Twain. He and wife Mimi retired to Marvin's grandparents' farm in Candler.

Another book by Marvin Cole:

Cole, Marvin M., *The Coke Candler We Knew*. Enca, N.C.: Colonial House Publishers, 2013.

# JOB HISTORY FOR MARVIN MALLONEE COLE

1994- President Emeritus of DeKalb College which became Georgia Perimeter College and now merged with Georgia State University. Presently I am a lawn mower, garden tender, house custodian, and part-time Sunday School Teacher.

1981-1994 President of Dekalb Community College of the University System of Georgia in Atlanta, Georgia. The college had four campuses and over 16,000 students.

1974-1980 Executive Dean of the South Campus of DeKalb College.

1973-1974 Academic Dean of the South Campus of DeKalb College. While in this position, and because of a keen interest stimulated by an Interdisciplinary Program in Humanities which included my participation in sessions on Adventures of Huckleberry Finn, the English Faculty encouraged me to do a one-person show like the one given by Hal Holbrook that began my thirty-eight years of performing and lecturing the works of Mark Twain.

1970-1973 Advisor to the President of Kabul University, Kabul, Afghanistan under the auspices of Indiana University and the United States Agency for International Development.

1968-1970 Dean of Students helping to establish Atlanta Baptist College which is now a Pharmacy Campus for Mercer University.

1966-1968 Dean of Institutional Programs at Morehead State University, Morehead, Kentucky.

1966 Completed requirements for Doctor's Degree at Indiana University, receiving EdD in a split major of Higher Education and Psychology and Sociology.

1965-1966 Assistant to Dean of Education at Indiana University while completing requirements for the doctor's degree.

1963-1965 Administrative Assistant at the Institute of Education and Research at the University of the Punjab, Lahore, Pakistan under the auspices of Indiana University and The United States Agency for International Development. This program was developing and implementing the first Master's Degree program in Education in Pakistan and I collected data for my doctoral dissertation.

1961-1963 Administrative Assistant to a Professor at Indiana University while a student in the doctoral program.

1958-1961 Instructor of Psychology of Adjustment (Freshman Orientation) and Director of Student Center while studying for Master's Degree.

1955-1958 Student at Western Carolina University majoring in Business Administration. I was elected President of the Study Body and Senate my senior year and this experience determined my life's vocation.

1951-1955 Served four years as Military Policeman in the US Air Force with three years in London, England. Because my father made me take typing in high school I was given a wonderful job of obtaining security clearances for personnel working in high security areas.

1950-1951 Freshman at Mars Hill College (University), Mars Hill, NC.

1950 Graduated from Candler High School, Candler, NC.

## AND SO!

This book was an attempt to provide answers to questions descendants may have about the Mimi and Marvin Cole family. I have long wished I would have asked my grandparents about their life and where they obtained their values and way of life. In a serendipitous fashion, this book may have clarified the life of the contributors also, as well as some cathartic value.

It has taken two years to process the writing and editing. I want to thank all the contributors for their time, effort, and thought in attempting to complete the book's mission.

Much appreciation is offered to the publisher, Dr. Micki Cabaniss for her extraordinary patience, expertise, and encouragement in the months of work taken getting the book ready for printing. She insisted on doing things right even when I thought the commas were all right where they were.

In the end, I feel better about her way. Thank you, Micki.

www.ingramcontent.com/pod-product-compliance
Lightning Source LLC
Chambersburg PA
CBHW041156290426

44108CB00003B/88